The United States Occupation of Haiti, 1915–1934

Hans Schmidt

 RUTGERS UNIVERSITY PRESS
New Brunswick, New Jersey

INSTRUCTIONAL RESOURCE CENTER
HILLSBOROUGH COMMUNITY COLLEGE

Copyright © 1971
By Rutgers University, The State University of New Jersey
Library of Congress Catalog Card Number: 70–152721
Manufactured in the United States of America
by Quinn & Boden Company, Inc., Rahway, N.J.
ISBN: 0–8135–24–0690–5

To Lloyd C. Gardner, Jr.

Contents

Acknowledgments

Except for several articles dealing with special topics, this study is the first to be based on archival materials that have been opened over the past fifteen years. The new sources used in this study include State Department papers; Navy Department and Marine Corps papers, especially the Naval Records Collection in the National Archives; articles and memoirs written by high-ranking military officers where permission to publish had been denied previously by the Navy Department; personal papers of military and State Department officials.

I am indebted to many people for help in the research and writing of this study. Lloyd C. Gardner, Jr., of Rutgers University helped me with advice and encouragement through every phase. Warren I. Susman of Rutgers University made many helpful suggestions in the earlier stages and provided a penetrating critique of a portion of the final manuscript. Professors Emeritus L. Ethan Ellis of Rutgers and Dana G. Munro of Princeton University graciously shared their knowledge and insights with me; I thank them both for their interest and their example of historical scholarship. Sidney W. Mintz of Yale University read an early draft of the manuscript and made excellent detailed criticisms. Adam D. Horvath, currently at Case Western Reserve University Press, gave me sound advice at a crucial stage. Colonel Robert D. Heinl, Jr., United States Marine Corps (Ret.), steered me to important source materials and read a portion of the manuscript. My colleagues at State University College, New Paltz, New York, David Krikun, J. Ignacio Mendez, Donald Roper, and

Joseph d'Oronzio read portions of the manuscript and made useful suggestions.

Many librarians and archivists have contributed to this study. I especially thank Mr. Schwartz of the National Archives Naval Records Collection, François-Xavier Grondin of Rutgers University Library, Serge Corvington of the New York Public Library, and the staffs of the Marine Corps Headquarters Historical Section, Alexandria, Virginia, and the Marine Corps Museum in Quantico, Virginia.

I am grateful to the following archives and libraries for granting me access to source materials and assisting me in their use: The National Archives for the State Department Papers, the Francis White Papers, the Naval Records Collection, the General Records of the Navy Department, the Marine Corps Records, the Forbes Commission Papers, the Records of the Bureau of Insular Affairs, and the records of the Bureau of Foreign and Domestic Commerce. The Library of Congress for the W. Cameron Forbes Papers, the Josephus Daniels Papers, the Cordell Hull Papers, the John A. Lejeune Papers, and the Woodrow Wilson Papers. Yale University Library for the Henry L. Stimson Papers. Columbia University Oral History Research Office for the Frank A. Vanderlip Papers. The Franklin D. Roosevelt Library, Hyde park, New York, for the Franklin D. Roosevelt Papers.

The following have graciously provided me with or granted me permission to use photographs: The United States Marine Corps Combat Pictorial Section, Washington, D.C.; the Marine Corps Museum, Quantico, Virginia; Mrs. Virginia A. White; and *National Geographic* magazine.

My graduate school colleagues Richard Brody of Queens College, Tom Hulbeck of Auburn Community College, Terry Major of the University of Maryland, Bob Mayer of Newark State College, and Jeff Safford of Montana State University buoyed me with their enthusiasm, friendship, and many helpful insights during the early research phase. Morris Garber of Rutgers University made my life as a teaching assistant simpler and happier so that I was able to concentrate more intently on this project.

The State University of New York Research Foundation granted me a faculty research fellowship to pursue my work in this area.

My wife Joan has shared the rewards and frustrations throughout.

Hans Schmidt

The United States Occupation of Haiti, 1915-1934

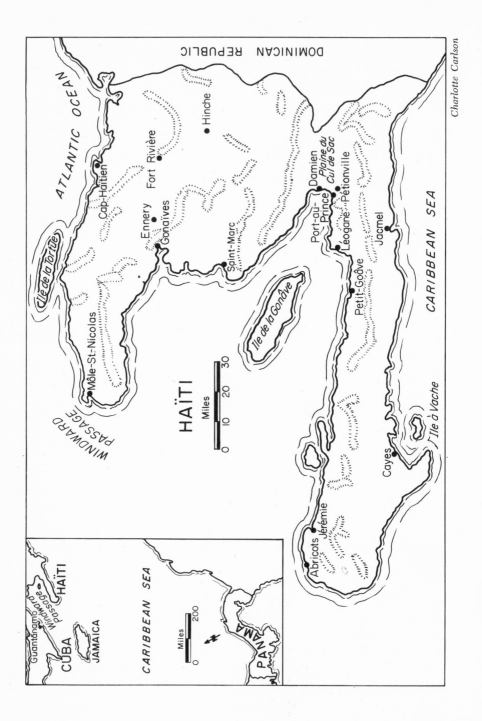

Charlotte Carlson

1

Introduction

United States foreign expansion after the Civil War was characterized by an intensified interest in establishing American political and
military control in the Caribbean and the Pacific. Previous American
interests in these areas had centered around commercial expansion,
focusing on the China trade and various official and private efforts
to procure trading advantages such as the activities of Commodore
Perry in Japan and Cornelius Vanderbilt in Nicaragua. Immediately
after the Civil War, Secretary of State William Seward began the
quest for an American empire by purchasing Alaska in 1867, by
occupying Midway Island in the Pacific, and by attempting to annex
Santo Domingo in the Caribbean.

The new tendency toward militant imperialism and territorial
acquisition reflected the emergence of the United States as an industrial power competing with European nations in an intense rivalry
for world markets and overseas possessions. American expansionists
James G. Blaine, Henry Cabot Lodge, and Theodore Roosevelt
pointed to the economic necessity of foreign markets to relieve the
glut of industrial production in the United States. Military strate-
gists, notably Captain Alfred Thayer Mahan, promoted the construction of a mighty navy, acquisition of foreign naval bases and
coaling stations, the building of an isthmian canal, and procurement
of foreign colonies. Given the pressures of international rivalry and
nascent imperialistic ambitions, American diplomatic maneuvers
during the late nineteenth century exhibited a new stridency as

indicated by Marine Corps landings in Formosa, Japan, Uruguay, Mexico, Korea, Colombia, Hawaii, Egypt, Haiti, Samoa, Argentina, Chile, Nicaragua, and China. Military preparations, featuring the construction of a modern fleet of warships begun in the 1880s and the creation of a general staff in the aftermath of the Spanish-American War, provided the United States with the requisite force for participation in world power politics. In an era when national success was measured in terms of imperialistic conquest, the challenge of European rivalry and the example of French, British, and German successes in winning new colonial possessions served as potent stimuli to the United States. Of the European rivals, Germany constituted both the most immediate threat to American interests and the most compelling example of expanding national greatness. American naval ambition paralleled that of Germany, and German and American interests clashed frequently in the Pacific and Latin America. After the Prussian victory over France in 1870, the United States Marine Corps, in a remarkable testament to American aspirations for a place in the sun, adopted the Prussian spiked helmet as dress uniform headgear.

The immediate objectives of American expansion were to achieve hegemony in the Caribbean and the Pacific. During the period from 1867 to 1900 the United States annexed Alaska, Midway, Hawaii, Guam, Tutuila, the Philippines, Wake, and approximately fifty smaller islands in the Pacific. Acquisition of these territories provided coaling stations along the sea lanes to the Orient and strategic bases from which American naval forces could operate effectively in the Pacific. Most of the islands were governed by naval officers responsible to the Navy Department. The taking of the Philippines made the United States an Asiatic power.

In the Caribbean, American interests were strategically bound to developments in the Pacific and Asia. The lengthy voyage of the battleship *Oregon* from the West Coast around the tip of South America to the Caribbean, where the ship was needed for action during the Spanish-American War in 1898, dramatized the urgent need for an isthmian canal. President Theodore Roosevelt, himself a strong advocate of sea power, "took" Panama in 1903 and the United States proceeded to stake out a Caribbean sphere of influence that pivoted around strategic concern over the security of the new Panama Canal and extensive economic interests in Mexico and Cuba. The canal, completed in 1914, became the vital military and commercial link connecting the East Coast of the United States with the West Coast, the Pacific empire, and Asia.

As had been true in the Pacific, the American expansion into the Caribbean began with commercial adventures and culminated in territorial acquisitions and military invasions. Spain ceded Puerto Rico to the United States in 1898, Roosevelt took Panama in 1903 and established a customs receivership in the Dominican Republic in 1905, American troops occupied Cuba in 1898, Nicaragua in 1909, Haiti in 1915, the Dominican Republic in 1916, and the United States purchased the Virgin Islands in 1916. Marine interventions in the so-called banana wars were primary instruments of American control in the area, and in several cases were of extended duration, lasting intermittently from 1909 to 1933 in Nicaragua and consecutively from 1915 to 1934 in Haiti.

The pattern of diplomacy in the Caribbean and Pacific contrasted sharply with American diplomacy elsewhere in the world. Historians, focusing on relationships with European powers and policies regarding their colonial spheres of influence, frequently characterize American diplomacy as having evolved within the broad framework of the liberal political tradition. Both those historians who defend American policy and the revisionists who are generally critical assume, from their respective vantage points, that liberalism has been the key historical factor. Revisionists have argued that the United States pursued an Open Door policy in the twentieth century, and that this policy was rooted in an ideology of "liberal internationlism" that envisaged capitalist economic expansion in an open world. The United States, exercising its financial and industrial strength in a free-trade world economic system, would thrive and dominate within the framework of liberal values and without ugly use of force or the encumbrances and expenses of colonialism. One leading revisionist has characterized the policy as "imperial anti-colonialism" inasmuch as it involved American economic imperialism sustained in part by the destruction of other nations' colonial spheres of influence.[1] Thus the United States sought to destroy trade barriers, colonial enclaves, and economic spheres of influence established by rival powers on the premise that the United States could best realize its full political and economic potential in an open world. Traditional historians, defending American foreign policy, see in liberal internationalism the embodiment of American values of democracy, freedom, and equal rights guaranteed by law.

In view of American activities in the Caribbean and Pacific, this liberal, open-door characterization must be severely qualified to the point of denying the plausibility of seeing liberal internationalism as a basic or pervasive factor in the formulation of American policy. The United States practiced liberal internationalism only in those areas where it could not set up its own exclusive spheres of influence. Thus we see an open-door policy used as a ploy to further American interests in China, where the United States did not enjoy predominant politico-economic power, but an exclusive closed-door policy in the Caribbean and the Pacific, where the United States exercised sufficient military power to enforce its own absolute hegemony. The subject of this study, the United States occupation of Haiti, obviously entailed a complete departure from any principles of liberal internationalism. While the United States sought an open order elsewhere in the world, this was not the case in the Caribbean, which in the early twentieth century became the "American Mediterranean." The occupation of Haiti clearly was a case of closed-door, sphere-of-influence diplomacy, as illustrated by the systematic deportation of German businessmen from Haiti by United States military authorities in the early 1920s.

It has been argued that the subsequent evolution of the Good Neighbor policy in Latin America, exemplified by the American withdrawal from Haiti, was an indication of dominant liberal internationalist tendencies in United States foreign policy. This is dubious. The Good Neighbor policy always assumed United States control over the entire area as a special sphere of influence. The acid test of the Good Neighbor policy was the much-belabored posture of noninterventionism. As soon as the United States perceived a serious threat to its hegemony in the Caribbean, as in Guatemala in 1954, Cuba in 1961, and the Dominican Republic in 1965, it scuttled noninterventionism. The Johnson Doctrine, enunciated during the 1965 Dominican intervention, was a direct extension of the Monroe Doctrine and the Wilsonian banana wars. While the circumstances of the Cold War are in many ways new, the exclusive domination of the Caribbean region against incursions by outside powers, by force if necessary, remains an axiom of United States foreign policy.

The precedents for the United States intervention in Haiti were not the Open Door policy in China or Woodrow Wilson's crusade to make the world safe for democracy, but rather the long series of guerrilla wars waged against alien races and cultures in western North America, the Pacific, and the Caribbean. The abrasive contacts with alien peoples outside the United States occurred at the same time that alien peoples within the United States were being subjected to nativist and racist harassment marked by brutal treatment of Indians, lynchings of immigrants, Ku Klux Klan bigotry, oriental exclusion, and systematic suppression of blacks. Internal nativist and racist tendencies were carried abroad when, as a facet of continuing national growth and vitality, Americans mastered weaker neighboring peoples who occupied the contiguous areas in continental North America and overseas. This expansion entailed a long history of bloody military confrontations, first with the American Indians and subsequently with Mexicans, Filipinos, Cubans, Dominicans, Haitians, Nicaraguans, and others. These wars involved racism and American disdain for "savages" and frequently degenerated into torture, systematic destruction of villages, and military tactics tantamount to genocide. The military logic of guerrilla warfare, where superior forces equipped with modern weapons were pitted against elusive, poorly equipped guerrillas who were physically indistinguishable from noncombatants, dictated vicious hunt-and-kill tactics which were most conveniently rationalized in terms of racial and cultural prejudices. Americans came equipped with a store of such prejudices to go along with their superior firepower. This was a world apart from "civilized" Western wars and the refinements of European diplomacy. A United States Army general who commanded troops during the suppression of the Philippine insurrection in 1900, when questioned about American violations of the "ordinary rules of civilized warfare," replied simply, "These people are not civilized." [2]

The prolonged experience of hostile contact with alien peoples had a cumulative effect. Each new encounter was conceived partly in terms of past experience and almost always as being outside the framework of mutual respect which characterized United States relations with European nations. This was especially true after 1898, when increased American activity in the Caribbean and Pacific resulted in the creation of a core of career personnel who served successively at various colonial outposts. By the time of the occupation of Haiti, the United States had a wealth of such experience to draw upon. Many marines had fought in earlier banana wars; Major Smedley D. Butler, first commandant of the American-sponsored Gendarmerie d'Haïti, had previously campaigned in the Philippines, China, Honduras, Nicaragua, Panama, and Mexico; and Colonel Littleton W. T. Waller, commander of the Marine Expeditionary Forces in Haiti in 1915, had commanded the marine landings in Cuba in 1906 and before that had achieved notoriety in connection with the Samar atrocities in the Philippines. Many American civilian administrators also came to Haiti with previous colonial experience; three of the four financial advisers, the most important civilian officials, had held similar posts in Peru, Persia, and Liberia, and the head of the agricultural-technical service had held a similar position in Indochina.

Given the increasing trend in the twentieth century toward respect for the dignity of all men and the new postures of liberal internationalism and progressivism that were being promoted by the Wilson administration, the prior colonial experience of individuals and the larger tradition of condescension to alien races and cultures had a baneful effect in Haiti. Americans came to Haiti equipped with racist concepts and stereotypes that included such characterizations as "gook" and "nigger," which were handed down from previous contacts with alien peoples.[*] The past experience of governing these peoples had all too often involved routine patronization punctuated by occasional brutality. As a student of the 1906–9 United States military occupation of Cuba has observed, the army, in its encounters with American Indians and Filipinos, had gained "little meaningful education in governing complex alien societies."[3]

[*] The term "gook" is still in common usage among American troops in Vietnam. Admiral Daniel V. Gallery refers to North Koreans as "gooks" in his book *The Pueblo Incident* (New York, 1970). Common use of the term "nigger" remains symptomatic of white American racism within the United States. The derisive term "greaser," elsewhere applied to Latin Americans, especially Mexicans, was not current in Haiti.

While American attitudes toward Haitians derived from nine-teenth-century Indian wars, previous banana wars, and experience with blacks in the United States, the circumstances of the interven-tion were related to the emergence of twentieth-century America as the dominant power in the Caribbean. The United States had achieved naval supremacy in the Caribbean upon the withdrawal of the larger units of Britain's West India squadron in 1905. Never-theless, American hegemony in the area was considered susceptible to challenge by European rivals, principally Germany, which pos-sessed greater overall naval strength. State and Navy Department officials felt the possibility of Germany's acquiring a naval base in the Caribbean to be a grave threat to American hegemony and to the security of the Panama Canal. Largely because of this postu-lated military danger, United States troops occupied Haiti, the Dominican Republic, the Virgin Islands, and parts of Cuba in 1915, 1916, and 1917, thereby completing the American garrisoning of the Greater Antilles with the exception of British Jamaica. In 1917 American troops, plus the British in Jamaica, controlled all the major islands in the Caribbean from Cuba in the west to Puerto Rico and the Virgin Islands in the east, thereby securing the several sea lanes approaching the Panama Canal against possible German attack during World War I. The occupation of Haiti, which had been considered most likely to fall into German hands, was thus conceived as an important short-term measure to ensure American military hegemony in the Caribbean. In the context of long-term American expansion in the Pacific and the Caribbean, the occupa-tion of Haiti constituted another sequent step in the continuing formation of exclusive American spheres of influence.

The intervention in Haiti took place at a time when, irrespective of the relentless progression of American military incursions in the Caribbean, the official posture of United States foreign policy was one of conciliation and respect for the rights of smaller nations. President Wilson and Secretary of State William Jennings Bryan were both anti-imperialists insofar as they abjured the use of force in international relations. Wilson's public statements about never again seeking "one additional foot of territory by conquest," about treating Latin-American countries on "terms of equality and honor," and about making the world "safe for democracy" created a compelling scenario which served as background for the intervention. More indicative of the coercive tendencies in United States policy were Wilson's remarks about teaching South American republics to "elect good men," and his frequent insistence that the United States had a moral responsibility to promote constitutional, democratic government in the Caribbean area. In Haiti the reality of American actions sharply contradicted the gloss of liberal protestations, however self-righteously sincere these protestations may have been. Racist preconceptions, reinforced by the current debasement of Haiti's political institutions, placed the Haitians far below levels Americans considered necessary for democracy, self-government, and constitutionalism. The generous and even noble narcissist compulsion to bestow American civilization was stymied by self-defeating ethnocentric prejudices, cultivated during several centuries of domination over Indians and black slaves, which stigmatized the subject peoples as genetically and culturally inferior. Moreover, the Occupation in Haiti always gave first priority to United States political, military, and economic interests.

The belief that Haitians were inherently inferior, coupled with the dictates of State Department diplomacy in the Caribbean, led to grotesque perversion of the declared missionary ideal of spreading liberal democracy. Indeed, the Occupation, in the process of exercising unwelcome foreign military domination, consistently suppressed local democratic institutions and denied elementary political liberties. Wilson's obsession with order, stability, and constitutionalism, implying government by law and the sanctity of legal contracts, was translated into rigid authoritarianism based on the assertion that Haitians were incapable of self-government. This assertion was in part an apology and a rationalization for United States military dictation, but it was also basic to American prejudices regarding blacks and Latin Americans. Instead of building from existing democratic institutions which, on paper, were quite impressive and had long incorporated the liberal democratic philosophy and governmental machinery associated with the French Revolution, the United States blatantly overrode them and illegally forced through its own authoritarian, antidemocratic system. One might have expected, given Wilson's passion for constitutionalism, that the new American-sponsored Constitution of 1918 would have been an exemplary, enlightened document. It was not. Its most important provisions were the legalization of alien landownership, indefinite suspension of the elected bicameral Haitian legislature, temporary suspension of the irremovability of judges, and legalization of all acts of the American military occupation. The new Constitution, clearly a device to serve American ends, was rammed through by means of an illegal, marine-supervised plebiscite after the Haitian legislature, the only body legally competent to tamper with the constitution under existing Haitian law, was summarily disbanded because it refused to consider any alteration of the long-standing precept which outlawed alien landownership as a bulwark against recurrence of white foreign domination. The elected legislature was henceforth replaced by a Council of State appointed by the occupation's client-president, and did not sit again until after the anti-American strikes and riots of 1929. Respect for law and legal contracts applied only in cases which suited American purposes. The Haitian-American Treaty of 1915, in effect a unilateral document executed by the State Department, was frequently cited as justification for continuing the occupation, a binding commitment by which the United States was morally and legally obligated to continue the occupation until 1936. That the treaty could have been abrogated at any time in exactly the same way that it was originally imposed, with the enthusiastic approval of Haitian nationalists, was ignored until after the 1929 uprisings, when the United States decided on early termination of the occupation as best serving American ends. At that stage the 1915 treaty was neatly jettisoned. Legal contracts involving the interests of American bondholders were another matter; these were rigorously and exactingly enforced.

Perhaps the most telling indications of the extent to which liberal democratic missionary impulses were distorted under the pressures of racist colonial realities were the massive forced-labor corvée used by the marines to build roads, and the basic policy, operative in many occupation programs, that economic development should come about through plantation agriculture financed by private American investments. The establishment of foreign-dominated plantation agriculture necessitated destruction of the existing minifundia land-tenure system with its myriad peasant freeholders, and implied converting these independent farmers into latifundian peons. The American liberal democratic tradition was historically rooted in the Jeffersonian ideal of independent yeoman farmers; introducing plantation agriculture in Haiti would have destroyed such a system and substituted a socioeconomic system characteristic of oligarchic, antidemocratic political regimes. Likewise, the corvée, in which unpaid conscripts were sometimes roped together in gangs, had its parallel in the corvée employed by the British in nineteenth-century Egypt and was obviously antithetical to the development of liberal values.

The perversion of professed American liberal democratic intentions was, of course, the function of a whole constellation of unfavorable circumstances, as well as of the racial and cultural prejudices of the invaders. That the occupation was imposed and maintained by force effectively precluded democratic elections, since elections would have resulted in humiliation and defeat for the United States. When free elections were finally held in the aftermath of the 1929 uprisings, all pro-American and moderate candidates lost decisively. Maintaining the occupation by force involved heavy reliance on military personnel who, following patterns established in prior colonial experience, were often inclined toward military dictation. United States priorities, reflected in the posting of a marine general as supreme commander of all phases of the occupation and in the rigorously conservative, extractive fiscal management of Haitian government money, consistently placed the interests of the United States above those of Haiti and correspondingly narrowed opportunities for introducing meaningful Haitian participation. Economic policy was linked to anticipated American economic expansion into Haiti, and consequently focused on development of plantation agriculture and manual-technical education for the Haitians; literacy and familiarization with democratic privileges and processes were neglected. Adding to all the built-in handicaps on the American side was the absence of viable, organic roots for democratic liberalism in Haiti. Behind the façade of democratic constitutions and the national credo *Liberté—Egalité—Fraternité* lay a century of political despotism, militarism, and class exploitation. The vast majority of Haitians had learned to distrust and avoid contact with the government, which always took and never gave.

Despite all the apparent difficulties realized from the outset, United States officials persisted in publicly maintaining the rhetorical illusion that the occupation was a noble and self-sacrificing mission to plant democratic liberalism. This is not to say that the idealists were hypocrites. Doubtless most Americans would have liked to introduce democratic liberalism into Haiti, but the sentiments were, under the circumstances, simply irrelevant. The rhetoric of liberal internationalism, based on relations with European powers and so much a part of all American foreign policy, was wildly out of place with respect to Haiti, where so many contradictory factors were operative.

The dominant theme of the American presence in Haiti was materialistic rather than idealistic. American efforts to uplift and "civilize" Haiti emphasized material achievements, technological modernization, organizational efficiency, and the cultivation of pragmatic as opposed to esthetic or spiritual attitudes. The Occupation excelled at the construction of roads, hospitals, and public buildings. The materialistic approach fit the methods and priorities dictated by selfish American purposes and also conformed to American prejudices, which held that Haitians were incapable of political and intellectual achievements. It was hoped that Haiti, despite the alleged inferiority of Haitians, would be developed into a prosperous country with the help of American leadership and technological genius. The United States would first create what were thought to be the prerequisite material bases for advanced civilization, so that Haitians at some undetermined future time might attempt the subtleties of American political institutions.

The American policy of pragmatic, materialistic uplift in Haiti was conceptually rooted in aspects of the Progressive reform movement in the United States and in models taken mainly from enlightened British colonial experience. The Progressive movement in the United States had a strong technocratic orientation, based on the belief that progress would come about through increased technical efficiency and rationalization of existing institutions.[4] With respect to blacks in the United States, the Progressive, pragmatic approach involved Booker T. Washington's 1895 Atlanta Compromise, with its abnegation of intellectual, cultural, and social aspirations for blacks in favor of manual-technical education and material betterment through efficient performance at low-status trades. These concepts were employed by the Occupation in Haiti. The technocratic, materialistic aspects of Progressivism had persisted into the 1920s and were even accelerated, as for instance with the efforts of Secretary of Commerce Herbert Hoover to increase government efficiency in assisting United States foreign commerce by posting active commercial agents to American diplomatic missions. In Haiti the materialistic, technical Progressive impulse was given free rein, since the human objects, Haitian "Negroes" * whose culture was held in contempt, had no rights and were not permitted to interfere with the more enlightened designs of the occupiers. Haiti thus became a test case of isolated technocratic Progressivism, devoid of its liberal democratic trappings, with all the stops pulled.

American commitment to efficiency, technical expertise, and rational organization can be seen in the methods and models drawn upon in setting up the Occupation. The most important decision in this respect was the granting of overall authority to an American military officer instead of a civilian official. The marine general who served as American high commissioner had absolute authority over both the military and the civilian facets of the Occupation. The effect of this system was to rationalize the chain of command by eliminating civilian-military feuding, to strengthen military control of the country, and to emphasize command authority as opposed to a consensual or participatory relationship with the Haitians. The model for American actions most frequently cited was the British occupation of Egypt, which was similarly a rigid authoritarian system run by an all-powerful high commissioner. American officials also drew analogies with British rule in India and the "benevolent" dictatorship of Porfirio Díaz in Mexico. The intention was to set up an authoritarian regime that would exercise power for the good of people who, because of their alleged inferiority and backwardness, did not know what was good for themselves.

In selecting a Haitian to serve as client-president under the authority and protection of the American high commissioner, the

* In American racial discrimination the term and social category "Negro" included people of all proportions of Negroid ancestry, while in Haiti and elsewhere in Latin America important distinctions were made between mulattoes and blacks. The United States applied its own racial ideology in Haiti, disregarding local distinctions.

United States settled upon an individual who shared a materialistic, technocratic concept of progress. Louis Borno, client-president during the eight-year period when the American uplift program was in full swing, was an avowed admirer of Mussolini and an advocate of complete American domination as the fastest way to modernize Haiti and reconstruct viable economic and efficient governmental institutions. Borno saw salvation for Haiti in American technological prowess and disciplined technical efficiency. As a self-styled nationalist, he had no sympathy for Haitian nationalists who opposed the occupation as offensive to national pride. Borno repeatedly denounced the Haitian nationalist opposition, which included most politically aware Haitians except a minority of collaborators, as traitors who were conspiring against the best interests of the Haitian masses. The masses, in turn, were deemed too ignorant to participate in political processes or to appreciate the benefits that the occupation was bringing them.

Therein lay one of the principal ironies of the occupation. While the technical, materialistic approach to reform was quite modern and enlightened in the sense of being comparable to the latest developments in advanced industrial countries, the Occupation in Haiti, already assured of absolute power by virtue of American military presence, lacked precisely those elements which indigenous technoprogressive political movements relied upon to achieve and maintain power. Fascism in Italy and Germany, also dedicated to progress through technical efficiency,[5] was based on mass support achieved through modern, sophisticated public relations techniques, including nationalism, charismatic leadership, and ethnic or racial elitism. In the United States the Progressive movement was also associated with nationalism, the personal charisma of Teddy Roosevelt and Woodrow Wilson, and with ethnic and racial elitism exemplified by discrimination against blacks, immigration laws, and proposals for human genetical selectivity. In Haiti these elements were lacking: instead of nationalism, the Occupation entailed foreign military domination under an autocratic marine general; instead of appealing to ethnic and racial elitism, the Americans approached Haitians with ethnic and racial contempt; instead of charismatic leadership, the Occupation had client-President Borno, a man who publicly disparaged his countrymen and who was despised as a collaborator. In effect, the Occupation embodied all the progressive attributes of contemporary Italian fascism, but was crippled by failures in human relationships. For all the technical expertise, scientific agriculture, and modern rational organization, the Occupation's uplift programs achieved only marginal results. Borno and the Americans, aspiring to make the trains run on time, were precluded from achieving the successes of Mussolini, such as they were, because of the very circumstances through which the Occupation held power.

The irony of modern technological elitism failing because of an obtuse lack of complementary modern political techniques was compounded by other contradictions. Irrationalism in American racial and cultural prejudices consistently hampered the effectiveness of enlightened, rational uplift measures. The American-nurtured Haitian constabulary, rationally and plausibly conceived as an efficient, nonpartisan peacekeeping force, was irrationally stunted in its development by the American racist dogma, as expressed by a commander of the Occupation, that "you can never trust a nigger with a gun." [6] Educational policy, focusing on manual-technical training similar to contemporary functional education for blacks in the United States, was variously blighted by cultural and racial difficulties. When President Hoover sent a distinguished group of black American educators to Haiti to investigate Haitian education, they were stranded and humiliated because the United States Navy refused to transport them. American agricultural ventures, utilizing the latest developments in scientific agriculture, were plagued by a series of disastrous failures attributable to an irrational disdain for the agricultural experience of local peasants. In 1929 the head of the American Service Technique reported that Haitian peasants were growing cotton more successfully than American plantations which employed the latest scientific methods; the Americans produced healthier plants, but the amount of cotton in the bolls was less than that obtained by Haitian farmers using local methods. Likewise, the policy of Jim Crow racial segregation served to undermine efforts by American governmental administrators to train Haitian subordinates in efficient, rational, bureaucratic methods. Racial and cultural antagonisms severely limited the effectiveness of progressive development programs. Instead of modeling after the

Americans, many Haitians were alienated by American arrogance and condescension.

Within the United States, political controversy over the occupation of Haiti raised questions about the American free enterprise system, American democratic ideals, and the very nature of American political and social institutions. Anti-imperialists argued that imperialism profited a privileged minority of American businessmen, while the expenses of conquest and military occupation were borne by all the people. The invasion of foreign territories and subjugation of alien peoples contradicted basic American doctrines of democracy and individual liberty. Opponents of the occupation argued that an America bent on foreign conquest could not remain a free liberal democracy at home. Anti-imperialists Ernest Gruening, James Weldon Johnson, Senators William Borah, and William King, and Marine Corps General Smedley D. Butler charged that the marines invaded Haiti as bill collectors for the National City Bank of New York. Marine suppression of Haitian revolts and use of forced labor for military road building were denounced as atrocities by Republican politicians seeking to discredit the incumbent Democratic administration in 1920. The absolutely authoritarian character of the Occupation, the unchallenged military dictation, suppression of local democratic institutions, and jailings of Haitian newspaper editors prompted vigorous denunciations from American idealists who saw in the occupation a dangerous breach in American political morality. Imperialists answered denunciations of aggression and military conquest by alluding to the "white man's burden" and citing benefits that subject peoples would receive as part of America's enlightened crusade to spread democracy and progressivism by the sword.

In sum, the occupation of Haiti was both a logical extension of America's quest for empire and a clear example of many of the contradictions involved in that quest for empire. These contradictions were by no means successfully resolved in Haiti—indeed, the conflicts between American racism and rational progressivism, between democratic egalitarianism and military conquest, and between missionary zeal and economic exploitation were, in some ways, exacerbated. At the same time, American policy underwent perceptible changes during the course of the occupation, adapting to new pressures of nationalism abroad and opposition to military expansion at home. The occupation began as a military invasion and ended as a conspicuous and presumably final renunciation of interventionism. American withdrawal from Haiti in 1934 was hailed as a positive affirmation of the new Good Neighbor policy in Latin America.

2

Haiti before the Intervention

The Republic of Haiti occupies the western third of the island of Hispaniola, which lies sixty miles across the Windward Passage from Oriente Province in Cuba. Haiti shares Hispaniola with the Dominican Republic. The land area of Haiti is approximately one-third greater than that of the state of New Jersey. In 1915 Haiti's population was estimated at two million persons, the vast majority of whom earned their livelihood at small-scale independent farming. Port-au-Prince, the capital and only large city, had a population of about 100,000. From 95 to 97 percent of the population was illiterate.[1]

After the United States, Haiti is the oldest independent nation in the Western Hemisphere. Independence was achieved during the French Revolution after a protracted slave revolt led by Toussaint Louverture and Jean Jacques Dessalines, both of whom had been slaves. Under Dessalines, black slaves decisively defeated an impressive contingent of French troops commanded by Napoleon's brother-in-law General Leclerc. On January 1, 1804, revolutionary chiefs met at Gonaïves and proclaimed the new nation. The French colonial name of Saint Domingue was discarded in favor of the aboriginal term "Haïti," meaning land of mountains.

At the time of the French Revolution, Saint Domingue was the wealthiest European colonial possession in the Americas. As early as 1742 the sugar production of Saint Domingue exceeded that of all the British West Indies, and on the eve of the revolution the colony accounted for more than one-third of the foreign commerce of France.[2] In 1789 French trade with Saint Domingue amounted to £11 million, while the whole of England's colonial trade totaled only £5 million. In the same year the ports of Saint Domingue received 1,587 ships, a greater number than Marseilles, and France employed 750 ships exclusively for the Saint Domingue trade.[3] The chief exports of the colony were sugar, coffee, cotton, indigo, molasses, and dyewoods. The French built an elaborate network of roads, irrigation systems, and magnificent plantations. Wealthy French creoles had also established the rudiments of urbane French culture—Cap Français, later renamed Cap Haïtien, had been known as the Paris of the Antilles.

The population of Saint Domingue on the eve of the French Revolution was made up of over 90 percent black slaves, with whites numbering only about 40,000 out of a total population of 519,000. There were also about 20,000 free mulattoes, many of whom were educated and prosperous.[4] Slavery in Saint Domingue had been particularly brutal, with commonplace whipping, mutilation, and torture, and the war for independence was marked by atrocities on all sides. With the defeat and withdrawal of French troops, the white French colonists either emigrated, in part to South Carolina and Louisiana, or were massacred by the newly independent Haitians. The colonial period and struggle for independence left Haiti with a confused legacy of racial pride and antagonism, plus a persisting fear of white encroachment. The rigid colonial caste system, in which admixture of white blood determined social status, persisted to the extent that Haitian mulattoes continued to enjoy social and economic advantages over blacks.

Independent Haiti emerged as a segmented society.[*] The free *gens de couleur* of colonial Saint Domingue, mostly mulattoes but also including some blacks, had adopted the cultural values of dominant white French society despite their having been subjected to vicious racial discrimination by the whites. Wealthy *gens de*

* I am indebted for many of the concepts and some of the details in the following discussion to H. Hoetink, *The Two Variants in Caribbean Race Relations: A Contribution to the Sociology of Segmented Societies* (London, 1967).

couleur sent their children to France for education and sought to prove themselves by successful emulation of white society, while simultaneously exhibiting the same virulent race prejudice against black slaves that they themselves were subjected to by the whites. White racist values ascribed status according to lightness of skin pigmentation. In Saint Domingue, as in other areas where Europeans enslaved Africans, subtle differentiations were made according to degrees of white ancestry among half-castes. The physical norms of the dominant white segment of French colonial society were carried over into independent Haiti by the *gens de couleur,* who now constituted an educated elite among a much larger number of illiterate former slaves. As in colonial Saint Domingue, where the *gens de couleur* and black slaves hated each other, racial antagonism persisted between the elite and the black peasantry of Haiti.

Haiti's emergence as a "segmented" or "plural" society, with "different sections of the community living side by side, but separately, within the same political unit," was marked by a range of differences clearly separating the elite from the peasant masses.[5] American scholar James G. Leyburn, in his incisive study *The Haitian People* (1941), went so far as to describe the division between the elite and the masses as a "caste" system. While the term "caste" is probably not warranted since the elite are not strictly endogamous and Haiti has moved historically in the direction of homogenization, the use of the term by a scholar of Leyburn's stature testifies to the sharpness of the cleavage in Haitian society.[6] The key to segmentation was the retention of the previously dominant white French cultural orientation by the elite, including even white somatic norms which were all the more awkward since the elite included the whole range of skin pigmentation from white to black. While not an exclusive factor, lightness of skin pigmentation was a desired attribute among the elite, especially in marriage partners, and served as a physical criterion which distinguished the elite, which were largely mulatto, from the peasant masses, who were predominantly black.

The separation of the elite from the masses was defined and maintained by a whole series of contingent, interrelated distinguishing characteristics including language, education, religion, and life style. Basically, the elite, comprising about 3 percent of the population, looked to Europe and especially France for inspiration and disavowed all African and black associations, while the masses were involved in a unique acculturation of African and European heritages. Unlike the neighboring Dominican Republic and Puerto Rico, where language, religion, and elements of African culture were shared by the whole society regardless of color and class, Haiti was divided into two distinct segments. There were two languages, the official French used by the literate elite and Haitian Creole, a distinct language of obscure origins, based largely on Norman French, spoken by the masses. Until recently no effort was made to transcribe Haitian Creole into writing. Literacy, involving the French language, and formal education were the special preserves of the elite, which dominated urban, commercial, and governmental functions irrespective of the frequent political and military ascendancy of black peasant strongmen. The elite, emulating sophisticated European society, cultivated poetry, literature, and the learned professions, while disdaining any form of manual labor. Haiti became known as the land of poets. For a member of the elite to work with his hands was anathema. The masses subsisted by means of manual labor and were essentially rural in their life style as opposed to the urbanity of the elite.

Differences in religion epitomized the distance between the elite and the masses. The elite were practicing Catholics and maintained the Catholic church establishment, which was serviced by imported white French priests and teachers. The peasant masses practiced the folk religion *vodoun*, also known as vodun and voodoo. According to a popular anecdote, 90 percent of Haitians are Catholic and 100 percent are believers in vodoun. Vodoun is a fluid agglomeration of African and Catholic elements which has no organized priesthood, permanent church buildings, or documented liturgy. It was pervasive in the Haitian countryside despite the nominal allegiance that most Haitians had to the Catholic church, and, because of its African and black derivation, was considered (overtly at least) repulsive and vulgar by the elite. Vodoun has served historically as a bulwark of Haitian folk culture and as a rallying point for mass political action and resistance against foreign domination. In colonial Saint Domingue, vodoun was the medium by which slaves maintained their common identity and conspiratorial liaisons. Macandal, the precursor of Toussaint and Dessalines whose 1758 uprising was thwarted, achieved influence as a prophet and sorcerer who then conceived and organized a plan to poison all the whites. After his death at the hands of the French, Macandal lived on mystically as a vodoun Papa-Loa. Vodoun played a vital part in generating fervor and establishing communications between blacks during the war of independence. Haitian scholar Jean Price-Mars has stated that "1804 est issu du Vodou."[7] During the war for independence and again during the guerrilla war against United States Marines in 1919, Haitian soldiers, often conspicuous for their bravery, went into battle wearing vodoun charms which were thought to ward off enemy bullets. The white French clergy and later the American marines, realizing the importance of vodoun in the impervious resistance of the masses to foreign encroachments, tried unsuccessfully to prevent ceremonies and outlaw vodoun.

Because of cultural pluralism, the American occupation would cause a tremendous crisis in Haitian society, especially for the elite. In 1915 the elite still retained their European orientation and took pride in impressive emulation of refined white Western culture, while simultaneously scorning peasant Africanisms. Contact with white American marines, who treated all Haitians as "Negroes" or "niggers" according to American usage of the terms, making no categorical distinction between blacks and mulattoes or between educated and illiterate Haitians, came as quite a shock to the elite. In reaction to the occupation many elite, especially young intellectuals of the *génération de l'occupation,* renounced the former white French orientation and turned instead to the black African heritage embodied in the culture of the masses. The new black ethnic awareness, eventually culminating in the international phenomenon of *négritude,* has been a continuing factor in Haitian political and cultural life. Haitian president François Duvalier wrote articles on Haitian ethnology as a young man during the occupation and later emerged as a champion of black nationalism. Duvalier's adroit use of vodoun as a political force has been credited with having bridged the long-standing gap between the government and the masses. The segmentation of Haitian society, which has been the dynamic factor in so many of these events, was based upon the racial and cultural heritage left over from the French colonial experience.

The great wealth of colonial Saint Domingue was largely destroyed during the protracted war for independence. What remained gradually deteriorated through years of neglect under independent Haitian rule. Abandoned plantations and sugar mills crumbled to ruin. French roads, aqueducts, and irrigation systems fell into disuse. Large-scale agriculture, which had been the basis of colonial production, was replaced by independent subsistence farming. The great plantations were broken up into small plots and farmed by former slaves who became passionately attached to their individual holdings and were correspondingly unenthusiastic about working for wages.[8] Peasants, especially in the mountains, used their sometimes minute holdings to raise a wide variety of vegetables and fruits which were largely consumed within the household. Whatever surplus remained after home consumption was taken to market by the women, who, after the West African pattern, played the leading role in a complicated marketing system that featured punctual rotation of trading centers, an elaborate system of wholesale and retail commerce, and intense competition and pride in trading skills.[9] Agricultural production resembled West African practices, notably with respect to cooperative field work for heavy tasks such as cultivation and clearing land, but European tools and techniques were also employed. Peasants continued to pick coffee beans from bushes planted by the French, but cultivation was limited and most of the coffee crop was picked wild. Sugar and indigo production ceased.

Independent Haiti was generally isolated from the outside world. The country had no foreign sponsors or allies. Fear of French invasion and repossession dominated Haitian politics during the early nineteenth century, and a series of fortresses were built to repel the French. The most spectacular of these was the famous Citadel of Henry Christophe, one of the architectural wonders of the Caribbean, which has walls up to 30 feet thick and 270 feet high. All the costly military preparations proved unnecessary as the expected invasion failed to materialize, and Haitian rulers shifted their energies to civil wars and periodic incursions into neighboring Santo Domingo. The threat of French military invasion was finally laid to rest with the signing of an agreement between Haiti and Charles

X of France in 1824. France recognized Haitian independence in return for the granting of extensive commercial concessions and payment of a 150-million-franc indemnity to compensate former colonists. The indemnity was eventually adjusted to a more reasonable sum and was refunded by a series of loans, but indebtedness to France continued to shackle the fiscal operations of Haitian governments. The initial indemnity, extracted as the price of independence from France, was the basis of perennial financial crises in Haiti for the next century.

From the outset, independent Haiti found itself in difficult circumstances. Unlike the United States, which emerged from its war for independence with stable political institutions, a fundamentally sound economy, and with an immediate colonial history of quasi independence during which the requisites of national unity and viability had been firmly established, independent Haiti enjoyed almost no advantages and was faced with myriad obstacles. Not only had the Haitian war for independence resulted in widespread death and near total physical devastation, but the departure of French colonists left Haiti without trained administrators and skilled craftsmen.

Leadership of the northern half of the new nation devolved upon black military strongmen who lacked experience in political administration, while in the south mulattoes replaced the French colonists as the dominant political force. In effect, the death and expulsion of the white colonials eliminated the entire governing class and left a largely uneducated slave population, which had been deliberately held in the most menial and brutal servitude, to fend for itself. The small, educated elite dominated urban and administrative functions.

The legacy of French colonialism included a tradition of hostility to political authority, a tendency toward corruption and immorality in public and private life, the example of ostentatious display of wealth, and a notorious lack of concern for sanitation and cleanliness in colonial urban centers. Moral decadence in white colonial social and political life, plus frequent scandals in the Catholic church establishment and the colonial inclination to revolt against the authority of the mother country, established a heritage of political instability and corruption that survived the war for independence. Evidence of similar characteristics in independent Haiti were cited by European and American observers as indications of Haitian racial inferiority. The colonial system of racial discrimination served as the basis for mulatto-black rivalry and social stratification that figured prominently in subsequent civil wars and periods of political turmoil.

Haiti faced additional disadvantages and obstacles in foreign commerce and international diplomacy. Commercial ties with France and Europe were broken during the war for independence. Haitian export trade, which had been based on the large-scale plantation agriculture of the colonial period, was destroyed. The heavy indebtedness to France was an overwhelming burden for a new nation that was barely viable in any case, and served to drain off any surplus revenues. In international relations Haiti faced a hostile world which disparaged Haitians as Negroes and former slaves, and feared the example of the Haitian slave revolt. For their part, Haitians were extremely jealous of their independence and refused to allow foreigners to reestablish the old plantation economy. From the beginning, foreigners were forbidden to own land in Haiti. The Haitian economy remained stagnant, while the population multiplied.

Haitian internal politics lacked cohesiveness and direction. While the democratic and egalitarian ideology of the French Revolution was officially adopted by the infant nation, the ideals were never translated into reality. The Constitution of 1806 established legislative, executive, and judicial branches of a government styled the Republic of Haiti. This basic form of government was retained thereafter, except for one instance in the mid-nineteenth century when President Faustin Soulouque proclaimed himself emperor. The slogan *Liberté–Egalité–Fraternité*, taken from the French Revolution, appeared on Haitian government proclamations up to and including the time of the American occupation. In reality Haitian politics were dominated by the numerically small elite, and by a succession of military strongmen who controlled the presidency.

The series of strongmen who ruled the country after independence were usually preoccupied with maintaining themselves in power by beating off numerous rivals. During the early period several presidents, most notably Jean Pierre Boyer (1818–43), held office for prolonged periods and achieved a measure of political stability. Thereafter, however, governments were increasingly unstable and fell easily to revolutionary movements. In the period from the founding of the Republic in 1806 to the American intervention in 1915, seventeen of twenty-four presidents were overthrown by revolution. Only two of the twenty-four retired peacefully at the ends of their terms, and eleven served for less than one year each.

Haiti figured prominently in United States foreign policy and internal sectional conflicts, and in fitful attempts to resolve the American race problem. The attitude of the United States toward Haiti during Haiti's struggle for separation from France and early years of independence was heavily influenced by the revulsion and fear with which Southern Americans viewed the specter of a successful slave revolt. Despite the misgivings of Southern planters, President John Adams gave decisive naval aid to Toussaint Louverture during Toussaint's civil war against Haitian mulattoes in 1800. Adams's policy was determined not by sympathy for the Haitian slave revolt but by the circumstances of America's quasi war with France and efforts to maintain American neutral rights during the War of the Second Coalition. United States Marines participated in the naval engagements which ensured the defeat of Toussaint's mulatto rival, foreshadowing a prolonged series of future involvements in Haitian affairs. While American intervention in 1800 helped to establish the independence of Toussaint, the United States neither recognized this independence nor supported it. The reestablishment of peace between the United States and France in 1800 caused American relations with Toussaint to cool.

American interest in the fate of the Haitian slave revolt increased sharply with Napoleon's dispatch of a 30,000-man French army of reconquest under General Leclerc in 1801. As President Thomas Jefferson knew, this army was to proceed to Louisiana after it had regained Saint Domingue. Napoleon's attempt to establish a western empire based on Spain's cession of Louisiana to France in 1800, was, of course, a grave threat to the United States. Success of the French venture depended upon the speedy recovery of Saint Domingue, which would again become the French stronghold in the New World. Toussaint Louverture, despite the continued hostility of Southern planters, became America's first line of defense. Toussaint himself was captured and died in a French prison, but Leclerc's army eventually succumbed to yellow fever and defeat in battle. The defeat of French troops in Saint Domingue, coupled with French difficulties in Europe, caused Napoleon to abandon his effort to establish a New World empire. In 1803 France sold Louisiana to the United States. The success of the Haitian slave revolt was a critical factor in Napoleon's decision to sell Louisiana, and thus figured as an important event in American history.[10]

The question of what attitude the United States should assume toward newly independent Haiti was the subject of a bitter political contest between New England traders and Southern planters. New England merchants, concerned with selling fish and buying molasses, were the Americans most directly involved with colonial Saint Domingue and independent Haiti. New England interests argued for the recognition of Haiti and the establishment of diplomatic relations and commercial ties. Southern planters, appalled by the example of a successful slave revolt, sought to use American diplomatic pressure to quarantine Haiti. The Southern view prevailed, despite continuing agitation by New England interests, until the Civil War. Abolitionists, led in the House of Representatives by John Quincy Adams, used the issue of Haitian recognition as one of their devices for keeping constant pressure on the South in House debates.

Southern spokesmen reacted to the agitation for recognition by pointing to Haiti as a dangerous threat to internal order in the United States. Senator Robert Y. Hayne of South Carolina stated in 1825: "Our policy with regard to Hayti is plain. We never can acknowledge her independence . . . which the peace and safety of a large portion of our Union forbids us to even discuss."

In a similar vein, Senator Thomas Hart Benton argued that the honoring of Haiti by recognition and the acceptance of black ambassadors and consuls would appear to be a reward for the murder of masters and mistresses by black slaves.[11] The specter of a successful slave revolt was raised again and again by Southern planters and, despite an effective alliance of Northern merchants and abolitionists, diplomatic recognition of Haiti was never a serious possibility so long as the South remained in the Union.

The United States was the only major maritime power to persist in ostracizing Haiti, although other nations were slow in establishing full-scale diplomatic representation. France recognized Haiti almost a quarter century before officially abolishing slavery in French colonies, and Britain established relations shortly after the Emancipation Act of 1833. The United States continued to trade with Haiti but persisted in denying formal recognition. The Haitian government retaliated by imposing a discriminatory 10 percent surcharge on duties payable by American vessels entering Haitian ports.

American refusal to accord recognition to Haiti was based upon American postures regarding the institution of slavery and the status of free blacks. The same considerations led to attempts by Americans to use Haiti as a site for colonization of former slaves. Since freedmen were considered unassimilable in the United States because of white racial prejudices, some Americans, notably Thomas Jefferson, argued that they should be encouraged to emigrate. The American Colonization Society, founded in 1817, made a significant effort in this direction by dispatching free blacks to Liberia. Haiti was a logical alternative to Africa as a site for colonization, especially since the Haitian government at various times actively sought to encourage the immigration of American freedmen. During the 1820s, 13,000 black Americans emigrated to Haiti, but the experiment failed as the emigrants discovered that Haiti, with its exploitive, exclusive elite and xenophobic peasantry, offered few advantages over the United States. Many of the emigrants returned to the United States, and plans for further colonization were dropped. A second major effort at colonization in Haiti was undertaken in the 1860s by the Lincoln administration. President Lincoln, a longtime advocate of colonization, agreed to a contract committing the United States government to pay $50 per person to an American concessionaire for settling up to 50,000 freedmen in Haiti. Five hundred freedmen sailed from Fortress Monroe in 1863 and settled on Ile à Vache off the southern coast of Haiti, but the venture turned into a fiasco because of mismanagement and unscrupulous attempts to exploit the emigrants by the American concessionaire. A special agent sent by the Lincoln administration to investigate rumors of maltreatment discovered grossly inadequate provisions for food and shelter, but an ample supply of stocks, leg chains, and handcuffs.

Those freedmen who survived were rescued by a United States Army transport and returned to America. After the Ile à Vache debacle, the Haitian government lost interest in colonization schemes, and American policy shifted to retention and assimilation of blacks.

With hostile Southern planters absent by virtue of secession, the United States finally granted diplomatic recognition to Haiti, along with Liberia, in 1862. The North proceeded to use Haiti to advantage during the Civil War, establishing a coaling station at Cap Haïtien and procuring special privileges in Haitian ports. Despite Haiti's technical neutrality, Union warships were allowed to use Haitian ports as bases for operations against Confederate raiders and blockade runners.

While racism had been the most important factor in United States Haitian policy, the strategic importance of the West Indies, and of Haiti, became manifestly apparent during the Civil War, especially given the attempts by France, Britain, and Spain to capitalize on temporary American weakness by intervening in Mexico and the Dominican Republic. Actually, the United States had been interested in obtaining a West Indian naval base as early as 1849. In the years following the Civil War a number of attempts were made to secure a base at Samaná Bay in the Dominican Republic. In 1868 President Andrew Johnson proposed the annexation of both Haiti and the Dominican Republic, and the following year President Ulysses Grant signed an agreement calling for the annexation of the Dominican Republic, but Grant's treaty was rejected by the Senate. While American efforts to procure a Caribbean naval base in the late 1860s had focused mainly on Samaná Bay, the Haitian harbor at Môle-Saint-Nicolas also came up for consideration. In 1869 Grant ordered a naval officer to survey the Môle as a possible site for an American base, and the resulting report was favorable. Môle-Saint-Nicolas had a deep and well-protected harbor, and in the eighteenth century had been known as the Gibraltar of the Caribbean. Despite its many advantages, both Johnson and Grant administrations declined repeated offers by Haitian revolutionaries to cede the Môle to the United States in return for assistance in Haiti's civil wars of 1866–69. Instead, American policy was directed toward keeping clear of Haiti's myriad internal problems while simultaneously making sure that neither Britain nor France procured the Môle.

In the late 1880s, after a twenty-year lapse, American interest in a Haitian base was revived by proponents of American "big navy" sea power. Secretary of State James G. Blaine, a strong advocate of commercial expansion and the development of an American merchant marine, made a vigorous attempt to obtain lease of Môle-Saint-Nicolas as a naval base. During the years 1889–91, Blaine engaged in a number of intrigues with Haitian revolutionaries and maintained constant pressure on the Haitian government to cede the Môle to the United States. Despite Blaine's elaborate plans, which at one point contemplated a display of American naval forces holding target practice in Port-au-Prince Bay while the Haitian Cabinet deliberated, the Haitian government adamantly refused to bow to American threats. Blaine failed to take the Môle because he was unwilling to use force and because his unsavory diplomatic intrigues in Haiti were hampered by the presence of Frederick Douglass as American minister to Haiti.

With increasing emphasis on American naval expansion in the 1890s and the subsequent building of the Panama Canal, the United States retained a strong interest in Môle-Saint-Nicolas and in the strategic importance of Haiti. In 1897 Captain Alfred Thayer Mahan, mastermind of American sea power, surveyed the Caribbean and pointed to the strategic importance of the Windward Passage, but selected Guantánamo Bay, Cuba, rather than the Môle, as the most desirable site for a navy base. While the United States did not establish a resident military presence in Haiti prior to 1915, American warships were active in Haitian waters throughout the late nineteenth and early twentieth centuries. Navy ships visited Haitian ports to "protect American lives and property" in 1857, 1859, 1868, 1869, 1876, 1888, 1889, 1892, 1902, 1903, 1904, 1905, 1906, 1907, 1908, 1909, 1911, 1912, and 1913.[12] Despite the establishment of diplomatic relations, the American attitude toward Haiti was not cordial. In 1888 Assistant Secretary of State Alvey A. Adee referred to Haiti as "a public nuisance at our doors."[13] Disdain and concern over Haiti's strategic position in the Caribbean were the main features of United States policy in the late nineteenth and early twentieth centuries. These tendencies culminated in the 1915 intervention.

Both principal spheres of United States foreign expansion, the Caribbean and the Pacific, were hotly contested by other powers. The intense rivalry characteristic of modern imperialism applied especially to the Pacific and the Caribbean, which, as marginal areas, were among the last places open to incursions by foreign powers in the late nineteenth century. The United States clashed with European rivals, especially Germany, which paralleled the United States as a late entry in the scramble for imperial power and prestige, in Samoa in 1889 and in the Caribbean throughout the several decades preceding World War I. In Haiti the contest for domination involved the United States, France, and Germany.

The French had retained a strong influence in Haiti. The 1824 Franco-Haitian agreement, whereby France recognized Haitian independence in return for payment of a large indemnity, placed France in a dominant position in Haitian commerce and finance. The 1824 indemnity was refunded by French loans in 1875, 1896, and 1910, with Haiti maintaining a remarkable record of payment of this burdensome debt, never defaulting until after the American intervention in 1915. Haiti's diligence in meeting debt payments despite a weak economy, frequent revolutions, and the example of numerous instances of default by other Latin-American countries may be attributed to its continuing fear of foreign intervention. Haiti's foreign debt, held mainly by French bondholders, amounted to about $21.5 million in 1915.[14]

The 1824 Franco-Haitian agreement had provided for generous commercial privileges in addition to the indemnification. French merchants enjoyed a 50 percent preferential reduction in Haitian duties. French commercial privileges in Haiti were deeply resented by the United States, which was trying to establish the most-favored-nation principle as the basis of foreign trade in Latin America. The special French position in Haitian commerce continued until the various privileges were rescinded during the American occupation. Under the 1907 Franco-Haitian commercial convention Haiti granted France special tariff preferences, while receiving in return only most-favored-nation treatment.[15] French advantages in

Haitian finance and commerce were augmented by French owner-ship and control of the Banque Nationale, chartered in 1880, which became the country's leading commercial bank and also served as the government treasury.

Haiti was also dependent upon France as a market for the lead-ing Haitian export commodity, coffee. Haitian coffee, which had a distinct aroma, strength, and smoothness, was especially appreciated in France. The Haitians, for their part, preferred French over American tobacco. In the years immediately preceding the American intervention roughly half of Haiti's total exports went to France, while French products accounted for only about 10 percent of Haitian imports. In the years 1911 to 1913 Haitian exports to France amounted to $21 million for the three years, as against $2.2 million of imports from France.[16] Haiti's heavy dependence on the French market and the relatively inconsequential amount of French sales in Haiti gave France a strong bargaining advantage in procuring preferential commercial privileges.

Insofar as European civilization prevailed in Haiti, French cul-tural influence was predominant. French was the official language of the country and was used with care and precision by the elite. Correct French was a mark of education and status which separated the user from the vast majority of the population. Haitian Creole, spoken by the masses, was based largely on Norman French vocabu-lary and syntax. The elite followed French fashions and sent their children to France for education. Haitian literature, up to the time of the American intervention, followed styles set by French writers of preceding generations. The Haitian Catholic church, after a con-cordat with the Papacy in the 1860s, was staffed by French priests who also served as educators and missionaries. Up to the time of the American occupation, educated Haitians prided themselves on their French culture and repudiated African associations.

The Haitian elite shared French inclinations toward official pomp, conversation, and politics. Members of the elite took an active inter-est in politics and aspired to high political office irrespective of their vocational backgrounds. Haitian political institutions were modeled after those of France, and Haitians looked to the French Revolution as the birthplace of Haitian liberty. One prominent Haitian stated that France was the mother country of the black race, because the first time that a man of the black race was ever a citizen, he was a French citizen; the first time that a man of our race was ever an officer, he was a French officer. And our national birthright, where is it found? Was it not in France, in the Declaration of the Rights of Man? [17]

While Haiti remained sensitive to any threat of French encroachment on Haitian independence, France held a special place of affection for the Haitian elite, which ignored and suppressed their own historical identification with the horrors of slavery in colonial Saint Domingue. Indeed, the elite sought to achieve international respect for Haiti and the Negroid race by successfully emulating French culture.

The French were firmly established by virtue of strong historical ties, but after 1900 German merchants became increasingly important in Haitian internal commerce. Germany, as a nascent and aggressive imperial power, was considered by the United States as its chief rival in the Caribbean. German entrepreneurs come to Haiti and established themselves as traders and wholesale merchants. The Germans married Haitian women in order to circumvent the Haitian prohibition against alien landownership and founded resident German colonies in Port-au-Prince and several other Haitian cities. As was the case with the few resident Frenchmen, the Germans intermingled socially with the Haitian elite. This racial and cultural fraternization gave the Germans a strong advantage over potential American commercial competition. Haitians were generally received into German and French society, while contacts with Americans, especially painful when Haitians visited the United States, were blighted by racial prejudice and Jim Crow social barriers.

By intermarrying the Germans created a progeny of Germano-Haitians that ensured a continuing tie with the fatherland. In 1912 a German school, supported by funds from the Imperial Foreign Office, was established in Port-au-Prince. According to a speech made by the German minister at the school opening, the intent was to "Germanize the descendants of Germans established in Haiti," and to inculcate attachment to the emperor.[18] Children of Germano-Haitian parents were sent back to Germany for their education. By

1915 there were 210 Germans and Germano-Haitians in Haiti, and many German business houses and private residences.[19]

The Germans in Haiti engaged mainly in wholesale merchandising, but branched out into finance and public utilities. In 1914 a State Department officer estimated that Germans controlled 80 percent of the commercial business in Haiti.[20] Germans also controlled the public utilities in Port-au-Prince and Cap Haïtien, along with the only wharf at Port-au-Prince. The Hamburg-American Line dominated shipping to and from Haiti. About two-thirds of coffee exports were carried away in German ships.[21]

After 1908 German merchants became active in financing Haiti's increasingly frequent revolutions.[22] Loans were apparently made both from local German resources and from Berlin.[23] Germans would float loans at high prices to presidential candidates forming armies in the north, and then be repaid handsomely after each successful revolutionary campaign. Germans also made loans, again at high rates of interest, to incumbent Haitian governments which found themselves in desperate financial straits.[24] Involvement in financing various political factions in Haiti was apparently motivated by the lucrative profits obtainable to individual German merchants, rather than by machinations of the Imperial Foreign Office. In any case, the growing frequency of revolutions and obvious German complicity increased the apprehensions of the State Department and opened the way for American military intervention, which was anathema to German interests.

American commercial interest in Haiti quickened at the same time that the Germans were stepping up their activities. Few Americans lived in Haiti and, except for the fascination of some Haitians with American efficiency, technical expertise, and commercial initiative, cultural contacts were negligible. American exports to Haiti in 1890 totaled $5.3 million, while Haitian exports to the United States amounted to only $2.4 million. Although American products accounted for more than one-third of Haiti's total imports, they constituted only $\frac{4}{10}$ of 1 percent of total American exports.[25] American trade was actively sponsored and furthered by the State Department, which, between 1865 and 1890, had negotiated the elimination of discriminatory trading conditions for American commerce. The increasing interest and attainment of more favorable trading conditions did not materially increase American trade and by 1890 the American advantage based on proximity was being challenged effectively by enterprising Germans. The State Department, responding to the new competition and also seeking to compensate for the decline of American merchant shipping in the Haitian trade, attempted to further American interests by obtaining exclusive competitive advantages for American products. The Haitian government refused to lower its duties on American imports, and the United States, in 1892, imposed retaliatory tariffs on Haitian goods. Haitian imports to the United States fell drastically, but the attempt to create an exclusive market for American products by pressuring the Haitians into granting preferential concessions failed.

A more successful approach was undertaken by the McKinley administration, which appointed William F. Powell as minister to Haiti. Powell encouraged American manufacturers to adapt their products to the Haitian market and grant more liberal credit terms. American imports, which had consisted of codfish and other staple foodstuffs, were expanded and diversified through salesmanship to include a variety of manufactured goods. The value of American imports depended upon fluctuations of the Haitian economy, but by 1910 the United States had cornered about 60 percent of the Haitian import market. In 1913, the last year before the disruption of Haitian commerce by World War I, American imports amounted to $5.9 million out of $8.1 million total imports, while Haitian exports to the United States were $1 million out of $11.3 million total exports.[26]

The first significant American investments in Haiti were in concessions to build railroads. An 1876 concession resulted in an American construction effort that floundered before it got beyond the city limits of Port-au-Prince. The concession was eventually taken over by German interests, who used it to extort half a million dollars from the Haitian government in 1901.[27] A second effort by Americans finally resulted in the construction of the 40-mile Plaine du Cul-de-Sac (P.C.S.) Railroad in 1904. The P.C.S. Railroad was subsequently taken over by German interests.

In 1904 the Haitian government granted another railroad concession to a Haitian national who promptly sold his rights to two Americans for $50 cash and $62,500 in stock.[28] The Americans persuaded the Haitian government to extend their concession to include the development of a comprehensive network linking major ports with the interior, but nothing came of the new project until it was taken over by American entrepreneur James P. McDonald. Through bribery that was rumored to have included the gift of a string of fake pearls to the daughter of Haitian President Antoine Simon, McDonald obtained a renewal and expansion of the earlier concession. Although McDonald himself was chiefly interested in developing fig-banana plantations and never achieved any real results, his railroad concession became the basis of future construction work and expensive claims against the Haitian government by American investors. The concession, dated April, 1910, called for the Haitian government to guarantee, upon failure of the railroad company to meet its expenses, 6 percent interest and 1 percent amortization on National Railway of Haiti bonds, which were to be issued at the rate of up to $33,000 per mile of track constructed.[29] The concession also granted McDonald 12 miles of land on either side of the track on which to grow fig bananas, for which he was given an export monopoly, but McDonald failed to develop any land and the Haitian government foreclosed that part of the contract dealing with fig bananas, thus depriving the railroad of its most promising revenue possibilities.[30]

The frivolous character of the entire venture changed sharply when McDonald's railroad concession was taken over in 1911 by a formidable New York syndicate headed by W. R. Grace and Company with participation by two Wall Street firms, National City Bank and Speyer and Company. Speyer and National City Bank had been involved in Haitian railroads since 1909, when, at the suggestion of a large German mercantile house in Port-au-Prince, the two firms bought $800,000 par value of P.C.S. Railroad bonds.[31] W. R. Grace and Company sold $870,000 of the new National Railway bonds in France and advanced $2 million as part of its underwriting obligation, borrowing $500,000 of this from National City Bank.[32] The list of stockholders in the National Railway included W. R. Grace and Company, National City Bank, Speyer and Company, the Ethelberga Syndicate of London, Vice-President Samuel

McRoberts of National City Bank, and Frank A. Vanderlip, president of National City Bank.[33]

Construction work on the new National Railway began in 1911 and continued, with interruptions, until the Haitian government refused to make further payments to the railroad in 1914. The government claimed that it had contracted for a complete railroad connecting Port-au-Prince with the northern city of Cap Haïtien, while the company had built only three disconnected sections totaling 108 miles. A gap of 40 miles between Saint Marc and Gonaïves and another gap of 30 miles over the mountains between Cap Haïtien and Ennery made through traffic impossible and necessitated the maintenance of three separate sets of rolling stock. The railroad, represented by National City Bank, claimed that it had been prevented from fulfilling the contract by frequent revolutions. The railroad claimed costs of the full $33,000 per mile constructed, although the sections actually completed ran through level country and the sections left out were those that would have gone over mountains. Moreover, the work was badly done and the main station at Port-au-Prince was located two miles out of town in a swamp.[34] Claims against the government for this railroad, which were eventually paid in full during the American occupation, were a continuing source of grief to Haiti. The most important immediate effect of the National Railway venture was to draw powerful American banking interests into participation in Haitian internal finances.

An even more important sphere of American economic penetration was in banking. Haitian scholar Leslie F. Manigat has argued convincingly that the United States achieved preponderance in Haiti by defeating French and German interests in the 1910 struggle for control of the Banque Nationale.[35] In 1905, following the discovery of extensive frauds, the Haitian government had suspended the government treasury service operated by the French-owned Banque. In November, 1909, Speyer and Company and National City Bank sent a representative to Haiti in an attempt to secure control of the Banque, but the American firms were outmaneuvered by German interests, represented by the German ambassador in Paris and the German minister in Port-au-Prince, which were trying to reorganize the Banque and float a new loan to the Haitian government.[36] The German interests, cooperating with the French directors of the existing Banque, procured a contract for reorganization of the Banque and flotation of a 65 million franc loan. The bonds were taken by the Franco-German interests at 72.3 percent, while National City Bank later claimed that it had offered 80 percent but had been turned down because of failure to include graft.[37] The contract for the reorganized Banque Nationale provided that the Banque would have sole right of note issue and would serve as the government treasury, charging 1 percent on money received and 0.5 percent on money disbursed. The Banque also retained 10 million francs of the loan as a reserve fund to redeem paper currency.[38]

The State Department, objecting to "plainly unconscionable" exploitation of the Haitian government and to the absence of American participation, refused to sanction the contract.[39] In response to State Department objections, the Franco-German interests agreed to 50 percent American participation and control in the new Banque, including National City Bank and Speyer and Company with 10 percent each. Amendments were made in the contract to remove some of the provisions objected to by the State Department, notably the clause providing for Banque collection of Haitian customs duties. In an agreement signed in January, 1911, the American bankers assured the State Department that they would retain at least 50 percent control of the Banque and would also attempt to bring to Haiti the benefits of American enterprise and capital.[40] On the basis of this agreement, Secretary of State Philander Knox consented to drop the department's objections to the contract but did not waive his reservations about the fairness of the contract terms. In future years the State Department would, of course, be called upon to back the American interests in their conflicts with the Haitian government, even though Article XXIII of the 1910 contract prohibited diplomatic intervention.

The initiative for procuring American participation in the 1910 contract was exercised concurrently by the State Department, by the American bankers, and by the Franco-German interests which hesitated to close a deal without State Department approval. The American bankers, who had sought to gain control of the Banque

Nationale, expressed primary concern over their railroad interests. Frank A. Vanderlip, president of National City Bank, wrote Secretary Knox:

A fact that determined us to take this participation [in the 1910 Banque contract] more largely than any prospective profits was the desire to have the loan matters out of the way, so we could go on with the building of the National Railroad of Haiti, our negotiations in that direction being interfered with by the pending negotiations in regard to the loan and the establishment of the bank.

Vanderlip had personal investments in a Haitian mining syndicate as well as in Haitian railroads.[41] The State Department demanded American participation in the Banque Nationale as a means of preventing exclusive Franco-German control but persisted in dilatory tactics after American participation had been ensured in hopes of ameliorating the contract in Haiti's favor.[42] When challenged by the department, the American bankers vigorously denied having had any knowledge of the extensive payments of bribes to Haitian government officials that took place in early 1911 after the contract had been closed, claiming that French interests had handled all negotiations.[43] In sum, the 1910 contract involved compromises by the department, the American bankers, and the Franco-German interests, but American interests, backed by the full commitment of the State Department, emerged in control of the Banque. After 1911 American personnel replaced Frenchmen in the management and direction of the Banque.

Because of the high flotation discount, the Haitian government realized only 47 million francs from the 65 million franc loan. Of the 47 million francs, the Banque Nationale retained 10 million francs as cash reserve for redemption of paper currency to be accomplished at some undetermined future date. The contract made the Banque sole depository for all government receipts and also granted the Banque control over the service of Haiti's external debt to French bondholders. According to the contract, the Banque held government receipts until the end of each fiscal year, paid the external debt, and then turned over the remaining funds to the government. Provisions for payment of monthly advances to the government by the Banque provided for by separate annual conventions gave the Banque an added element of control over the government's purse strings; the monthly advances, made at the discretion of the Banque, were necessary to meet government operating expenses.

Much of the rivalry between American, German, and French interests was based on political considerations and expectations of future economic development, rather than on prospects of spectacular short-term profits. Haiti was a poor country, and was insignificant in terms of the overall Latin-American investment market. During the decade preceding 1914 there had been a boom in foreign investments in Latin America, which, unlike previous booms in 1820 and 1860, had included French, German, and United States capital as well as British. The total nominal value of foreign investments in Latin America in 1914 was about $8.5 billion, or about one-fifth of worldwide long-term foreign investments. The Latin-American total of $8.5 billion was broken down as follows: Britain $3.7 billion; United States $1.7 billion; France $1.2 billion; Germany $.9 billion; and others $1.0 billion.[44] Foreign investments in Haiti in 1915 consisted mainly of the $21.5 million owed to French bondholders as a result of the 1875, 1896, and 1910 loans. German and British direct investments were of little consequence. United States investments in Haiti in 1913 amounted to about $4 million as against $800 million in Mexico and $220 million in Cuba. The $4 million invested in Haiti constituted only 0.32 percent of total United States investments in Latin America.[45]

3

The Decision to
Intervene

Revolutions and insurrections in Haiti became more frequent during the late nineteenth century and by 1910 followed well-established patterns. A candidate for the office of president would form a caco * army in the north of Haiti, capture the port of Cap Haïtien, declare himself a legitimate rival of the incumbent president, and march on Port-au-Prince. As the caco army approached Port-au-Prince, plundering as it moved along, the incumbent president often would leave the country with part of the treasury funds. The caco army would then capture Port-au-Prince, surround the legislature, and oversee the election of the insurgent candidate by the Haitian Senate. From 1888 to 1915 no Haitian president served a complete seven-year term and only one died a natural death while in office; the other ten were either killed or overthrown, seven of them during the chaotic period after 1911. The main prize for successful revolutionaries was control of the customhouses, which accounted for all government revenues.

With increasingly frequent revolutions, government administration deteriorated and graft became blatant. Payments on Haiti's foreign debt, which amounted to $21.5 million in 1915, continued to be made, but the payments placed a tremendous strain on Hai-

---

* A "caco" army consisted of part-time military adventurers and conscripts recruited and loosely organized by local military strongmen.

tian government finances. On the eve of the American intervention, 80 percent of government revenues were pledged to debt service.[1] Periodic financial crises forced the government to borrow at exorbitant rates, realizing as little as 59, 56, and 47 percent cash return for internal bonds which the government pledged to redeem at 100 percent plus interest.[2]

Despite the precarious character of Haitian finances and the frequent revolutions, Haiti continued to meet external debt obligations up to the time of American intervention and the coincidental loss of Haiti's coffee market in France as a result of World War I. Indeed, Haiti's record of debt payment was exemplary compared to that of other Latin-American countries: in 1915 Ecuador was $2 million in arrears, Mexico was $15 million in arrears, and Honduras was more than $100 million in arrears.[3] Haiti's desperate efforts to meet foreign debt obligations did not, however, provide the hoped-for guarantee against United States intervention. The degeneration of Haitian finances and politics was of itself cause for concern to the State Department, since weak, impoverished Haitian governments were considered susceptible to manipulation by European financial interests. This possibility of European subversion, rather than the nominal hazard of actual default, was the factor that caused anxiety in Washington. American policy in the Caribbean during the early twentieth century was specifically directed toward averting exactly the type of situation that was developing in Haiti.

Coinciding with the political and financial deterioration in Haiti, United States interest and involvement in the Caribbean area increased dramatically with the construction of the Panama Canal. From 1900 onward, successive administrations in Washington committed the United States to a policy of maintaining political stability in the Caribbean as a means of preventing foreign encroachment that might threaten the developing American military, political, and economic hegemony in the area. In 1905 Secretary of State Elihu Root wrote: "The inevitable effect of our building the Canal must be to require us to police the surrounding premises. In the nature of things, trade and control, and the obligation to keep order which go with them, must come our way." [4]

The Monroe Doctrine, which had declared the United States intention to prohibit further European colonization of independent

Latin-American countries, was no longer adequate to cover the new strategic importance of the area. Even limited, short-term intervention by European powers in the affairs of Latin-American countries would no longer be tolerated.

The impetus for such foreign intervention in Latin America, as in the case of Venezuela in 1902–3, was generally a syndrome of economic exploitation whereby foreign financial interests would float loans at exorbitant rates to an unstable and often corrupt Latin-American government. That Latin-American country would eventually default on its loan payments, and the foreign financial interests would apply to their governments for diplomatic assistance in collecting. If diplomatic pressure and intervention succeeded in forcing a settlement of the debt, the foreign investors would enjoy high-risk rates of return on their loans where there was actually no risk involved at all, thanks to their government's intervention.[5]

The United States, while refusing to permit foreign military intervention in the vicinity of the Panama Canal, continued to recognize the legitimacy of European financial claims on Latin-American countries. Thus the Roosevelt Corollary of 1904 stated that the United States would ensure against European intervention by assuming the burden of policing Latin-American countries which were delinquent in honoring their international debts. President Theodore Roosevelt defined America's new Caribbean policy in his dealings with Cuba, Venezuela, and with the Dominican Republic, where he established an American customs receivership in 1907. This policy of guaranteeing foreign financial investments by American police action served as a precedent for subsequent interventions. The new policy manifested itself in American concern for order and stability in the internal affairs of Caribbean countries, since stable governments were capable of the efficiency and responsibility necessary for the paying off of debts, while unstable, transient governments tended to be irresponsible in paying debts, unresponsive to American diplomatic pressures, and corrupt enough to contract new, exorbitant loans with foreign investors.

Roosevelt's Big Stick policy of intimidating Latin-American countries with the threat of American intervention was given new dimensions by President Taft. Taft and Secretary of State Philander Chase Knox, attempted to remove the sources of European claims by encouraging American financial interests to replace their European counterparts as the creditors of various Caribbean countries. It was hoped that this policy would yield the double advantage of curtailing European influence while simultaneously opening new markets for American capital and commerce. In 1909 Secretary Knox attempted to conclude a treaty with Honduras that would have called for the consolidation and refunding of the Honduran debt by American bankers and the setting up of an American customs receivership. Such an agreement was concluded with Nicaragua in 1911, but only after a pro-American government had been established with the help of a landing of American marines. Within a year it became necessary to station a permanent marine contingent in Nicaragua (it remained until 1925 and returned again from 1927 to 1933) in order to sustain the pro-American government and the customs receivership.

The Taft administration's Haitian policy was similarly oriented toward introducing American financial participation as a means of limiting European influence. The State Department refused to sanction the 1910 Haitian bank concession until 50 percent participation by American bankers had been included and certain exploitive features had been removed from the contract. The department's activities in connection with the 1910 transaction indicated the stabilization of several policy criteria including: a desire to limit the extent of European interests in Haiti; a refusal to permit foreign influence in a Haitian customs receivership; a desire to promote American participation in Haitian finances; and a concern over the viability of Haitian finances, as demonstrated by the department's efforts to secure a contract that would be constructive and therefore less likely to result in a repetition of the loan default-intervention syndrome.

The Taft administration was also becoming increasingly concerned about internal order and stability in Haiti. In 1912 Secretary Knox, speaking pointedly at a banquet given in his honor at Port-au-Prince, said:

At a time when the obligation which my country has assumed as the agent of the interest of all America and of the world in creating a highway for international commerce [the Panama Canal] is about to be realized, we are impressed with the conviction that the fullest success of our work is, to a notable degree, dependent on the peace and stability of our neighbors and on their enjoying the prosperity and material welfare which flow from orderly self-government. A community liable to be torn by internal dissension or checked in its progress by the consequences of nonfulfillment of international obligations is not in a good position to deserve and reap the benefits accruing from enlarged commercial opportunities, such as are certain to come about with the opening of the canal. It may indeed become an obstruction to the general enjoyment of those opportunities.[6]

In emphasizing order and stability the United States of course assumed that the existing political balance favored American interests and that disorder might result in political changes unfavorable to the United States. Concern for peace, stability, and orderly political processes in the Caribbean was a continuing facet of American policy in the early twentieth century. Indeed, by the time the Wilson administration entered office, this concern had become axiomatic, and the terms "order" and "stability" had become cliches. Disorder and instability in the Caribbean were considered threats to United States security in and of themselves, irrespective of immediate European involvement.

The Wilson administration continued the Caribbean policy of seeking to dominate and stabilize the area, and was even more active than preceding administrations in exercising military force and diplomatic pressure to achieve these ends. This was true despite the fact that the Democrats had severely criticized the Republicans for imperialism and that both Woodrow Wilson and Secretary of State William Jennings Bryan tended to be more rhetorically idealistic on foreign policy issues than their blatantly materialistic predecessors had been.

In his 1913 Mobile speech, Wilson, while emphasizing the need for economic expansion, disclaimed government-sponsored economic exploitation and envisioned a policy of dealing with Latin-American countries "upon terms of equality and honor."[7] Bryan had a long record of opposing imperialism and special governmental assistance to privileged financial interests. In the 1900 presidential election campaign, he had said:

Trade cannot be permanently profitable unless it is voluntary. When trade is secured by force, the cost of securing it must be taken out of the profits, and the profits are never large enough to cover the expense. Such a system never would be defended but for the fact that the expense is borne by all the people, while the profits are enjoyed by a few.[8]

In approaching the Caribbean situation as secretary of state thirteen years later, Bryan understood that the principal threat to American control came from European financial involvement, and he sought new tactics with which to attack the problem. He first proposed that the United States refund the foreign debts of Caribbean countries. This plan would have eliminated both European and American financial interests and would have ensured reasonable and manageable terms to participating Latin-American countries. The plan would decrease the need for American military interventions, since interventions were often precipitated by the exploitive machinations of private financial interests. President Wilson rejected this debt-refunding plan as too radical.[9] In 1915 Bryan suggested another plan for freeing Latin-American countries from the problem of financial exploitation and attendant evils: Latin-American governments would issue bonds drawing 4 percent, and deposit them as security with the United States government; the United States would then market its own bonds at 3 percent to cover the Latin-American bonds, with the 1 percent difference creating a sinking fund which would retire the Latin-American bonds. Bryan asserted that "by loaning our credit to these sister republics we would hasten development, and render them a great service without incurring any real risk ourselves, for we need not fear that any of these Governments would default in the payment of such obligations." [10]

It is clear that Bryan would have liked to eliminate both European and private American interests from the Caribbean loan-sharking business, in favor of a nonexploitive governmental system, but his plans were politically and ideologically unacceptable. He reverted to the policy of promoting the interests of private American capital, as his predecessors had done, in an effort to supplant European interests.

The formulation of an adroit Haitian policy by the Wilson administration was impeded by the initial ignorance of both Wilson and Bryan concerning Caribbean affairs.[11] The Secretary of State, who was to be responsible for formulating the details of policy, knew almost nothing about Haiti. In 1912 Bryan summoned John H. Allen, the American manager of the Banque Nationale in Port-au-Prince, to Washington and asked Allen to tell him everything there was to know about Haiti. After Allen had described the country to him, Bryan exclaimed, "Dear me, think of it! Niggers speaking French." [12] Bryan's own ignorance was compounded by the scarcity of knowledgeable Caribbean specialists within the State Department.

Upon taking over the department, Bryan dismissed many incumbent Latin-American agents and replaced them with political appointees.[13] In a 1913 letter to a State Department officer posted to the Dominican Republic, Bryan inquired:

Now that you have arrived and are acquainting yourself with the situation, can you let me know what positions you have at your disposal with which to reward deserving Democrats? . . . You have had enough experience in politics to know how valuable workers are when the campaign is on, and how difficult it is to find suitable rewards for all the deserving.[14]

The personnel situation in Haiti was especially unfortunate on the eve of the intervention because American Minister Arthur Bailly-Blanchard, although a professional diplomat, was neither trusted nor considered competent by either Bryan or State Department Counselor Robert Lansing.[15]

Under these circumstances Bryan was forced to seek competent advice wherever he could find it. Roger L. Farnham was one of the few people available to Bryan who was thoroughly familiar with Haitian affairs. Farnham, who was more than willing to offer his services, was a vice-president of National City Bank of New York City and of Banque Nationale in Haiti, and, after 1913, president of National Railway of Haiti. In spite of Farnham's potential conflict of interests and Bryan's reputed hostility to Wall Street, Bryan leaned heavily on Farnham for both formulation and execution of State Department policy in Haiti.[16] Bryan even followed Farnham's lead on the appointment of some of the personnel sent to Haiti, on one occasion first accepting Farnham's recommendation for a special agent, then weakly complying as Farnham changed his mind and substituted a different man.[17]

Farnham's role as Bryan's man in Haiti was neatly complemented by his position as mentor of the Banque Nationale. While the 1910 Banque reorganization provided for American participation and control, the American role became even more important during the war in Europe, when all questions of routine management were handled by a New York committee chaired by Farnham.[18] After the 1910 Banque contract went into effect, two sources of difficulty developed between the Banque Nationale, represented by Farnham, and successive Haitian governments: (1) the Banque persisted in its efforts to secure a customs receivership and (2) the Banque, which held the concession for the government treasury service and was the sole repository of government funds, attempted to restrict government income and thereby force the government into financial destitution and concomitant default on the French debt. Default on the debt would, in turn, result in further borrowings from German merchants and thus lead to American intervention.

Despite the facts that the provision for customs control had been deleted from the 1910 Banque contract on the insistence of the State Department and that American bankers had assured the department that Haitian customs would not be collected by the Banque, Farnham approached successive Haitian governments trying to induce them to agree to a customs receivership.[19] He threatened the Haitians with American intervention and also offered loans to financially desperate Haitian governments on condition that the United States government be granted customs control. He also offered loans as bait for further railroad concessions.[20] Because Farnham's 1911 efforts to procure a receivership were considerably in advance of those of the State Department, he was forced to play a double game, informing the department that no receivership was in prospect while simultaneously refusing to close a loan until the Haitian government agreed to American customs control.[21] In pressing the Haitian government for a receivership and trying to force the department's hand, Farnham and the New York bankers were opposed by American Minister to Haiti Henry W. Furniss who repeatedly pointed out Farnham's duplicity and was, in turn, denounced to the department by National City Bank as being hostile to American interests.[22] In any case, Farnham's many attempts to negotiate a receivership were foiled by unresponsive Haitian governments, which refused to give up national sovereignty even though Farnham, by pledging financial support, offered survival as bait to a series of ephemeral regimes. Relinquishment of customs, which were the sole source of government revenues, would have meant complete American control of all Haitian government funds from collection through expenditure, since the Banque Nationale already controlled all funds once they were deposited in the treasury service. With the advent of the Wilson administration, Furniss was replaced as minister and Farnham, whom Bryan seems to have trusted completely,* became the leading State Department adviser on Haitian affairs. United States policy was thenceforth directed toward the achievement of a customs receivership, and the State Department proceeded to work in concert with the Banque Nationale.

While Farnham and the State Department attempted to procure a negotiated customs receivership in 1914 and early 1915, the Banque Nationale simultaneously employed a second stratagem designed to force the Haitian government into a receivership—withholding a 10 million franc monetary reform fund.

The 1910 Banque contract and contingent 65 million franc loan included a provision that 10 million francs be set aside and held by the Banque for future monetary reform intended to bolster the Haitian gourde, which had been severely inflated. Before any plan could be put into effect, the gourde made a vigorous recovery, and the contemplated total redemption of paper gourdes was obviated.[23] The Banque refused to agree to several partial redemption plans offered as alternatives by the government, insisting that the new plans would violate the 1910 contract, which called for the complete elimination of government currency and gave exclusive right of note issue to the Banque. In 1914 the Banque and President Michel Oreste executed a redemption scheme in which one-fourth of the 10 million franc monetary fund was used; but the plan failed,

* I have found no indication, either in the Bryan-Wilson correspondence or in the State Department papers, that Bryan had any misgivings about working with Farnham.

and payments were suspended when Oreste was overthrown. The remainder of the 10 million franc fund remained in the hands of the Banque and was used for routine banking purposes, drawing up to 12 percent interest, while the Haitian government received, after a protracted dispute, only 1.5 percent interest.[24] A search made by a Haitian examining magistrate in December, 1914, revealed that only $162,050 of the redemption fund was actually in the Banque's vaults in Port-au-Prince, where there should have been $1 million.[25] The Banque, despite the abandonment and redundancy of plans for monetary reform, refused to allow the government access to the money, claiming that it was a trust fund.

In 1914 the Banque took a decisive step toward the financial strangulation of the Haitian government by defaulting on the *convention budgétaire*, by which the Banque had agreed to advance government funds on a monthly basis instead of holding all government receipts until the end of each fiscal year, as called for by the 1910 Banque contract. The Banque claimed that it was forced to take this step because of the condition of the European money market at the outset of World War I.[26] The Haitian government, left without money for operating expenses, was forced to float internal loans at disastrous rates and to seek financial remedies as best it could. American Minister Madison R. Smith summed up the situation in a report to Bryan:

There is nothing in the loan contract providing for advancements by the bank, and the convention budgétaire has been in the nature of an accommodation extended by the bank. As before stated, the suspension of the convention budgétaire most likely would bring the Government to a condition where it could not operate. It is just this condition that the bank desires, for it is the belief of the bank that the Government when confronted by such a crisis, would be forced to ask the assistance of the United States in adjusting its financial tangle and that an American supervision of the customs would result.[27]

The Banque, claiming *force majeure* as justification for stopping the *convention budgétaire*, refused to consider pleas of *force majeure* from the Haitian government with respect to releasing the redundant monetary reform fund.[28] In spite of the difficulties in the European money market which allegedly prevented the Banque from fulfilling the *convention budgétaire*, the Banque continued to offer a single recourse to the Haitian government—an immediate advance of funds contingent upon government acceptance of a customs receivership.[29]

The Banque engaged in various other schemes, such as blocking non-Banque foreign loans and supporting revolutions, in its efforts to drive the Haitian government into a receivership and bring about United States intervention.[30] Conversely, in its relations with the State Department the Banque depicted itself as being solicitous toward corrupt and irresponsible Haitian governments. In 1915 Farnham informed the State Department that, from 1911 on, "The American interests in the bank have, during this period, rather led their French colleagues in extending assistance." [31]

Farnham's main stratagem in serving as Bryan's adviser on Haitian affairs was to play up Franco-German activities while simultaneously pointing to increasing disorder in Haitian politics.[32] Farnham reported that French and German interests were conniving to take over the Banque Nationale and the National Railway, that American interests were unable to hold out against the French and Germans without State Department assistance, that Germans were dominating Haitian finance and commerce, and that Haitian revolutions were becoming increasingly violent and destructive to American property.[33] Farnham's alarming reports about French and German intrigues, partly corroborated by dispatches from the American legation in Port-au-Prince, created grave anxiety within the department. A 1914 Division of Latin-American Affairs memorandum to Bryan stated that Germans were seeking "almost complete control of the financial and commercial affairs of the island," that Germans were going to set up a coaling station at Môle-Saint-Nicolas under the guise of a general commercial store, that the French had set up a 3,000-ton store of coal in a steel hulk at Port-au-Prince, and that Germans were trying to buy the National Railway.* The assessment

---

* SD 838.00/1667, Stabler to Bryan, May 13, 1914. The extent of German influence and activity in the Caribbean during this period remains a subject of historical controversy. A recent study indicates that contemporary reports of German interest in bidding for canal rights in Nicaragua in 1914 were spurious and were contrived by Nicaragua in order to increase interest in the United States. Robert Freeman Smith, "A Note on the Bryan-Chamorro Treaty and German Interest in a Nicaraguan Canal, 1914," *Caribbean Studies*, IX, No. 1 (April, 1969), 63–66.

of German commercial penetration as being ascendant was largely justified, although German investments were negligible.[34] The specter of German penetration, assiduously overdrawn by Farnham, was compounded by an obverse tendency to demur on the part of American business interests. American investors who expressed interest in Haiti, such as the United Fruit Company, refused to go in unless the United States government took over the country and stopped revolutions.[35] In 1915 Farnham added a final element of stress by threatening Bryan with an exodus of all American interests if the administration failed to intervene.[36]

Bryan was greatly alarmed by Farnham's reports of Franco-German activities and was apparently taken in by even the more implausible stories. In 1915 Bryan reported to Wilson that Farnham had told him some things that could not be put into writing, but that

It seems that the German and French Ministers acted simultaneously—if not together—and there seems to be some sympathetic cooperation between the French and German interests in Haiti. There are some indications that their plans include taking advantage of Môle St. Nicolas.[37]

Since France and Germany were then at war, it seems absurd to reason that they would cooperate in establishing a naval base in Haiti. In any case, Bryan and Wilson were determined that French and especially German interests should not be permitted to take over Haiti.

In response to Farnham's threat to withdraw American business interests, Bryan agreed that the United States must act to protect the Americans against the French and Germans, and requested that the American interests acquire the French shares in the Banque Nationale.[38] Farnham insisted on United States control of Haitian customs, and Bryan acceded, even though the department's efforts to secure a receivership through diplomatic means had failed. In a note to Wilson in April, 1915, Bryan stated:

The American interests are willing to remain there, with a view of purchasing a controlling interest and making the Bank a branch of the American bank—they are willing to do this provided this Government takes the steps necessary to protect them and their idea seems to be that no protection will be sufficient that does not include a control of the Customs House.[39]

Bryan was reluctant to use force to achieve control in Haiti, but felt, at this point, that force was necessary and probably unavoidable. Wilson, commenting on the "sinister appearance" of the Haitian situation, agreed that American interests should be sustained and assisted.[40]

In resisting French and German advances in Haiti, Wilson and Bryan were continuing the established American policy of limiting European interests and insisting on peace, order, and stability in the Caribbean, while simultaneously furthering American economic interests. The broad strategic interests of the United States in the Caribbean, which of course had economic implications, were the primary factors, rather than specific economic interests in Haiti. The major emphasis of the Wilson administration's Haitian policy was on negative interdiction of foreign interests, rather than on positive promotion of American economic imperialism.

American economic interests in Haiti, despite the energetic efforts of Farnham and others, were of limited scope. United States investments in Haiti in 1913 amounted to only $4 million as against $220 million across the Windward Passage in Cuba and $800 million in Mexico. Relative to the overall thrust of United States imperialism in the Caribbean, Haiti was strategically crucial but economically of little consequence. Some Americans thought Haiti had great potential for future economic development because of abundant and cheap labor coupled with what appeared to be fertile land; but no serious investigation had ever been made, and few businessmen were even aware of the country.[41] Those few American entrepreneurs who had attempted to start agricultural projects in Haiti, such as J. P. McDonald of the 1910 fig banana concession, failed miserably. The only significant American economic interests in Haiti were the capital investments in railroads and the Banque. These and previous American capital investments depended on lucrative government concessions rather than on general economic development.

Bryan, while favoring American economic expansion in Haiti, subordinated the promotion of American economic interests when these conflicted with strategic and political goals. In 1915, when the Haitian government offered concessions for economic exploitation as a counterproposal to an American attempt to negotiate a customs receivership, Bryan rejected the concessions, replying:

While we desire to encourage in every proper way American investments in Haiti, we believe that this can be better done by contributing to stability and order than by favoring special concessions to Americans. American capital will gladly avail itself of business opportunities in Haiti when assured of the peace and quiet necessary for profitable production . . . we shall give all legitimate assistance to American investors in Haiti, but we are under obligation just as binding to protect Haiti, as far as our influence goes, from injustice and exploitation at the hands of Americans.[42]

Long-term stability, which was thought to be of crucial importance for strategic reasons, was given precedence over short-term economic exploitation. Stability was also prerequisite to the massive American investments that would be required to develop Haiti into a lucrative economic satellite, as was the case in Cuba. Past experience had shown that exploitive concessions, as opposed to sustained agricultural development, were continuing sources of trouble and contributed to political demoralization and instability.

It is true that the American business interests in Haiti, represented by Farnham, were particularly influential in the formulation of State Department policy and that the business interests received full diplomatic support from the department in their conflicts with the Haitian government, but this does not mean that Bryan and Wilson were acting predominantly in their behalf. Rather, Bryan and Wilson sought to use the American interests as instruments of State Department policy, which remained focused on the restriction of Franco-German influence and the establishment of orderly and stable government amenable to the United States and capable of maintaining political independence against European encroachments. Concurrent American economic penetration in Haiti was an extra benefit, rather than the pivotal consideration in the formulation of policy. Farnham, however, was more than just an instrument of State Department policy. His exploitation of his special position as Bryan's man in Haiti, along with the machinations of the Banque Nationale, constituted the important and perhaps crucial factor that American economic interests played in the Wilson administration's decision to intervene in Haiti.

The main considerations in the decision to intervene in Haiti were strategic and, more specifically, military. With the construction of the Panama Canal and large-scale investment of American capital in Cuba, the maintenance of United States military security demanded control of the Caribbean. Wilson and Bryan both felt that foreign financial control of Caribbean countries would be as dangerous as outright control by foreign governments.[43]

In Haiti, where Wilson and Bryan were led to believe that foreign capitalists were controlling the government, the situation was further complicated by the existence of Môle-Saint-Nicolas as a potential coaling station and naval base.[44] At the outset the Wilson administration wanted the Môle as an American base, as had several previous administrations. In 1913 Bryan suggested and Wilson approved a plan by which the United States would procure the Môle and a strip of land 20 miles long and 10 miles wide extending into the interior, with Haitian residents being given the option of either selling their land to the United States or becoming American citizens if they wished to remain.[45] By this time, however, the Navy Department, which already had an excellent base across the Windward Passage at Guantánamo Bay, Cuba, had come to regard the Môle as obsolete and superfluous for its own purposes, but insisted that no other nation be permitted to acquire it.[46] In 1914 and 1915 the State Department, convinced that the Germans had serious designs on the Môle but itself no longer interested in establishing an American base there, dropped the plan for outright acquisition and sought instead guarantees from the Haitian government that the Môle would not be ceded to any foreign power. The Wilson administration ultimately came to the conclusion that, because of political instability and domination by foreign capitalists, Haitian guarantees were insufficient and that United States intervention was required to eliminate the threat of European encroachment.[47]

The strategic importance of Haiti to the United States lay in its location along the Windward Passage and in the relative weakness of the United States Navy before World War I. In 1903 the American navy ranked sixth in size among the world's navies, and by 1914 had suffered a severe decline in efficiency as a result of prolonged concentration in Mexican waters. The United States had developed a strong position in the Caribbean by building the Panama Canal and establishing a naval base at Guantánamo Bay but, given the weakness of the fleet, the American position was vulnerable. Britain, which possessed a number of Caribbean naval stations, had abandoned the area to the United States and concentrated her fleet against Germany, while France and Germany were preoccupied with activities in their home waters.[48] Nevertheless, any of the three powers could conceivably have challenged the United States in the Caribbean and, in terms of naval strength, have dominated the area. The Wilson administration especially feared the Germans, who would theoretically have been formidable opponents had they been able to procure a Caribbean base and then station their fleet there.

Môle-Saint-Nicolas, Samaná Bay in the Dominican Republic, and the Danish West Indies were considered vulnerable to German seizure because the United States lacked firm control over local politics in each case. The United States had made a series of attempts to secure the three strategic harbors, dating from Secretary of State William H. Seward's designs on Samaná Bay in the 1860s. The Wilson administration took over all three by establishing military occupations in Haiti in 1915, in the Dominican Republic in 1916, and by purchasing the economically worthless Danish West Indies in 1916. The offer to purchase the Danish West Indies was accompanied by threat of American seizure to prevent German control in the event that the Danish government turned down the offer.[49]

Wilson's Secretary of the Navy, Josephus Daniels, and Robert Lansing of the State Department were especially fearful of German activities in the Caribbean. Lansing, first as counselor and after June, 1915, Bryan's successor as secretary of state, was suspicious of National City Bank's machinations in Haiti and did not trust Farnham, who he felt was not liked by the Haitians and had been arrogant toward them.[50] Despite Farnham's falling out of favor with the departure of Bryan, the momentum toward intervention was in no way diminished since Lansing was an ardent Germanophobe in his own right. Discussing German operations in Mexico, Haiti, the Dominican Republic, and elsewhere in Latin America several weeks after taking over as secretary of state, Lansing stated, "Everywhere German agents are plotting and intriguing to accomplish the supreme purpose of their government," and argued for "the prevention by all means in our power of German influence becoming dominant in any nation bordering the Caribbean or near the Panama Canal." [51]

In a 1922 letter to a Senate committee investigating the intervention in Haiti, Lansing stated that the reason for intervention was the imminent threat of Haiti's falling into German hands. [52] He said that the Germans were financing revolutions, dominating local politics, and were about to take over exclusive control of Haitian customs and the Môle-Saint-Nicolas. He also referred to a "mysterious action" in 1914, when a landing party from the German cruiser *Karlsruhe* was reported turned back by the German minister on the pier at Port-au-Prince just as the war broke out in Europe.* Lansing's assertions in this 1922 letter were, however, gross exaggerations; the letter was written with the connivance of the State Department which in 1922 was defending the occupation of Haiti against partisan political attacks and which arranged that Lansing should stress the German threat as having justified the original intervention. [53] In his 1935 *War Memoirs*, Lansing said that fear of Germany's establishing submarine bases along the approaches to the Panama Canal had prompted the intervention in Haiti and the purchase of the Danish West Indies. [54]

In a 1915 memorandum to Wilson, Lansing advocated an extension of the Monroe Doctrine to constitute a new "Caribbean Policy" in which forcible United States intervention would counter the danger of European financial control of Caribbean countries. [55] Lansing believed, as did Wilson and Bryan, that European financial control constituted as great a menace to United States security as did outright cession or occupation. Lansing argued that American

---

* Shortly after Lansing's statement, the German government informed the State Department that the alleged *Karlsruhe* incident had not taken place. SD 838.51/1294, Aide-Memoire from German Embassy, Washington, June 10, 1922.

national safety demanded the establishment of stable and honest governments in the Caribbean by taking control of public revenues and thus removing the prize sought by revolutionaries and foreigners who financed them. Lansing stated emphatically that the primary purpose of his "Caribbean Policy" was nationalistic, rather than Pan-American, saying:

The opposition to European control over American territory is not primarily to preserve the integrity of any American state. . . . The essential idea is to prevent a condition which would menace the national interests of the United States. . . . I make no argument on the ground of the benefit which would result to the peoples of these republics by the adoption of this policy.[56]

Attendant benefits for the Caribbean countries, such as prosperity and "intellectual development," were of secondary importance. Wilson responded favorably to Lansing's memorandum, saying, "The argument in this paper seems to be unanswerable, and I thank you for setting it out so explicitly and fully." [57]

Secretary of the Navy Josephus Daniels was concerned with preventing the Germans from establishing a submarine base in Haiti. Even before the United States entered the war in Europe, Daniels had sent men to inspect all potential sites for submarine bases from Maine to Panama, and the possibility of a German base in Haiti caused him special anxiety. Writing a private letter to William Allen White in 1930, Daniels recalled:

Outside of getting the soldiers to France in safety, my greatest anxiety always was that German submarines might come over to the Caribbean or to the Gulf and sink tankers on the way to Europe. You will recall that they sunk very many tankers on the other side and if we had not been very vigilant with our ships south of Florida they would undoubtedly have secured a base and come over on this side and sunk tankers. You know, they did come over to our coast later and ravage merchant shipping. From the very day the first U boat sunk a merchant ship I was nervous and distressed for fear they would get into the Caribbean or the Gulf of Mexico and do what they later attempted to do off the Delaware coast.[58]

At the time of the American intervention in Haiti in July, 1915, the military potential of the submarine and the outcome of the European war were both unknown factors. In retrospect it seems that Lansing and Daniels were unduly alarmed over the German threat in the Caribbean, but had Germany somehow procured a base in Haiti and then won the war, the United States position in the Caribbean would have been seriously compromised.

While the decision to intervene in Haiti was part of the long-term development of United States hegemony in the Caribbean, the threat of German incursion was a more immediate factor and ultimately the decisive one. State Department tactics for executing the intervention evolved over two years, beginning with diplomatic efforts to obtain a customs receivership and ending with the landing of marines in July, 1915.[59]

The Wilson administration consistently supported American business interests in Haiti from the outset, interceding on behalf of Farnham's National Railway in March, 1913, by urging the Haitian government to accept three sections of badly constructed track. The State Department, despite contract clauses prohibiting diplomatic intervention, supported both the railway and the Banque Nationale in all subsequent disputes with the Haitian government. The department had apparently committed itself to support the Banque during the 1910 Banque contract transaction, when department representatives arranged for American participation. Farnham stated in a 1915 memorandum to Bryan and Wilson:

While no specific statements were made by the then officials of the State Department to such effect, it never-the-less was generally understood by the American interests involved that, should the occasion arise, the American interests would receive from their Government such prompt and full support as the Department might deem necessary in the circumstances.[60]

The most blatant instance of support was the *Machias* incident of December, 1914, when Bryan, after last-minute consultation with Farnham, dispatched the U.S.S. *Machias* to Port-au-Prince and landed a detachment of marines which removed $500,000 of Haitian government funds from the vaults of the Banque Nationale. The money was then transported to New York, where it was deposited with National City Bank for safekeeping.[61] In January, 1915, the Banque Nationale raised the United States flag in place of the French flag, signifying it would henceforth be under the protection of the United States.[62]

Farnham enlisted the State Department in his effort to achieve an American customs receivership in early 1914. In January he wrote Bryan that customs control was necessary and that two Haitian presidential candidates whom he was supporting were amenable to American control but required American intervention to achieve power.[63] In March, 1914, Bryan and Wilson, hoping that the Haitian government would request an American customs receivership, decided that Germany and France, both of whom had expressed interest in joining in any American receivership, should not be allowed to participate.[64] In July Bryan accepted a scheme known as the "Farnham Plan," which envisioned a United States customs receivership and which Farnham, assisted by the American consul at Cap Haïtien, attempted to negotiate with Haitian politicians.[65] At this time Bryan sent to Port-au-Prince a proposed draft of a Haitian-American convention that was modeled after the 1907 Dominican receivership but included provisions for an American financial adviser as well as for a customs receivership.[66]

The Farnham Plan and subsequent attempts to negotiate a receivership failed because no Haitian government, no matter how desperate its financial or political situation, could afford to surrender national sovereignty. One Haitian minister of foreign affairs who suggested a deal with the United States was denounced by the Haitian Senate, which rose in a body and attempted to assault him physically.[67] Instead of a customs receivership and outright cession of Môle-Saint-Nicolas, successive Haitian governments offered economic concessions and guarantees not to alienate the Môle to any foreign power.[68] These were insufficient to placate the State Department, which, by November, 1914, was demanding: (1) a customs convention; (2) settlement of claims made against the Haitian government by the American railroad; (3) settlement of claims made by the Banque Nationale; (4) full protection of foreign interests; and (5) the guarantee not to alienate the Môle.[69]

The State Department dispatched two special commissions to Haiti in early 1915 in continued efforts to negotiate a receivership, but it was becoming apparent that diplomatic efforts would not succeed. Commissioner Paul Fuller reported in June, 1915, that no Haitian politician could afford to sign an agreement because he would be accused of selling the country to the United States and that armed intervention was the only way to carry out American policy.[70] Possible complications that might result with Germany and France because of unilateral American action were smoothed over successfully, probably because neither country wished to alienate the United States at that stage of the European war. The German chargé in Washington assured the department that Germany understood that the United States could not agree to German customs participation for internal political reasons and that the Imperial Foreign Office persisted in its claim to participation only because of public opinion in Germany.[71] At the time of the intervention the French expressed approval and hoped that the United States would be "energetic" in its revamping of Haiti.[72] In April, 1915, Bryan wrote Wilson that the only questions left to be determined about American intervention were the time and the method. At this point Bryan suggested that the United States control Haiti through a "resident Adviser" similar to the system used by the Netherlands in Java and the British in India.[73]

In the development of the intervention policy little consideration was given to the rights of the Haitians. The only instance when Haiti's right of self-determination was given token recognition was a 1914 suggestion by Lansing that the Wilson Plan, by which the United States had supervised elections in the Dominican Republic, be applied to Haiti.[74] Even this plan, which proved to be impracticable, was to have included customs control by the United States. State Department officials, confident of American superiority and reflecting the racial prejudices of the period, tended to disparage Haitian achievements and capabilities, as had most foreign observers throughout Haitian history. Lansing remarked:

The experience of Liberia and Haiti show that the African race are devoid of any capacity for political organization and lack genius for government. Unquestionably there is in them an inherent tendency to revert to savagery and to cast aside the shackles of civilization which are irksome to their physical nature. Of course there are many exceptions to this racial weakness but it is true of the mass, as we know from experience in this country. It is that which makes the negro problem practically unsolvable.[75]

Haitians, for their part, were aware of the lack of respect Americans had for Haitian sovereignty. The French minister at Port-au-Prince reported to the French government in April, 1915, that "for the Haitian the Americans are the Whites, and among the Whites those who have the most insulting contempt for Blacks." [76]

Assistant Secretary of State William Phillips, writing a memorandum summing up recent developments in Haiti at the time of American intervention, pointed to Haitian lack of public opinion, lack of public responsibility, "complete political incompetence," and growing demoralization. Phillips stated: "These facts all point to the failure of an inferior people to maintain the degree of civilization left them by the French, or to develop any capacity of self government entitling them to international respect and confidence." [77] Phillips recommended complete forcible intervention and the establishment of military government presided over by a United States Army general.

4

The Intervention

The immediate occasion for United States intervention was the overthrow of Haitian President Vilbrun Guillaume Sam in July, 1915. Declarations issued by the State Department that intervention was undertaken for humanitarian reasons to prevent anarchy and bloodshed were spurious and misleading. American warships had been maintaining a close vigil in Haitian waters throughout the unsuccessful attempts to negotiate an American customs receivership, and had been alerted for possible landing operations as early as July, 1914.[1]

Plans for military occupation of Haiti were drawn up well in advance, showing that intervention was not precipitated by a single, anarchic revolution. A detailed Navy Department "Plan for Landing and Occupying the City of Port-au-Prince," drawn up in November, 1914, begins:

Situation—The government has been overthrown; all semblance of law and order has ceased; the local authorities admit their inability to protect foreign interests, the city being overrun and in the hands of about 5,000 soldiers and civilian mobs.[2]

This description could pass for a news report of the actual landings which took place nine months later. Another contingency plan, constructed in the summer of 1914, contained sample letters for notifying Haitian authorities of American intentions: one such, under a 1914 dateline with the day and month left blank, stated that "the

purpose of the President of the United States is solely for the establishment of law and order." This same plan stipulated that naval
landing forces at Port-au-Prince should not be used against organized armed troops ashore, which would instead be subjected to
gunfire from American warships standing out in the harbor.[3] The
Haitian army's capacity for resistance was correctly judged to be
negligible, with one 1914 intelligence report describing Haitian
soldiers as a mob armed with worthless rifles.[4] When it became clear
that the Haitians would not agree to a negotiated customs receivership and that military force was necessary to achieve American
ends, the only missing detail in the military invasion plans was an
appropriate Haitian revolution that would justify United States intervention on the customary pretext of protecting American lives
and property. In fact, there was no record of any American life
having been lost or property destroyed prior to the intervention.[5]

The overthrow of President Guillaume Sam provided the United
States with the requisite opportunity. Not only were Haitian politics
becoming increasingly chaotic, with seven presidents in the preceding five years, but the overthrow of Sam was exceptionally
bloody and repugnant to public opinion both within Haiti and in
the United States. Sam, in office less than five months, was impli-
cated in the massacre of 167 political prisoners who were murdered
by Sam's army commander as Port-au-Prince was being taken by
revolutionary forces. After the massacre of prisoners, many of whom
were members of prominent elite families, Sam took refuge in the
French legation, and chief executioner General Oscar Etienne in the
Dominican legation. Enraged mobs violated the legations and
killed both Sam and Etienne. Sam was dragged from the French
legation and publicly dismembered. Portions of his body were then
paraded around the streets of Port-au-Prince in a grotesque spec-
tacle accompanied by vindictive cries from the mob.[6]

Even before learning of the unprecedented violation of foreign
legations, the State Department ordered marines under the command of Rear Admiral William B. Caperton to land at Port-au-
Prince. Unlike previous revolutions, when French, German, and
sometimes British marines were landed for short periods to protect
their nationals, this time the United States intended to go in alone.
Admiral Caperton was instructed to request the captains of British

and French warships in the area to abstain from landing forces, and to assure them that the United States would protect all foreign interests.[7] The French minister had, in fact, requested a French landing party after the violation of the French legation, but a navigational error delayed the French cruiser *Descartes* and helped avert possible Franco-American complications.[*] The *Descartes* remained in Haitian waters for several months, until the French received a satisfactory response to their protest over the violation of the legation.

The macabre overthrow of Sam was cited as justification for intervention by subsequent apologists for American policy. The United States, as the self-appointed trustee of civilization in the Caribbean, was obligated to maintain minimal standards of decency and morality. The weakness of this argument was readily demonstrated by opponents of the intervention. A prominent Haitian writer, referring to an incident in a Southern United States town where a black man was dragged from the local jail and burned alive in the town square, pointed out that barbarity also existed in the United States.[8] In a 1929 United States congressional debate, several congressmen noted that the number of Haitian presidents assassinated over the years was almost the same as the number of American presidents assassinated and that since 1862, the year of the American recognition of Haiti, the number was identical—three presidents killed in each country.[9] Likewise, the frequent overthrow of governments was not unique; France had eleven governments from 1909 to 1914.

Whatever the moral implications of American intervention, the missionary impulse did not figure prominently in the deliberations of United States policy makers in the Wilson administration. Policy discussions centered around strategic considerations, with the sensational demise of Sam serving only to make intervention more palatable to moralists outside the government, and to those administration officials, notably Secretary of the Navy Daniels, who

[*] The *Descartes* had landed French marines at Cap Haïtien several weeks earlier, but these were withdrawn upon the arrival of Admiral Caperton, who undertook the task of protecting all foreign interests during a revolutionary outbreak there. Pierre Girard, "La Révolution d'Haïti, Juillet, 1915," *La Revue Hebdomadaire* (Paris), Année 34, VII (July, 1925), 428–32. Girard was the French minister at Port-au-Prince in July, 1915.

had qualms about the moral rightness of military incursions into friendly neighboring countries. Secretary of State Lansing took a decidedly cynical approach, writing Wilson a few days after the intervention:

We have no excuse of reprisal as we had at Vera Cruz, to take over the city government and administer the offices. There would appear to me to be but one reason which could be given for doing so, and that is the humane duty of furnishing means to relieve the famine situation. If our naval authorities should take over the collection of customs on imports and exports these might be expended on the ground of dire necessity for the relief of the starving people.[10]

Since food shortages were caused by Haitian guerrillas cutting off roads to marine-occupied cities as a part of their military resistance to American intervention, Lansing's humanitarian argument was doubly specious.

Three hundred thirty United States sailors and marines landed at Port-au-Prince on July 28, 1915, and were quickly reinforced by troops dispatched from Guantánamo Bay, Cuba. As the *New York Times* remarked on July 31, "The force being sent to Haiti is much larger than is necessary for mere protection of foreign interests." The intervention was immediately sanctified by the spilling of American blood as two American sailors, one of whom was a nephew of Samuel Gompers, were killed in action. The two men were described in American diplomatic and newspaper reports as having been killed by Haitian snipers.[11] President Wilson expressed his personal condolences, but even these first casualties proved to be lacking in the romantic battlefield pageantry that was to be conspicuously absent in many of the American military skirmishes in Haiti. Subsequent military reports disclosed that there were no indications of enemy fire in the area where the two sailors were killed and that they were accidentally shot in the night by rifle fire from their comrades in the Seaman Battalion, which was untrained for shore action and under severe nervous strain in unfamiliar surroundings.[12] The Americans were intimidated by the sound of constant firing in the city throughout the night, but there was no danger since the firing was just a traditional form of celebration at the fall of a tyrant.[13]

Many of the American troops that landed in Haiti were unfamiliar with the abject poverty and unsanitary conditions which now surrounded them. Port-au-Prince, with its background of picturesque mountains, was one of the most beautiful harbors in the world when viewed from the sea, but first impressions on landing were unfavorable. One young marine, anticipating exotic adventure in a tropical paradise, later described his first day ashore as follows:

It hurt, It stunk, Fairyland had turned into a pigsty. More than that, we were not welcome. We could feel it as distinctly as we could smell the rot along the gutters. . . . In the street were piles of evil-smelling offal. The stench hung over everything. Piles of mango seeds were heaped in the middle of the highway, sour-smelling. It was not merely that these, mingled with banana peels and other garbage, were rotting—the whole prospect was filthy. . . . Haitians of the working class have the ugliest feet in the world. In my bewilderment I somehow blamed them for the horrid things on which they stood. We were all annoyed.[14]

The hostility of the Haitians also tended to make things unpleasant for the newly arrived marines. Night curfew patrols were forced to march warily down the middle of the streets of Port-au-Prince in order to avoid being showered with household waste dropped from darkened second-story windows.[15]

Organized military resistance to the invasion, both at Port-au-Prince and at the other locations throughout the country where American troops were landed, was minimal. Admiral Caperton, the senior officer in charge of the intervention, cabled Secretary of the Navy Daniels and President Wilson:

U.S. has now actually accomplished a military intervention in affairs of another nation. Hostility exists now in Haiti and has existed for a number of years against such action. Serious hostile contacts have only been avoided by prompt and rapid military action which has given U.S. control before resistance has had time to organize.[16]

Faced with the overwhelming military superiority of American forces, those Haitians who were determined to resist the intervention took to the hills and there organized guerrilla bands.

At the time of the intervention American authorities found that the general economic situation, and especially the food supply in Port-au-Prince, was disorganized. Under the impact of military invasion, many additional economic functions were temporarily suspended. The situation was further complicated when Haitian guerrilla forces, erstwhile cacos, cut off the food supplies to major cities in an attempt to exert pressure on United States forces. The United States, which assumed a measure of responsibility along with military control, was thus called upon to provide relief for the destitute population of Port-au-Prince until such time as the food supply could be restored. Secretary Daniels, assessing the Haitians according to racial stereotypes of Negroes in the Southern United States instead of viewing them as a distinct foreign people, was skeptical about the effects that free relief might have upon them, and wrote to President Wilson: "It is very dangerous to begin to supply provisions because the Haitiens are like negroes in the South after the war and would quit work entirely, deserting plantations if our Government undertakes to feed them." [17]

This wholesale misapplication of the presumed lessons of white American historical experience with Negroes indicates the extent of misinformation and prejudice which typically clouded the minds of cognizant United States officials. Aside from the implicit racial slur, Daniels was badly confused, since the problem in Haiti involved feeding the urban population of Port-au-Prince and, moreover, there were no plantations in Haiti comparable to those in the American South during the Civil War era. In spite of Daniels' apprehensions, navy doctors and medical corpsmen undertook relief work among "a large population of sick and practically starving people" in Port-au-Prince in August, 1915.[18] The navy medical personnel, aided by the American Red Cross, which contributed a fund of $1,500 in January, 1916, gave medical attention to indigent Haitians in Port-au-Prince and distributed food on a regular basis to those who had been investigated and certified as destitute. This was the beginning of a long series of constructive humanitarian projects originated by the navy medical corps that was to continue throughout the occupation.

Shortly after intervening, the United States restored the Haitian treasury service to the American-controlled Banque Nationale, which had been deprived of the service by the Haitian government during a dispute earlier in the year, and assigned American naval officers to supervise the collection of all customs duties. These customs and financial adjustments fulfilled long-standing objectives of United States diplomacy and resulted in effective control of the Haitian government's purse strings. American officers who took over customhouses and local government administration were often appalled at the inefficiency and corruption characteristic of local institutions. The marine officer who took charge of the coastal town of Jérémie audited the mayor's books and found evidence of extensive graft.[19] A navy pay corps officer, under orders to assume "complete authority over all port activities and coastwise trade" at Petit Goâve, found that customs facilities included stones and pieces of iron used as weights to measure for duties.[20] Within several weeks of the landings United States forces were in control of all governmental agencies and revenues in the coastal towns of Haiti. Military control of the occupied towns and cities varied in style and emphasis according to the personalities of local commanders, but in all cases American authority was predominant. The marine officer at Jérémie, a veteran of other banana wars, remarked that "in Cuba we didn't have the absolute authority we had here." [21]

With American forces in effective control, the Wilson administration turned to the problem of developing suitable political machinery through which the United States could govern the country. Apparently little advance consideration had been given to the problem, since both Wilson and Lansing were uncertain as to how they should proceed. Both agreed on the necessity of prolonged military occupation but at the outset neither had any clear idea of how this could be done within the framework of international law. On the sixth day after the intervention, Lansing wrote Wilson that he was "not at all sure what we ought to do or what we legally can do." Wilson replied that he too feared that "we have not the legal authority to do what we apparently ought to do" but that the United States must send sufficient troops to subordinate local authorities and completely control the country. Excepting these irregularities, Wilson insisted that "constitutional government" be established and maintained, but he did not specify that the existing Haitian Constitution should be respected.[22] In keeping with the continuing interest the United States had in establishing order and stability in the Caribbean, Wilson's plans were to retain military control over Haiti until a strong and stable Haitian government could be set up under American auspices.[23]

Although American military leaders in Haiti favored outright military government, the Wilson administration decided to work through existing Haitian political machinery, including a Haitian chief executive. In deciding to set up a Haitian client-president, Lansing wrote Wilson: "I do not see why it would not be as easy to control a government with a president as it is to control the Haitian Congress and administrative officers."[24] The first important step in the political reconstruction of Haiti was the selection of a suitable client-president. By taking military control of Port-au-Prince in late July the United States had prevented the election of Dr. Rosalvo Bobo as the new president of Haiti. Bobo headed the caco army that precipitated the downfall of Sam and was about to appropriate the rewards of successful revolution by intimidating the Haitian legislature into electing him to the recently vacated presidency. Admiral Caperton, acting in accordance with advice given him by a prominent Haitian confidant, postponed the election and took measures to disarm the 1,500 caco troops who were demanding the election of Bobo.[25] Bobo's adherents hung together for several weeks, until he disbanded them after having been told by Admiral Caperton that the United States would forbid his candidacy if the troops remained in the city.[26]

Dr. Bobo was a man of considerable personal accomplishment. He had traveled widely, held degrees in law and medicine from the universities of Paris and London, and was fluent in many languages. Captain Edward L. Beach, Caperton's chief of staff who represented the admiral in all dealings with Bobo and who wrote a lengthy chronicle describing the various negotiations, commented that Bobo "was greatly beloved in Haiti because the poor and needy sick always had the first call on his services, and none of these ever received a bill from him," but Beach noted that Bobo was unbalanced and, as an "idealist and dreamer," was "utterly unsuited to be Haiti's President."[27] Moreover, Bobo had long been known to the State Department as an opponent of United States encroachments in Haiti. In 1911 Bobo had opposed the McDonald railroad and fig banana concessions, and as minister of the interior in 1914 he had worked to thwart the proposed American customs receivership.[28] The proclaimed object of his revolution against Sam was to prevent the "tremendous disgrace" of an American receivership.[29] On top of all his other liabilities, Caperton and Lansing believed that Bobo was bordering on insanity.[30] Given these grave misgivings about Bobo,* the United States began to look for an alternative candidate.

In seeking a suitable client-president, Admiral Caperton approached three of Haiti's most distinguished politicians: J. N. Leger, who for twelve years had been Haitian minister to Washington; Solon Menos, who was the current minister in Washington; and former president F. D. Légitime. Each declined, with J. N. Leger, whom Captain Beach recommended as "Haiti's most distinguished citizen," peremptorily refusing with this explanation: "I am for Haiti, not for the United States; Haiti's president will have to accept directions and orders from the United States and I propose to keep myself in a position where I will be able to defend Haiti's interests." [31]

Caperton's trusted Haitian confidant, referred to as "X" in Captain Beach's chronicle and probably J. N. Leger, also refused to form a provisional government because of the ignominy of holding office under American auspices.[32]

Faced with the reluctance of the foremost politicians to associate themselves with the Occupation, Caperton turned to Philippe Sudre Dartiguenave, president of the Haitian Senate, who was eager to volunteer his services. Dartiguenave, in declaring his candidacy to Captain Beach, insisted only that the United States guarantee to protect him if he were elected. He agreed to United States financial control and customs receivership, and offered to cede Môle-Saint-Nicolas outright, recommending to Beach a plan by which the United States would land troops at the Môle before the election, with a formal treaty of cession coming later.[33] In negotiating his candidacy with United States representatives, Dartiguenave also made specific commitments to settle outstanding difficulties between the Haitian government and the Banque Nationale and to

---

* The ambivalent reaction to Bobo is strikingly similar to United States treatment of Dominican President Juan Bosch in the 1960s. See John Bartlow Martin, *Overtaken by Events: The Dominican Crisis from the Fall of Trujillo to the Civil War* (Garden City, N.Y., 1966).

pay the various claims made against the government by the American-owned National Railway.[34]

Dartiguenave headed a faction of legislators and claimed to control the Haitian congress which, under strong pressure from Caperton (who made it clear that the United States insisted on effective control), was to elect the new president. Bobo's supporters, who controlled the guerrilla forces still active in the interior of the country and included the leading citizens who comprised the Committee of Public Safety through which Caperton governed Port-au-Prince, were still the dominant political group. Dartiguenave was threatened with immediate assassination if he did not withdraw his candidacy; he was then provided with a nine-man marine bodyguard by the Americans.[35]

With Dartiguenave and Bobo having emerged as the leading candidates, Captain Beach conducted a series of interviews with them in order to select the better man. Bobo's limitations as a long-time opponent of United States interests were well known, but Dartiguenave also had his drawbacks. Caperton's trusted Haitian confidant "X" did not think highly of Bobo, but preferred him to Dartiguenave whom "X" characterized as being "surrounded by grafters with whom he has grafted, which accounts for his candidacy." [36] Bobo, seeing his chances for selection deteriorate with each passing day, desperately offered to make any concessions the United States might demand, but Dartiguenave, in the series of interviews with Beach, made a much more favorable impression than did the temperamental Bobo, who became irate and impetuous.[37] Admiral Caperton recommended Dartiguenave to Washington, where Bobo was already viewed with disfavor because of his anti-American background, and Daniels replied, "Allow election of President to take place whenever Haitians wish. The U.S. prefers election of Dartiguenave." Daniels later confessed to William Allen White that, "Of course, you and I know that this was equivalent to America making Dartiguenave President." [38]

There were some qualms within the Wilson administration about the heavy-handed methods being employed by the United States in Haiti. Lansing wrote to Wilson: "I confess that this method of negotiation, with our marines policing the Haytien Capital, is high handed. It does not meet my sense of a nation's sovereign rights and is more or less an exercise of force and an invasion of Haytien independence." [39]

Secretary of the Navy Daniels, known as an anti-imperialist, was chided by his fellow Cabinet officers for his role in the intervention. Secretary of the Interior Frank K. Lane, with a wink toward President Wilson, addressed Daniels at a Cabinet meeting as "Josephus the First, King of Haiti," and another colleague, referring to the election of Dartiguenave, asked mockingly, "Will the candidate you and Lansing picked manage to squeeze in?" Daniels did not appreciate the situation and later wrote Franklin D. Roosevelt, who was Assistant Secretary of the Navy in 1915, that "You know that the things we were forced to do in Haiti was a bitter pill for me, for I have always hated any foreign policy that even hinted of imperialistic control." [40]

Dartiguenave was elected president on August 12, 1915, by the Haitian legislature, which convened under the protection of United States Marines instead of under the protection of a revolutionary caco army. Daniels later stated that Dartiguenave's election "was undoubtedly not the choice of the mass of the Haitian people but only of those who felt that intervention by America was essential." [41] After his election Dartiguenave personally thanked Caperton's chief of staff Captain Beach and insisted that Beach ride in the same car with him in the inaugural procession. Later Beach remarked that "Since his election, he [Dartiguenave] has repeatedly and publicly made known his intention, without reservation, to do everything the U.S. wishes." Beach felt that Dartiguenave, who was subsequently nicknamed "The Cat" by members of the American colony in Port-au-Prince, honestly believed that the interests of Haiti could best be served by complete cooperation with the United States. [42]

As had been anticipated by American authorities, the client-government established by Dartiguenave was unable to control political unrest without direct American military support. Because of this as well as increasing uneasiness in Port-au-Prince and inflammatory propaganda against the government and the American occupation, Admiral Caperton declared martial law on September 3, 1915. less than a month after Dartiguenave's election.* Along

* Much of the martial law proclamation was taken verbatim or copied from the same form as that used in 1914 at Vera Cruz, Mexico. Caperton to Daniels, Sept. 2, 1915. FR; 1915, pp. 484–85.

with the declaration of martial law, Caperton issued a contingent censorship promulgation which stated:

The freedom of the press will not be interfered with, but license will not be tolerated. The publishing of false or incendiary propaganda against the Government of the United States or the Government of Haiti, or the publishing of any false, indecent, or obscene propaganda, letters signed or unsigned, or matter which tends to disturb the public peace will be dealt with by the military courts.[43]

Martial law, by which Haitian political offenders were tried in United States military courts, continued in effect until the strikes and riots of 1929. Dartiguenave informed the Americans that the declaration of martial law would greatly facilitate the passing of the proposed Haitian-American treaty that was to legalize the occupation.[44]

Even with effective military occupation, control of all custom-houses and governmental revenues, and a handpicked client-president, the Wilson administration felt it necessary to legalize the occupation by means of a formal treaty with the client-government in Haiti. This treaty, in effect a unilateral declaration by the United States, was to be cited throughout the 1920s as a solemn moral and legal commitment to continue the occupation. Immediately after the election of Dartiguenave, Lansing instructed the American chargé at Port-au-Prince to negotiate a treaty that would incorporate all the demands made by Bryan during the unsuccessful negotiations which preceded the intervention. In addition, the United States took advantage of its greatly improved bargaining position and privileged relationship with Dartiguenave, who continued to live under the protection of a marine bodyguard, to exact new concessions. Lansing wrote to Wilson that the new treaty was "along the lines of the treaty which was sought to be negotiated a year ago last July [1914]. It, of course, makes several alterations and additions covering the ground far more thoroughly and granting to this Government a much more extensive control than the original treaty proposed." The additions included the appointment of an all-powerful financial adviser by the president of the United States, establishment of a constabulary organized and officered by Americans, settlement of foreign claims, and American control of public works.[45]

Despite the presence of a strong American military force and the cooperation of President Dartiguenave, Caperton experienced difficulties in getting the proposed treaty ratified by the Haitian legislature which, during the first two years of the occupation, was allowed to remain in existence. Caperton's patience and diplomacy were tried to the utmost, and at times he thought that the United States might have to set up a military government and abandon efforts to work through established Haitian political institutions.[46] Part of the difficulty was disappointment among the legislators in Dartiguenave's client-government, which had been unable to bestow offices and expend public funds because of American control over all revenue.[47] More than this, Caperton's repeated pledges of a loan and American financial aid were not backed up by the State Department.

In pressing for ratification of the treaty, Caperton had promised funds to alleviate the desperate financial embarrassment of the Dartiguenave government and made allusions to a bright economic future for the whole country.[48] Caperton's requests to the State Department for a loan and for the release of government funds held by the American-controlled Banque Nationale were denied. The American chargé also urged an advance of funds, saying: "I am convinced that the Government is using its best efforts to secure ratification by Congress but its efforts are being seriously hampered and ratification endangered by the withholding of the gourdes." [49]

Caperton urgently recommended a loan to bail out the Haitian government, which had unpaid salaries and was suffering sinking prestige, and, moreover, had incurred expenses "in educating country to realize necessity of ratifying treaty." He argued that unkept promises made by the State Department were weakening the position of the Dartiguenave government and that "enemies of the United States and of the treaty are taking advantage of this apparent lack of support. . . . American prestige is involved in this matter." [50] For its part, the State Department had decided to withhold funds as a means of forcing ratification of the treaty and advised Caperton and Chargé Davis that the embarrassment of the Dartiguenave government would only be temporary.[51] After passage of the treaty the State Department maintained that a loan could not be procured until after a settlement had been reached between the Haitian government and the Banque Nationale.[52] In playing the proffered loan for all it was worth Lansing, who earlier had suggested increasing the salaries of Haitian legislators "to avoid their being liable to graft temptations," was apparently being more cynical in his attitude toward Haitian politics than was Caperton.[53]

With the poor coordination in tactics employed by Caperton and the State Department and the breakdown of efforts to secure ratification by persuasion, Caperton employed threats and intimidation which proved successful. In early November, 1915, he asked Dartiguenave for the names of the senators hostile to the treaty so that personal pressure might be applied, and a week later he relayed orders from Daniels to inform the Haitian Cabinet that

Rumors of bribery to defeat the treaty are rife, but are not believed. However, should they prove true, those who accept or give bribes will be vigourously prosecuted. [Caperton had been instructed to make the threat of prosecution] . . . sufficiently clear to remove all opposition and to secure immediate ratification.[54]

The treaty was ratified by the Haitian Senate the next day, and went into effect as a *modus vivendi* pending action by the United States Senate, which ratified the treaty unanimously and without debate in February, 1916.[55]

The treaty provided that the United States would aid Haiti in economic development and establish Haitian finances on a firm basis. An American-appointed financial adviser and general receiver of customs would have extensive control over Haitian government finances, and Haiti was forbidden to modify its customs duties or increase its public debt without United States approval. The United States would organize and officer a Haitian gendarmerie, and the Haitian government agreed to execute an arbitration protocol with the United States for settlement of foreign claims. The treaty was to remain in force for ten years from the date of exchange of ratifications, which was May 3, 1916. Efforts by the Dartiguenave government to effectively participate in the drafting of the treaty were thwarted. A later State Department memorandum noted that "The Haitian Government attempted to make it appear that this treaty had been negotiated rather than dictated and suggested several changes in phraseology," but the department had insisted on its own phraseology.[56]

Admiral Caperton and Captain Beach, who had successfully completed their assigned mission of forming a client-government and procuring the treaty, left Haiti early in 1916. Caperton had been the senior officer in charge of the occupation for a year and in this capacity had attempted to rule by persuasion rather than force. He took great pains not to offend Haitian pride and was personally liked by the Haitian elite. One Haitian contemporary referred to him as a "beau vieillard svelte" and an indefatigable dancer who held his partners tightly.[57] Captain Beach, Caperton's representative ashore, spoke excellent French and paid social calls at Haitian homes where he made friends among the elite.[58]

Caperton's policy of sympathy and consideration toward the Haitians was officially encouraged by Daniels, who later stated that he had ordered "all officers to regard themselves as friendly brothers of the Haitians sent there to help these neighbor people." [59] Some effort was also made to instruct American troops that it was desirable to make a good impression. The detachments that landed at Cap Haïtien were ordered to treat Haitians with "utmost kindness and consideration" and to make friendly, if patronizing, gestures toward them. The troops were advised that "A cheerful word, a friendly pat on the man's back or the horse's rump, goes far to vitiate the sting of humiliation and will do much to change the natural feeling of resentment to one of respect and friendship." [60] Cursing and shoving were prohibited. In general, the problem of personal relations between occupying forces and Haitians was not acute at the time of the intervention.

With the departure of Admiral Caperton the occupation entered a new phase. Colonel Littleton W. T. Waller, who had been commander of the Marine Expeditionary Forces in Haiti and was now the commander of the First Marine Brigade, succeeded Caperton as the senior United States officer in Haiti. American Financial Adviser Addison T. Ruan later remarked:

We have used two policies in Haiti, one of force and one of conciliation. Admiral Caperton employed conciliation. He made personal friends of leading Haitians, by associating with them. General Waller, seconded by Colonel (now Brigadier General) Butler, adopted a policy of force.[61]

As Caperton's subordinate in charge of marines ashore, Waller had not gotten along well with the admiral, whom he referred to as "insane," complaining that, "Instead of backing up the men who are working for him, he knifes them when they do well." After Caperton's departure Waller asserted, "Since he left I have accomplished a great amount of work." [62]

Colonel Waller apparently recognized that tact was necessary in dealing with Haitians and once cautioned his impulsive friend and subordinate, Major Smedley D. Butler, not to be crude in his treatment of the elite because, "There is more harm done by such an act than can be remedied by months of work and labor." [63] Waller's own relations with Haitians, however, were difficult and strained. This was largely because of his racial prejudices, which approached outright scorn. He referred to one Haitian supplicant as "the blackest bluegum nigger you ever saw" and wrote to his friend Colonel John A. Lejeune * that "Thes people are niggers in spite of the thin varnish of education and refinement. Down in their hearts they are just the same happy, idle irresponsible people we know of." [64]

Waller disliked Haitians of the elite governing class, believed that client-President Dartiguenave was "as big a crook as any of the others," and stated that "There is not an honest men in the whole of Haiti of Haitian nationality." His racial prejudice precluded cordial relations even at the ceremonial level; he confided to Colonel Lejeune:

They are real nigger and no mistake—There are some very fine looking, well educated polished men here but they are real nigs beneath the surface. What the people of Norfolk and Portsmouth would say if they saw me bowing and scraping to these coons—I do not know—All the same I do not wish to be outdone in formal politeness. [65]

By undiplomatic behavior and insulting directives Waller quickly incurred the enmity of Dartiguenave. At one point Waller threatened to leave Dartiguenave unprotected in hostile Port-au-Prince

* Lejeune was at this time assistant to the commandant in Washington, and succeeded General George Barnett as commandant of the Marine Corps in 1920. Both Lejeune and Waller were promoted to brigadier general in 1916.

by withdrawing American forces for twenty-four hours if Dartigue-nave continued to complain to the State Department.[66]

Waller and many other marines made a sharp distinction between the masses of Haitian peasants and the elite, whose cultural accomplishments they derided. Toward the end of his stay in Haiti, Waller said, "I find myself intensely popular with the people but not on good terms with the ministers of the government." [67] Major Smedley D. Butler shared this bias. In 1916 he wrote his father, Congressman Thomas S. Butler,* concerning the death of an elite antagonist:

Last night the nephew of one of the prominent politicians attacked one of our Gendarme sentries, firing three shots at him. The Gendarme pursued him, and, finally blew a hole in him as big as your fist, thus ending the life of a miserable cockroach. This morning there is a big uproar among the prominent citizens over the "unjustifiable" shooting of this leader of society. However, if all the leaders will only get busy and attack sentries we will soon clean up this country.[68]

Butler divided the Haitian population into two categories: the 99 percent who went barefoot and the 1 percent who wore shoes. He expressed affection for the poor peasants but despised the elite, whom he "took as a joke," observing that "Without a sense of humor you could not live in Haiti among those people, among the shoe class." [69] Given the pride and sensitivity of the Haitian elite, Butler's sense of humor was not appreciated. Disdain for the educated elite and complementary expressions of affection for the uneducated, impoverished peasant masses paralleled contemporary racist values in the United States, where Negroes were accepted, sometimes with fondness, so long as they "stayed in their place," while those who exhibited wealth, education, or ambition were subject to attack as "uppity niggers."

Despite the fact that the client-government was completely dependent upon American military protection, relations between it and the Waller-Butler team deteriorated rapidly. In mid-1916, Butler wrote Colonel Lejeune:

* Thomas S. Butler was a member of Congress representing the Sixth and Seventh districts of Pennsylvania from 1897 to 1928. For part of this time he served as chairman of the Naval Affairs Subcommittee.

I have told these miserable ministers what I think of them and if I stay here [Butler remained in Haiti until March, 1918] they know exactly what to expect. . . . There will be a deadline drawn between me and the Haitiens, the same as there is in Egypt—between the British agents and the Egyptians. . . . This Government has lied to me two or three times, and I do not intend again to trust it or anybody in it.[70]

In fact, both Waller and Butler favored unimpaired military government to the client-government arrangement with Dartiguenave. Waller wrote the United States military governor of Santo Domingo that "There has never been any doubt in my mind that a just military government is the method of controlling Haiti." [71]

The arrogant treatment characteristic of the Waller-Butler period served to disillusion many Haitians, even some of those who had welcomed the American intervention as an opportunity for constructive reform. Dr. William W. Cumberland, the leading American civilian official of a later period, observed that "I regret to say that some of the earlier authorities were in constant turmoil with the Haitians, usually on racial and personal grounds." Cumberland described Butler * as a "misfit" and "a man with about as little tact as one could ever meet," and added that, "For years some of us had the job of trying to heal up the scars which that gentleman left." [72]

---

* In 1921 the *Nation* reported that Nicaraguan mothers invoked the memory of Butler when they wished to frighten their children; the expression "Hush! Major Butler will get you" had allegedly been a maternal warning in Nicaragua for years. *Nation* CXII, No. 2903 (Feb. 23, 1921), 278.

5

The Marines Take Charge

There had been little organized military opposition to the landing of United States forces in July, 1915. Those Haitians who were determined to resist the United States occupation withdrew into the interior of the country where a number of caco armies, supporting the revolution against President Sam and the candidacy of Dr. Bobo, were already in the field. Subjugating these bands of poorly equipped guerrillas was the original and continuing military objective of the marine forces in Haiti.

Caco armies consisted of peasant soldiers who were enlisted in short-term military adventures by regional military chiefs in the interior of Haiti, especially in the wild and mountainous north. The regional chiefs, self-styled "generals," were allied with urban politicians who provided funds and political leadership. Prior to the American intervention, cacos had provided the military punch behind the numerous Haitian revolutions, serving as mercenary armies on behalf of successive presidential candidates. They were armed only with machetes and obsolete rifles, but possessed great tactical mobility and were able to disappear into the countryside when pursued by superior forces. A caco soldier was indistinguishable from an ordinary peasant once he had discarded his weapon and removed a small identifying red patch from his clothing. Cacos continued to be characterized simply as bandits in American military reports, irrespective of the fact that caco efforts were eventually directed solely toward the nationalistic political objective of driving the Americans into the sea.*

While the marine landings and the establishment of American authority in the coastal cities were accomplished with ease, the problem of pacification in the interior was complicated and difficult. Numerous caco bands remained loyal to exiled presidential candidate Dr. Rosalvo Bobo. Cacos interfered with food supplies to American-occupied coastal cities, raided marine encampments, and impeded railroad communications. Pacification of these bands was achieved during the six months following the intervention. Thereafter, with the establishment of marine outposts throughout the interior, caco activities declined until the American forced-labor road-building program of 1918 and the massive Haitian uprisings of 1918–19.

The initial pacification in 1915 was carried out by the complementary devices of bribing cacos to turn in their weapons, and by forceful marine pursuit and extermination. Of the two alternatives Admiral Caperton at first preferred bribery and undertook negotiations with caco chiefs immediately after the intervention.[1] Caperton managed to disarm Dr. Bobo's supporters in Port-au-Prince by threatening not to consider him for the presidency, but the cacos in the interior were more difficult to handle, especially after the Americans had definitely rejected Bobo's candidacy. Negotiations with caco generals for surrender of troops and arms entailed dickering over the amount of money to be awarded as compensation, with the two leading generals, Zamor and Robin, at first demanding $200,000. Caperton stated that this sum was out of the question and that the proposition was "to a great extent an attempt to bleed the Americans." A number of chiefs eventually agreed to more modest terms, and Caperton, dispensing moneys collected from the Haitian customs receivership on behalf of the client-government, purchased large quantities of rifles and paid appropriate bribes to caco generals. The largest single transaction involved the purchase of 596 rifles at $5 each, plus the payment of $6,600 to three generals.[2]

Many cacos refused to accept offers of bribes and others violated

* In the 1960s, President François Duvalier outfitted his militia with red armbands reminiscent of caco insignia as an appeal to Haitian nationalism.

agreements signed by their chiefs and remained under arms. Those who did not come to terms with the Americans were subjected to vigorous pursuit and decimation by marine patrols; indeed, marine hunt-and-kill operations were sustained throughout the period of negotiations. In September, 1915, Admiral Caperton remarked that, while he regretted not having been able to pacify the north without bloodshed, the "severe lesson" to the cacos might "prove of greater benefit in the eventual settlement of affairs than buying them off would have been." [3] The military pressure also had the advantage of acting as a stimulus to the surrender negotiations by intimidating the cacos, but reports of Haitian casualties alarmed Secretary of the Navy Daniels and eventually caused him to restrict offensive military operations. In early September Daniels ordered that no offensive action be undertaken without first consulting Washington, and in November he informed Caperton that the department was "strongly impressed with number of Haitians killed" and that, "In view of heavy losses to Haitians in recent engagement department desires your offensive to be suspended in order to prevent further loss of life." [4]

One of the military skirmishes that had alarmed Daniels was the capture of Fort Rivière. This engagement was notable because two participating marines, one of whom was Major Smedley D. Butler, were later awarded the Congressional Medal of Honor for heroism.[*] In other respects, the capture of Fort Rivière was typical of marine campaigns against the cacos, who were difficult to hunt down but easily defeated once cornered. At the 1921 Senate Hearings on the Occupation of Haiti, General George Barnett, commandant of the Marine Corps from 1914 to 1920, was questioned about offensive operations against the cacos:

GENERAL BARNETT: One particular one was the capture of Fort Riviere. That was really quite an affair.

[*] The medals were awarded at the behest of Assistant Secretary of the Navy Franklin D. Roosevelt, who visited the site of Fort Rivière in January, 1917. Roosevelt was much impressed by Butler's account of the battle, and noted in his travel diary that Butler and 18 companions had killed over 200 cacos at Fort Rivière, whereas the official Marine Corps casualty list reported 51 killed. Franklin D. Roosevelt, "Trip to Haiti and Santo Domingo, 1917," unpublished travel diary; Roosevelt MSS, RG10, Box 155.

QUESTION: That was the affair when there were 51 Haitians killed but no casualties on our side?

GENERAL BARNETT: It was quite an affair. The Haitians were not well armed, but they stood up and fought to the best of their ability. [continues, reading the field commander's report of the engagement] All companies were in their position at the time specified and Butler and Low's companies made the assault, supported by five other companies. Hand-to-hand conflict in the fort lasted ten minutes. Twenty-nine killed and 22 jumped parapet, but all were killed by fire from the automatics, all avenues of escape being blocked.

QUESTION: Was that operation fairly characteristic of the operations in general conducted by our forces against the natives?

GENERAL BARNETT: I should say that was a sample. They had a little better protection there than they would have ordinarily, it being an old fort on a high mountain.

No prisoners were taken.[5] One marine officer who took part in the engagement, recalling that the only American casualty was a man who was struck in the face with a rock and lost two teeth, remarked that "We were fighting a people who did not know what sights were for, and in a tight spot they threw away their rifles and reached for rocks." [6]

Caco attacks and ambushes against marine patrols were generally unsuccessful, although they provided some tense moments in the early days of campaigning. Major Smedley Butler's group of twenty-seven marines, trapped in a nighttime ambush, was terrified by surrounding cacos who blew incessantly on their conch shells, but in daylight the Haitians were no match against superior marine firepower. Butler recalled that his men "went wild after their devilish night and hunted the Cacos like pigs," killing about seventy-five of them on the day following the ambush.[7] Marine casualties in this campaign were characteristically light, with Butler's group suffering only one man wounded. Butler's field commander, Colonel Eli K. Cole, had ordered vigorous pursuit of the guerrillas and was pleased with Butler's performance, stating: "Butler I am glad to say, as he is a very good officer, particularly in the kind of work we have to do in the mountains, takes my view, and that is that the only way to do the job is by a systematic cleaning up of the place." [8]

Faced with marine prowess on the battlefield and offered the alternative of amnesty and reward for surrender, caco resistance rapidly broke down in the fall of 1915. The first phase of pacification had been successfully completed, and the marines turned next to the problem of developing a permanent military agency with which to maintain order and institutionalize the authority of the occupation.

The Haitian-American Treaty of September, 1915, provided that the United States would establish and officer a Haitian gendarmerie. The practice of developing an American-controlled native military force had previously been employed by the United States in Puerto Rico and Cuba, and, while the Gendarmerie was being organized in Haiti, corresponding Guardias Nacional were being set up under American auspices on the other end of the island in the Dominican Republic and in Nicaragua. These constabularies were intended as efficient, nonpartisan, centralized forces sufficiently powerful to ensure continuity of pro-American political regimes and to eliminate the problem of instability caused by cyclical revolutions. After American withdrawal from Cuba, the Dominican Republic, and Nicaragua, the constabularies became bulwarks of the enduring Batista, Trujillo, and Somoza dictatorships.

The Gendarmerie d'Haïti was administratively a branch of the client-government, and marines who officered the force held official commissions from the Haitian government while simultaneously retaining their rank in the Marine Corps. The first commandant of the organization was Marine Major Smedley D. Butler, who took command in December, 1915, and assumed the rank of Major General, Gendarmerie d'Haïti. Under Butler's energetic direction the Gendarmerie rapidly took shape and legally began to perform police functions in February, 1916.

A major problem which Butler had to contend with was the recruitment of satisfactory personnel, both for the Haitian rank and file and for the American officer corps. Haitians, who were induced to enlist by pay ranging from $10 per month for privates to $25 per month for top sergeants, were generally uneducated and undernourished. Lack of physical stamina among the recruits necessitated lower standards of military discipline until health measures could take effect. Butler remarked: "I have frequently found a sentry on a post in front of an important building sound asleep, standing up with the sun shining in his face. That is not his fault. He was diseased. An examination showed that 95 percent of them had blood diseases and 85 percent had intestinal worms." [9]

Educational deficiency also was characteristic of recruits, the great majority of whom came from the illiterate poorer classes. As was the case across the border in the Dominican Republic, members of the educated upper class shunned service in the American constabulary, partly because of nationalistic reluctance to collaborate with the Occupation and partly because of the low social status associated with subservient police work.* Early attempts to set up an officer-candidate program for the Haitian elite failed because of the difficulty in obtaining volunteers and because of elite hostility to the demeaning aspects of American-style military training. Elite volunteers, who became social outcasts by enlisting, resented having to wear privates' uniforms and refused to perform menial duties, such as grooming horses, which were facets of American officer indoctrination. An initial effort to train ten elite officer-candidate volunteers in 1915 failed completely, and, although infrequent attempts were made in subsequent years, there was no effective officer training program until the establishment of the Ecole Militaire in 1928.[10] Up to 1929 the predominant source of Haitian officers for the Gendarmerie was promotion from the ranks. While such promotions were relatively few in number and limited to the lowest officer ranks, they provided an important new avenue of social mobility for lower-class Haitians, who received formal schooling within the Gendarmerie.[11]

During the early years, when the Gendarmerie officer corps was exclusively American, finding suitable marine volunteers was also a difficult problem. The war in Europe resulted in a sevenfold increase in the enlisted strength of the Marine Corps (from 9,968 in

* In 1927 the name "Gendarmerie d'Haïti" was changed to "Garde d'Haïti" at the request of Haitian client-President Louis Borno in order to remove the social stigma associated with the French word "gendarmerie." SD 838.00/2376, C. Gross to F. B. Kellogg, Aug. 22, 1927.

For a description of similar difficulties in recruiting officer candidates in the Dominican Republic, see Marvin Goldwert, *The Constabulary in the Dominican Republic and Nicaragua: Progeny and Legacy of United States Intervention* (Gainesville: Univ. of Florida Press, 1962), pp. 10–11.

1915 to 72,370 in December, 1918) and filled the ranks with inexperienced men. In 1918 the commandant of the Gendarmerie characterized the problem of finding "suitable material" for the Gendarmerie officer corps as "grave." [12] Even with the improvement in personnel after the European war was over, the officer corps of the Gendarmerie remained less than satisfactory. In 1922 Major General Wendell C. Neville wrote the State Department: "We have found that most of our troubles in Haiti, for instance, were due to noncommissioned officers given commissions in the Gendarmerie, this, notwithstanding the fact that they were amenable to our laws and regulations." [13] In order to attract the best caliber of marines for duty as Gendarmerie officers, volunteers were offered extra remuneration and the privileges of higher rank.

Most of the American officers in the Gendarmerie were marine enlisted men who were given special commissions by the Haitian client-government. All Americans continued to receive their regular pay and allowances as marines and in addition received pay from the Haitian government. Rank equations between the Marine Corps and the Gendarmerie varied, with some marine privates serving as captains in the Gendarmerie while some marine sergeants were only second lieutenants in the Gendarmerie. Pay also varied according to differences in family allowances and such. A representative rank/pay roster, dating from December, 1918, follows: [14]

Rank		Pay	
Marine	Gendarmerie	U.S.*	Haitian Govt.
LT COL	MAJ GEN	$5,814	$3,000
1st SGT	CAPT	1,500	1,800
SGT	CAPT	1,308	1,800
CPL	1st LT	1,296	1,200
PVT	2nd LT	1,100	720

* includes allowances.

President Wilson vetoed a suggestion that the Haitian government also be required to reimburse the United States for the regular salaries of marines serving in Haiti.[15]

The extra pay received by marines serving in the Gendarmerie was by no means entirely gratuitous, since the duty could be hard and often involved prolonged periods of deprivation at isolated interior posts. Smedley Butler, commandant of the Gendarmerie, complained about an initial delay in the payment of the bonus money to his officers, stating:

Non-commissioned officers performing duty in the "bushes" are certainly working like dogs for these wretched people, and I consider it an outrage that this Government [the Dartiguenave client-government] is not required to sign this agreement, and let them get their pay. Serving with Marines is a matter of duty with us—an honor—serving with Haitians is entirely different, and these men should be paid.[16]

In addition to pay and rank benefits, volunteers for Gendarmerie service received forty-five days' leave per year outside Haiti. Other factors, by no means inconsequential, in attracting volunteers were the exotic character of the duty and the opportunity to be of help to the Haitians. Gendarmerie Commandant Butler expressed his attitude toward duty in Haiti:

We were all embued with the fact that we were trustees of a huge estate that belonged to minors. That was my viewpoint; that was the viewpoint I personally took, that the Haitians were our wards and that we were endeavoring to develop and make for them a rich and productive property.[17]

Years later, Butler changed his perspective on the American occupation of Haiti and stated that the marines had been used as "a glorified bill-collecting agency" and that he had personally been "canned" in Haiti because he had refused to cooperate with New York banking interests, but this was not what he was saying at the time he organized the Gendarmerie. In recruiting marine officers for Gendarmerie duty Butler appealed to sympathy for Haiti and emphasized Haiti's need of American help.[18]

The Gendarmerie rapidly became the instrument of American authority in Haiti. The separate First Marine Brigade remained as a substantial garrison force in Port-au-Prince and Cap Haïtien but acted as a reserve force to back up the Gendarmerie in times of crisis. The ordinary, day-to-day governing of the country was the responsibility of the Gendarmerie officers, who were omnipotent in their assigned localities. Brigade Commander Eli K. Cole reported in 1917:

For a long time to come the White Officers of the Gendarmerie d'Haïti will form the only organization on which we can rely for honest and efficient administration in all parts of the country: my policy has been to extend our influence throughout the country by utilizing in all possible ways their activities, and I believe that through them we are going to be able to get a very strong hold (moral and physical) over the people of this country.[19]

Gendarmerie officers exercised authority over most local governmental and military matters and, according to personal inclinations, dominated their respective regions completely. One young American officer was referred to as *papa blanc* * (white father) by the Haitians in his district, and he addressed them in turn as *mon fils* (my son) and *ma fille* (my daughter).[20] Another Gendarmerie officer, a marine sergeant, became the crowned king of the island of La Gonave in Port-au-Prince Bay.[21] An American civilian, Dr. S. G. Inman, observed:

The marine who becomes an officer in the gendarmerie finds himself clothed with practically unlimited power, in the district where he serves. He is the judge of practically all civil and criminal cases, settling everything from a family fight to a murder. He is paymaster for all funds expended by the national government, he is ex-officio director of the schools, inasmuch as he pays the teachers. He controls the mayor and city council, since they can spend no funds without his o.k. As collector of taxes he exercises a strong influence on all individuals in the community.[22]

Under Butler, the Gendarmerie was powerful also at the national level. An American who went to Haiti in 1917 as traveling companion to Assistant Secretary of the Navy Franklin D. Roosevelt noted that "the actual running of the Government comes pretty near being vested in General Butler and his young colonels and majors." [23]

The development of the Gendarmerie as an effective military force, made difficult by the poor health and illiteracy of the Haitian recruits, was complicated by the language barrier. Few marines knew French and fewer still understood Haitian Creole. The English comprehension of Haitian gendarmes was limited to the march-

---

* The term "blanc" came to have a disparaging racial connotation in Haiti corresponding to the American term "nigger," but this does not necessarily apply in the above case.

ing commands barked out by their marine drillmasters. The resulting weaknesses and failings of the Gendarmerie were of little consequence until the force was challenged by the major caco uprisings of 1918–19. Prior to these uprisings, the Gendarmerie, along with the First Marine Brigade, performed the relatively easy tasks of suppressing plots against client-President Dartiguenave and maintaining security against possible German activities during the period of United States involvement in World War I.

The European war had immediate and important consequences in Haiti. A primary purpose of the American intervention in 1915 had been to counteract the presumed threat of German encroachment. Early American efforts to curtail German influence were intensified after the United States declared war against Germany in April, 1917, after which fear of German submarines and espionage activities kept the Gendarmerie and the marines on the alert until the end of the war in November, 1918. By means of wartime confiscation of property and internment of German nationals, along with postwar deportations, the United States deliberately and effectively eliminated German interests from participation in Haitian commerce. The war thus served as a perfect opportunity for the United States to supplant its leading rival in Haiti.

At the time of the American intervention there were approximately 210 Germans in Haiti, including Germano-Haitian wives and children of German nationals, while there were only about 50 Americans.[24] The German element was hostile to the intervention, realizing that the profitable business of financing revolutions was now at an end and that the Americans would discriminate against them in commerce and politics. From the very beginning of the occupation, Americans suspected that local Germans were intriguing against them.[25]

Marine Brigade Commander Waller linked Germans to the first serious attempt to assassinate President Dartiguenave in early 1916, while the *New York Herald,* bemoaning the "German menace in the Caribbean," contended that Germans were fomenting revolution in Haiti:

The German scheme is to arm the natives in the mountains and in the coast cities and bring about a general uprising in the event President Dartiguenave does not make good his threat to resign the Presidency.

Those German interests control every man who is in opposition to Dartiguenave and are supplying the brains of the rebellious faction in Congress.[26]

The *Herald* stated that "the fact was definitely established" that German financiers were negotiating in New York City for arms and ammunition to be used in Haiti. At about this time the War Department received an alarming dispatch about a mysterious Japanese agent, J. A. Ichicawa, who was reported to be headed for Haiti posing as a rice merchant. According to United States intelligence, Ichicawa had previously been involved in anti-American insurrections in the Philippines and might attempt to overthrow Dartiguenave in Haiti in order to procure a Japanese coaling station.[27] Speculation about enemy intrigues in Haiti became more clearly focused and pertinent after United States entrance into the war against Germany.

After the American declaration of war the marine commander in Haiti instructed the Gendarmerie to maintain close surveillance over all Germans in Haiti but not directly interfere with them unless they did something prejudicial to the United States. Brigade Commander Cole reported to Washington in February and March, 1917, that he was sure that local Germans were receiving secret instructions and that they were "in secret ways trying to block us where ever possible," current rumors having it that "a German raider will land forces near Leogane, march on Port-au-Prince, destroy the Americans, put the Germans in control, and then re-embark."[28] Cole's personal estimation of the German threat varied from time to time. In early April, 1917, he wrote that the local Germans would cause no trouble because "they realize that what they could do here would not affect the outcome of the war . . . but if they mix in the affair they are going to stand in a great danger of losing all their property." Shortly after Cole wrote this, his intelligence sources reported that Germans were plotting bombings, riots, and assassination attempts on prominent American officers.[29]

All the investigations of rumors, surveillance of German firms, censoring of letters, and other counterespionage work failed to turn up much concrete evidence of German intrigue.[30] The most substantive indication of complicity by resident Germans was a message from the German minister in Port-au-Prince to the imperial chancellor that was intercepted and turned over to the State Department by the British ambassador at Washington in June, 1917, apparently having been obtained in much the same way as the famous Zimmermann telegram of January, 1917.* The message from the German minister at Port-au-Prince, dated March 31, 1917, told of propaganda work undertaken by a local German newspaper, L'Echo, which was distributed gratuitously throughout Haiti and told the "truth" about the German war cause.[31] It is doubtful that this propaganda effort, if it existed at all, amounted to much. There is no mention of L'Echo in American reports, and, given the strict American press censorship of all local newspapers and the careful surveillance of German activities, it is not likely that such a paper would have gone unnoticed. Local Germans were incarcerated for much more innocuous activities than propaganda work, as, for instance, the case in January, 1918, when two Germans were sentenced to five years in prison for trying to leave Haiti in a small boat, with allegedly incriminating maps of England and the eastern United States and a small chart of the Atlantic Ocean in their baggage. In another incident, close surveillance of German residents resulted in the disclosure that several of them had sung the German national anthem at the home of Herr Lucas on Christmas Eve, 1917; Lucas was threatened with trial before a marine provost court if the incident was ever repeated.[32]

A more dramatic threat than possible machinations by the German colony was the possibility of enemy attacks by German raiders and submarines. Most of the marine career officers stationed in Haiti were eager to take part in the European war and were frustrated at being stuck in Haiti. Gendarmerie Commandant Butler, for instance, wrote in June, 1917, that duty in Haiti was "becoming more and more detestable every day and the knowledge that I am not to be allowed to fight for my country, makes it even more unbearable." [33] Under the circumstances any opportunity to engage the German war machine in Haiti was more than welcome. The American officer

* The British had broken the German diplomatic code and, after February, 1917, provided the State Department with copies of certain transatlantic radio messages emanating from the imperial chancery in Berlin and the various German diplomatic posts in Latin America. Barbara Tuchman, The Zimmermann Telegram (New York: Dell Publishing Co., 1965), originally published in 1958.

commanding the Gendarmerie in the south of Haiti wrote that "war fever" took hold in Haiti in early 1917, when marines were ordered to make coastal reconnaissances in search of enemy submarine bases.[34] Brigade Commander General Cole * felt that no German raider would risk being bottled up in Port-au-Prince harbor and that the danger of submarine bases was "almost infinitesimal," yet Cole was eager to do his part in the war against Germany and recommended elaborate defense measures for Haiti. Cole once reported an unverified rumor that the French ship *Montreal* had been sunk in Port-au-Prince Bay by a German submarine convoyed by two fishing smacks, and requested 5-inch guns for harbor defense.[35] In fact, the *Montreal,* which had taken on a load of coffee at Petit Goâve, was sunk while nearing the coast of France.[36] Marine defense measures against German invasion included plans for resistance by United States troops and the Gendarmerie and for the arrest of all local Germans appearing on a blacklist. American businessmen were organized and drilled as a civil defense force. No submarine bases were ever discovered and there were no German invasions.

By far the most significant facet of the anti-German campaign in Haiti was the sequestration of German property and the internment of leading German merchants following the declaration of war against Germany by the Dartiguenave client-government in July, 1918. Gendarmerie Commandant Butler had long since urged that the State Department "'cook up' some scheme to drive the German influence out of this country, now that the 'open season' for Germans is upon us, as after the war we should control this island." Butler noted that "A declaration of war would permit us to take most any step we saw fit towards the German holdings here." [37] The Haitian legislature had originally refused to declare war against Germany, in what General Cole referred to as "a deliberate slap at the U.S.," but this obstacle was removed by the permanent dissolution of the legislature in June, 1917.[38] Shortly after the formal declaration of war in 1918 all German property was sequestered, twenty-two leading Germans were interned, and all remaining members of the German colony were required to register and report daily at local Gendarmerie offices.[39]

---

* Cole, previously mentioned as a colonel, was promoted at the outbreak of the European war along with Butler, Waller, and other career marines.

German property and commercial enterprises had been impinged upon long before outright sequestration. The American military commander received and enforced a British blacklist of sixteen Haitian firms in August, 1917, and an American blacklist of twelve firms in December, 1917. Even before America entered the war General Cole took steps to expunge German interests from participation in the Haitian-American Sugar Company (HASCO). Under pressure from American authorities, HASCO later shifted its business from a private German bank to the American bank.[40] HASCO also took over the German-owned public utilities at Port-au-Prince. The German ice plant at Port-au-Prince was commandeered, incidentally causing considerable friction between the marines and local residents because, despite the shortage of ammonia during the war and resulting curtailment of production, officers' families continued to be supplied while Haitians and American civilians went without.[41] The sequestration of German property in July, 1918, while a serious blow to German interests, was ameliorated by the fact that some Germans, anticipating the move, had transferred their property to Haitians to avoid sequestration.

The internment of the twenty-two leading Germans lasted from July, 1918, to July, 1919. Conditions at the internment camp in Port-au-Prince were generally comfortable and the prisoners were treated humanely, but their ordeal did not end with the return of peace. Upon their release in 1919 following the signing of the Germano-Haitian peace treaty, the prisoners were not given complete freedom but were restricted to Port-au-Prince and required to continue reporting daily to the Gendarmerie. The United States was determined that the Germans should not be allowed to regain their former position in Haitian commerce. Colonel John H. Russell, brigade commander most of the time from 1918 to 1922 and subsequently American high commissioner, remarked in 1919: "The recent war has afforded an opportunity for the elimination of this class [Germans] from commerce and politics, and it is hoped that by this time this has been effected." [42] At the time the Germans were released from internment, Brigade Commander Louis McCarty Little earnestly recommended to Washington that they be repatriated to Germany for fear that "they will undoubtedly if allowed to remain shortly control all the business of this island to the exclusion of the present budding native enterprise." [43]

Colonel Russell, who resumed command of the brigade in late 1919, was "most anxious" that the Germans be hastily deported, and by January, 1920, orders had been issued by the Dartiguenave government for the deportation of fifty leading Germans. [44] Deported Germans were required to sign agreements not to return to Haiti unless granted specific permission by the marine brigade commander. Russell also took steps to restrict new German immigration by making an arrangement whereby the Dutch steamship line connecting Amsterdam with Port-au-Prince refused passage to Germans, regardless of passports visaed by the Haitian consul at Amsterdam, unless special permission had first been obtained from Russell. In December, 1920, Russell stated that "Haiti now well cleared of them [Germans] and I am strongly of the opinion that they should not be allowed to return except in special cases." [45] The State Department colluded in this policy, with the proviso that permission to enter Haiti not be denied to "bona fide German immigrants who settling in Haiti will contribute to the prosperity of the Republic and commercial development." [46] Russell made the subsequent decisions on which Germans were "bona fide" and which were dangerous to American interests; Germans never did regain a prominent place in Haitian commerce and politics.

Germans had originally created their strong commercial position in Haiti by marrying Haitian women and thus circumventing the long-standing prohibition of alien landownership. The Americans, rejecting this circuitous device, sought to open the way for American economic penetration by striking the alien landholding clause from the Haitian Constitution. This involved a major break with past Haitian efforts to prevent foreign encroachments and preserve the national patrimony from outside exploitation. Every one of Haiti's sixteen constitutions up to the time of the American intervention had prohibited alien landownership. A State Department official, writing in 1927, summarized the American legalization of foreign landownership as follows:

It was obvious that if our occupation was to be beneficial to Haiti and further her progress it was necessary that foreign capital should come to Haiti, in order to establish new industries and stimulate agricultural production in that country. Americans could hardly be expected to put their money into plantations and big agricultural enterprises in Haiti if they could not themselves own the land on which their money was to be spent. For this reason the United States Government caused the provision prohibiting the ownership of land by foreigners to be omitted from the new [1918] Constitution of Haiti. . . . The United States did use rather high handed methods to get the Constitution adopted by the people of Haiti.[47]

In drafting the new Constitution, the "most important change" made by the State Department in the proposals submitted by the Haitian client-government and the American officials in Haiti was the striking of a five-year residence requirement for alien land-ownership which "would have given unfair advantage to the Germans who were approximately the only ones who would have been resident in Haiti for five years." [48]

In 1917 a National Assembly, consisting of both chambers of the Haitian legislature, was convened to consider the adoption of the new American-sponsored constitution. According to the Constitution of 1889, then in effect, only the National Assembly could alter a constitution or replace it with a new one. The Haitian legislature, unlike the Dartiguenave client-government, had repeatedly demonstrated its political vitality and independence by protesting against and frustrating American designs. The 1917 National Assembly refused to pass the American-sponsored constitution. Instead, the Assembly drafted a new anti-American constitution of its own, and was in the process of passing this when proceedings were dramatically interrupted by Major Smedley Butler, who read a dissolution decree signed by President Dartiguenave. Butler observed privately that the Assembly had become "so impudent that the Gendarmerie had to dissolve them, which dissolution was effected by genuinely Marine Corps methods." * The obstreperous Haitian legislature did not sit again until after the strikes and riots of 1929.

* Butler added in the same letter that he would later give his correspondent, future Financial Adviser John A. McIlhenny, a "mouth to ear account of this dissolution, am afraid to write it, for fear the Department of State might get hold of this letter by means of the censors." Butler to McIlhenny, June 23, 1917; The Smedley Darlington Butler Papers, MARCORPS MUS.

The dissolution of the legislature was nominally achieved by the action of client-President Dartiguenave, but Dartiguenave, who was himself beginning to become recalcitrant by this time, had been browbeaten by Butler.[49] In any case, American authorities had agreed to dissolve the Assembly by force if Dartiguenave did not cooperate. The American minister reported to Lansing:

. . . the Assembly was in every way reactionary and opposed to the best interests of Haiti, refusing to adopt any article permitting foreign ownership of land in any manner whatsoever, and when matters in the Assembly had proceeded thus far . . . it was decided in a conference held at the legation on June 18 . . . to prevent the Assembly from passing such a Constitution by causing its dissolution, if occasion demanded it, preferably by a Presidential Decree, but if necessary by order of the Commander of the Occupation.[50]

A few days later Lansing, perhaps wary of Wilson's high regard for correct constitutional procedure, wrote the president that "You will observe that the Haitian Government is wholly responsible for the recent dissolving of the National Assembly. . . . I think that it is wise to allow the President of Haiti to work out this problem which is largely due to German residents in the island." [51] Scruples about constitutional procedures were completely disregarded in the subsequent promulgation of the new Constitution.

President Dartiguenave was left with little room for political maneuvering after the dissolution of the National Assembly, which had served as a bulwark of resistance to the Americans and had allowed Dartiguenave to attempt a middle position. General Cole reported: "There is no question but what the dissolution of the National Assembly has given us an absolute power over the President and has put us in such a position that whatever we demand will have to be executed by him—this he has promised completely." [52]

Dartiguenave quickly reverted to his earlier attitude of complete cooperation and himself suggested that the American-sponsored constitution be adopted by a plebiscite. According to a later State Department memorandum, the United States would have "greatly preferred" having the National Assembly pass the new constitution as required by Haitian law, but it was certain that new elections would result in another hostile assembly, so the department authorized the extralegal plebiscite, realizing that "The people casting ballots would be 97% illiterate, ignorant in most cases of what they were voting for." [53]

The plebiscite on the new constitution was held in June, 1918, and it passed by the overwhelming majority of 98,225 in favor as against 768 opposed.[54] The plebiscite was closely supervised by the Gendarmerie, which ran the polls and distributed the ballots. Prior to the election the commandant of the Gendarmerie issued instructions that barbecues and popular meetings, paid for out of Gendarmerie funds, be held to drum up support for the constitution, and that the American system of forced-labor road building be suspended for the week preceding the election. District Gendarmerie officers were also ordered to arrest any opponents of the constitution who publicly expressed their views.[55] Because of the suspiciously lopsided results of the plebiscite, in which 67 out of 96 polling places reported no negative votes at all, the marine commander felt compelled to write a special report to Washington.[*] He explained that, while there was no great enthusiasm for the new constitution, the impressive victory was caused by the fact that opponents did not vote rather than by marine interference in the election.[56] In fact, judging from contemporary population estimates, less than 5 percent of the population participated in the plebiscite. Years later Josephus Daniels wrote his former Assistant Secretary of the Navy, then President Franklin D. Roosevelt, that "I never did wholly approve of that Constitution of Haiti you had a hand in framing. . . . I expect, in the light of experience, we both regret the necessity of denying even a semblance of 'self-determination' in our control of Haiti." [57]

The new Constitution contained, of course, the desired provision granting foreigners the right to own property. Other features were the creation of a Council of State, appointed by the client-president, to perform all legislative functions until the elected legislature was

---

[*] Marine-controlled elections were not always devoid of favoritism. Smedley Butler described a marine-sponsored election in Nicaragua as follows: "The opposition candidates were declared bandits when it became necessary to elect our man to office. Our candidates always win. In one election nobody liked the fellow; . . . the district was canvassed, and 400 were found who would vote for the proper candidate. Notice of the opening of the polls was given five minutes beforehand, the 400 voters were assembled in a line and when they had voted, in about two hours, the polls were closed." Butler quoted in "The Hate of Haiti," *Literary Digest*, CIII, No. 12 (Dec. 21, 1929), 6–7. Also *New York Herald Tribune*, Dec. 7, 1929, p. 11, referring to the above statement made by Butler in a speech in Pittsburgh on Dec. 5, 1929.

reconstituted. Legislative elections would be held in "an even-numbered year" to be determined by the president. The irremovability of judges was suspended for a six-month period following promulgation of the Constitution. In a Special Article, all acts of the United States military occupation were validated.[58] In sum, the Constitution of 1918 served to consolidate the legal and constitutional position of both the Occupation and the client-government. It also presumably laid the bases from which Haiti would henceforth proceed along the enlightened paths of Wilsonian constitutionalism.

While the political machinery was thus being strengthened, the marines simultaneously were enhancing the military effectiveness of the Gendarmerie and the marine brigade by means of an extensive road-building program. At the time of the American intervention the only roads connecting major towns were the old French roads, which had fallen into disrepair and were impassable to modern vehicles. The commandant of the Gendarmerie noted that "This condition, principally from a military viewpoint, early drew the attention of American Marine officers whose military movements were hindered and sometimes defeated by the deplorable roads." [59]

Lacking adequate funds for a major road-building program because of the fiscal pauperage of the client-government, the Americans revived an 1864 Haitian law, discovered by Smedley Butler, by which peasants were required to perform labor on local roads in lieu of paying a road tax. This system, known as the corvée, had its historical roots in the unpaid labor which French peasants owed their feudal lords and was strikingly similar to the corvée employed by the British occupation to dredge canals in Egypt in the 1880s and 1890s. In Haiti the corvée resulted in the construction of an impressive network of roads connecting major towns, with the greatest achievement being a 170-mile unpaved highway between Port-au-Prince and the northern center of Cap Haïtien. The peasants, however, resented the forced labor, and resistance to the corvée soon developed into a full-scale revolt. In response to praise from Washington, Butler, who masterminded the system, wrote to Assistant Secretary of the Navy Roosevelt that "It would not do to ask too many questions as to how we accomplish this work." [60]

The corvée was inherently offensive to Haitian peasants, who prized their independence as small landholders and feared the return of slavery at the hands of white men. As the system became ridden with abuses, resistance increased proportionally. In 1920 Admiral H. S. Knapp, the military governor of Santo Domingo and the administrative commander in Haiti, reported to Secretary of the Navy Daniels that "it appears to be undeniable" that Haitians had been forced to work outside of their home districts, had been kept at work under guard, and had "been marched to and from their work bound together." [61] The corvée gangs were always kept under Gendarmerie guard, and native gendarmes practiced brutality on their charges.[62] The roping together of workers was especially upsetting to the peasants, since it recalled legends of French colonial slave gangs.

Because of rising hostility, the corvée was officially abolished in August, 1918. The brigade commander's August proclamation informed the citizens:

The time has come to put a stop to further bloodshed. . . . The Corvee has been done away with entirely. Work on the road is entirely voluntary and will be paid for daily. The workmen will be free to come and go when it pleases them. . . . Any injustices committed by native or American officials should be reported to American Military Officials and justice will be done and the offender punished.[63]

The succeeding brigade commander, Colonel Russell, decided on his arrival that, while the corvée had been a "source of continual trouble" and it was desirable to discontinue it, this would not be feasible until "certain roads, needed for military purposes, had been opened up." [64] A second and final order abolishing the corvée was issued in October, 1918.

Despite official termination, the corvée was continued illegally in the northern and central regions of Haiti by district marine commander Major Clarke H. Wells, who denied continuation of the corvée in his reports to headquarters.[65] This mountainous region had been the traditional center of caco activity and was the area where road construction was most difficult and most important to military accessibility. It became the center of the 1918–19 caco uprising and the region in which most confirmed atrocities were committed. In early 1919, a new brigade commander, General Albertus W. Catlin, personally investigated rumors of Gendarmerie malevolence in central Haiti, found the corvée still in existence and the countryside depopulated, and ordered all patrolling by gendarmes in the Hinche area to cease because of brutality.[66] Lieutenant Colonel Richard C. Hooker, conducting a special investigation ordered by Catlin, reported that the corvée was responsible for a "reign of terror" in the interior and that "indiscriminate strong-arm work being pulled off" had caused the local peasants to hide out in the hills for fear of the Gendarmerie. Hooker noted that he "got the impression that the officers higher up were approving these methods," and that "The situation in that whole district is, to say the least, out of hand." [67] After his investigation General Catlin relieved the district marine commander and caused the commandant of the Gendarmerie to issue a general order forbidding the killing of Haitian prisoners. Asked why the order was issued, the Gendarmerie commandant later stated, "it is a strong tradition in the military service that every offense is followed by the issuance of an order forbidding every one else to do the same thing." [68]

The corvée and associated brutality instigated a massive uprising against the Occupation. At one point the formidable caco leader Charlemagne Peralte organized a provisional government in the north and vowed to drive the Americans into the sea with his several thousand troops. Brigade Commander Russell estimated that Peralte had 2,000 "bandits" under his command in the fall of 1919, while Peralte earlier claimed to have had 30,000 to 40,000 followers.[69] Whatever the actual number of combatants, 1919 was a year of intense guerrilla warfare in Haiti, with official Marine Corps statistics listing 1,861 Haitians killed in that year out of a total of 2,250 for the first five years of the occupation.[70] Colonel Russell described Peralte's force as armed mostly with machetes, knives, pikes, a few pistols, and 200 or 300 rifles, and noted that they were very short of ammunition, using "our ammunition and the Krag by tying a piece of goatskin on a string around the base of the cartridge." [71] Charlemagne himself was eventually killed by two marines, disguised as blacks who sneaked into his camp at night and shot him. In an attempt to demoralize the guerrillas, the marines disseminated photographs of Charlemagne's body, but made the mistake of propping him up so that he looked like Christ on the cross. The photograph became a continuing source of inspiration to Haitian nationalists. Nevertheless, the 1919 insurrection declined after Charlemagne's death and was ultimately shattered in an unsuccessful direct attack on Port-au-Prince.

The cacos though poorly equipped and unsophisticated in the techniques of modern warfare, were more than a match for the infant Gendarmerie. Lieutenant Colonel Frederick M. Wise, who took command of the Gendarmerie in July, 1919, found the force in bad shape, with low morale and inferior equipment, and later recalled: "I discovered that my predecessors had discouraged target practice on the theory that it was dangerous to teach the native how to shoot. Some day they might possibly turn against us!" [72]

This failure to train the gendarmes dated back to the period when the marines were commanded by Colonel Waller, who once remarked that "you can never trust a nigger with a gun." [73] The question of how far Americans could trust their Haitian subordinates remained a problem at all levels of the occupation, and necessarily so since the relationship was ultimately based on force.

Given the unreliability of the Gendarmerie, the marine brigade was called upon to put down the caco revolt and, in early 1919, itself required reinforcements. The marines enjoyed marked superiority over the cacos in weaponry and training. They even had aerial support, with the cacos serving as targets for the first recorded instance of coordinated air-ground combat, in March, 1919. Cacos would be surrounded by marines in the bush and then have bombs dropped in their midst, causing them to panic and abandon their protective cover.[74] At the 1921 Senate Hearings on the Occupation, General George Barnett, commandant of the Marine Corps from 1914 to 1920, was asked to comment on the striking contrast in Haitian as opposed to marine casualties during the first five years of the occupation. According to a report made by Barnett, 2,250 Haitians were killed as against 14 or 16 marines.* The general replied:

* Earlier, Barnett had reported to Secretary Daniels that 3,250 Haitians had been killed. At the Senate Hearings, Barnett stated that the true figure was 2,250, and that the 1,000 mistake had been caused by an error in addition. Marine Corps records indicate that the original 3,250 figure was correct. Month-by-month casualty reports for the period from March, 1919, to November, 1920, total 3,071 Haitians killed. Barnett to Daniels, Sept. 18, 1920; NA, RG80, File No. 26283-3725:9. Barnett testimony; Senate Hearings, 1922, 433–34. "Election and Bandit Data" file, MARCORPS HQ Haiti MSS, Box 30.

It was largely like it was in the Philippines. There were a great many natives down there who would be friends today and so-called Cacos tomorrow. They had no uniform, and it was hard to distinguish one from the other, and they were not well armed. They were brave, but they would have no show against well-armed troops, especially with machine guns, and it is perfectly natural to suppose that the contrast would be very marked and that a very great number should be killed in comparison with the number of white people killed.[75]

Even so, the casualty statistics in Haiti were extraordinary; the kill ratio during the Philippine insurrection had been 25 to 1.[76] Despite the overwhelming advantages enjoyed by the marines, this, like most repressive guerrilla wars, was a frustrating and degrading experience for the superior, pursuing forces.

Considering the difficulties and frustrations encountered by the marines in hunting down elusive cacos, the almost unbearable living conditions in the brush, and American racial prejudices against "gooks," [77] it was almost inevitable that the marines allowed the rules of civilized warfare to lapse and that a number of atrocities were committed. The records of the 1921 Senate Hearings are replete with detailed atrocity stories, but much of the evidence was hearsay and relatively few allegations could be legally proved.[78] Relevant Marine Corps records and investigations deal mainly with the problem of illegal killing of prisoners, which was apparently widespread in northern Haiti in 1919. One American Gendarmerie officer, who had commanded a corvée detail of 3,000 Haitians, estimated from aggregate reports and rumors that there were at least 400 illegal executions, and Major T. C. Turner concluded an investigation undertaken in 1919 by stating:

Almost everyone stationed in Haiti during the early part of this year seemed to have some knowledge of the fact that both marines and gendarmes were killing prisoners. It was very difficult to get any witnesses to testify directly as, in the opinion of the undersigned, they were all equally culpable.[79]

Turner felt that Major Clarke H. Wells, a colonel in the Gendarmerie who commanded the District of the North in late 1918 and early 1919, was responsible for the killings and that subordinates had simply obeyed his orders. Marine Corps Commandant John A. Lejeune reported to Daniels in 1920 that there was specific evidence that Wells had knowledge of the illegal continuance of the corvée in his district, that he had given orders to his subordinates to "bump off" caco prisoners and to kill all suspected cacos rather than bring them in, and that Wells had ordered his juniors to suppress reports of unfavorable conditions in the district. General Lejeune recommended that Wells be tried by general court-martial, but marine investigations had been undertaken too late to build a concrete case, and court-martial charges were withdrawn for insufficiency of evidence. Lejeune also noted that there was evidence that Lieutenant Colonel Alexander S. Williams, commandant of the Gendarmerie, also had knowledge of the killing of prisoners but, again, there was insufficient evidence for a court-martial.[80]

A good indication of the actual extent of brutality can be gained by reading between the lines of a confidential order issued to the marines in Haiti by the Brigade Commander in October, 1919:

1. The brigade commander has had brought to his attention an alleged charge against marines and gendarmes in Haiti to the effect that in the past prisoners and wounded bandits have been summarily shot without trial. Furthermore, that troops in the field have declared and carried on what is commonly known as "open season," where care is not taken to determine whether or not the natives encountered are bandits or "good citizens" and where houses have been ruthlessly burned merely because they were unoccupied and native property otherwise destroyed.

2. Such action on the part of any officer or enlisted man of the Marine Corps is beyond belief; and if true, would be a terrible smirch upon the unblemished record of the corps, which we all hold so dear.[81]

This order was promulgated to all marines in Haiti, with the additional proviso that it would be read to each new marine as he arrived. The severe tone of the order and the explicit references to various types of misdeeds are evidence that the problems discussed were real and widespread.

Secretary Daniels later noted that "There were unquestionably some things done by the gendarmerie and some of the marines which deserved punishment and nobody could have been more distressed than President Wilson and myself." [82] Efforts to investigate and prosecute offenders were, however, foiled. Certain Gendarmerie records related to the investigation of atrocities mysteriously disappeared.[83] Daniels' order for a full investigation in August, 1920, was subverted by the assistant adjutant general of the Marine Corps with the approval of Major General Commandant George Barnett; Daniels remarked that this "stunned" him and caused him to call Barnett on the carpet.[84] Civilian control over the marines within the Navy Department was eroding as the lame-duck Wilson administration muddled through its last months in power. In November, 1920, Commandant John A. Lejeune informed Daniels that a report of a completed investigation by Brigade Commander Russell, dated March, 1920, "was never received, being apparently lost in the mail," a fact which was not discovered until September.[85] Daniels dispatched a court of inquiry, headed by Caribbean veteran Admiral Henry T. Mayo, to Haiti in the fall of 1920. This investigation resulted in the disclosure of only a small number of isolated atrocities, all of which, by suspicious coincidence, had already been prosecuted by previous general courts-martial.[86] While the Mayo court was in Haiti, it conspicuously neglected to call as a witness the commandant of the Gendarmerie, Lieutenant Colonel Frederick M. Wise, who was familiar with "rough stuff" that had gone on in the interior and had let it be known that "If they put me on the stand under oath I was going to tell the truth." [87]

Despite efforts to minimize the atrocities and killings, the brutal aspects of the occupation became a major national issue in the United States with the inadvertent publication, during the 1920 presidential campaign, of a 1919 letter in which Marine Corps Commandant Barnett had ordered the commander in Haiti to stop the "indiscriminate killing of natives." [88] In this letter Barnett wrote Colonel Russell that "The court-martial of one private for the killing of a native prisoner brought out a statement by his counsel which showed me that practically indiscriminate killing of natives has gone on for some time." [89] This letter and earlier assertions by Democratic vice-presidential candidate Franklin D. Roosevelt that he had had a hand in running several Caribbean republics and had written the 1918 Constitution of Haiti were exploited by Republican candidate Warren Harding, who used the episodes to denounce the Wilson administration. The publicity engendered by the 1920 presidential campaign resulted in a series of journalistic exposés and a reassessment of the Occupation, culminating in the 1921 Senate Inquiry and the subsequent reorganization of the Occupation by the Republicans.

6

Reorganization and Rationalization

Under the Wilson administration, which was preoccupied with the European war, the occupation of Haiti received little positive direction from Washington. The only high-level appraisal of the Haitian situation during the war years was a 1917 visit to Haiti by Assistant Secretary of the Navy Franklin D. Roosevelt. Roosevelt did little more than give an unqualified endorsement to marine activities, engage in ceremonial functions, and investigate possibilities of investment in Haiti for his own personal enrichment. Major American policy developments were limited to the passing of the new Haitian Constitution of 1918 and to a twenty-year extension of the 1915 treaty; both these moves were designed to legitimize the occupation in the legal sense and to open the way for American investments.

With the end of the European war, the military occupation was no longer necessary to safeguard American strategic interests; moreover, Wilson was faced with the embarrassing contradiction implicit in his championing the rights of small nations at the 1919 Versailles Peace Conference while simultaneously maintaining military control over Haiti. Wilson tried to withdraw American troops from Haiti in 1919, but found that this was impossible because the marines were tied down by a major guerrilla war. Instead of reducing American military commitment, the Wilson administration was obliged to reinforce the marines in Haiti, acknowledge the need for a prolonged occupation, and come to terms with the administrative confusion that had characterized the occupation from the outset. Possible efforts to reorganize the occupation were dropped when the Haitian situation became a political issue during the 1920 presidential election campaign, a development which silenced internal criticism within the administration. As a result of publicity generated during the election campaign, the United States Senate sent a special committee to investigate the occupation in 1921. This Senate Inquiry recommended that the United States reorganize the occupation to eliminate confusion and inefficiency.

The sequent reorganization of 1921–22 featured centralization and consolidation of authority in the person of an all-powerful American high commissioner. In related moves, Haitian finances were reorganized by the transfer of the Banque Nationale to the exclusive control of National City Bank and by a 1922 loan which consolidated Haiti's external debt to France in the hands of American creditors. Following the 1921–22 reorganization, the Occupation emerged as a static, internally disciplined institution capable of efficiently sitting on Haiti. There were few spectacular developments or changes in American policy until the strikes and riots of 1929.

That the Wilson administration had neglected Haiti during the years immediately following the American intervention in 1915 is not surprising, given the more pressing problems attendant to the war in Europe.[1] For the same reason the occupation received scant public notice in the United States, as indicated by the fact that the *New York Times Index* for the years 1917 and 1918 contains no entries for Haiti. High-level discussions on the direction and purpose of the occupation were rare, and the marines in Haiti were left largely to their own devices. This lack of guidance from Washington reached the stage where the marines in Haiti, who usually resented interference from civilians, complained that they were being ignored. In December, 1917, Brigade Commander Eli K. Cole wrote to his immediate superior that "It is very unfortunate, from my point of view, that I have absolutely no knowledge as to the policy that our Government desires to follow in regard to Haiti."[2] Cole's superior endorsed the complaint by reporting to the Navy Department

that he shared "the uncertainty felt by General Cole." [3] The department responded to these criticisms from subordinate officers by
weakly trying to shift the blame on them, blasting them for "the
scarcity of, and at intervals the lack of reports, regarding conditions
in Haiti," and ordering them to be more diligent in keeping Washington informed.[4] Positive direction from Washington remained
minimal until the end of the war.

Assistant Secretary of the Navy Franklin D. Roosevelt's January,
1917, visit did not alter this situation.[5] Roosevelt's visit, in style and
substance, was characteristic of the early years when the occupation
was a military enclave. Secretary of the Navy Daniels later wrote
Roosevelt that "Your trip of inspection (it was one of pleasant adventure too) gave to the President and the Navy Department actual
knowledge of the situation." [6] In fact, Roosevelt's endorsement of
the marines and recommendation that the Haitian client-government
and American civilian officials be dispensed with in favor of unim-
peded military government were little more than a reiteration of
what the marine commanders had been saying all along.[7]

Roosevelt's main efforts in Haiti were devoted to official ceremonies, during which client-President Dartiguenave was honored
by a naval salute from the assembled United States Caribbean Fleet,
and to the exploration of prospects for personal investment in Haiti.
The official ceremonies made a favorable impression on the Haitian
elite largely because of Roosevelt's careful observance of protocol,
his disregard of the color line, and his use of French in reading
formal speeches. Roosevelt made an especial effort to extend formal
courtesies to client-President Dartiguenave, as when he stepped
aside and insisted that Dartiguenave take precedence after Gendarmerie Commandant Smedley Butler had grabbed the president by
the collar and prevented him from entering a limousine ahead of
Roosevelt.* The elaborate observance of protocol by Roosevelt and
his party was not always backed by corresponding private sentiments. Roosevelt recorded in his travel diary that his friend and
traveling companion, John A. McIlhenny of New Orleans, who later

---

* Butler, who as commandant of the Gendarmerie was nominally subordinate to
President Dartiguenave, was not so scrupulous in the observance of protocol; while
traveling with Dartiguenave, Butler slept in a bed while the president slept on the
floor, and Butler enjoyed first use of their common bath water. Freidel, p. 279. Also
Marvin, *World's Work*, XXXIV, No. 1, 37. Thomas, *Old Gimlet Eye*, pp. 355–56.

became the occupation's leading American civilian official, had been unable to eat much at a luncheon given in honor of Dartiguenave because he was fascinated by the robust Haitian minister of agriculture who was sitting opposite him. McIlhenny told Roosevelt, "I couldn't help saying to myself that that man would have brought $1,500 at auction in New Orleans in 1860 for stud purposes." Roosevelt appears to have relished the story, and retold it to American Minister Norman Armour when he visited Haiti as President in 1934.[8]

While in Haiti, Assistant Secretary of the Navy Roosevelt took the opportunity to pursue a private investment scheme whereby he hoped to set up an agricultural plantation. In making investigations about possible sites for agricultural development, Roosevelt was anticipating the passage of the American-sponsored Constitution of 1918, which contained the foreign landownership clause designed to encourage an influx of American capital. Indeed, Roosevelt later claimed to have himself written this constitution, which was in the process of being drafted at the time he visited Haiti.* Roosevelt was assisted in his Haitian investment project by McIlhenny and by Roosevelt's distant cousin Major Henry L. (Harry) Roosevelt, who was serving as an officer in the Gendarmerie d'Haïti and who was himself to become an assistant secretary of the navy years later when Franklin was president.† Shortly after the Franklin Roosevelt party left Haiti, Major Harry Roosevelt wrote his cousin requesting that an anticipated shipment of boats for the Haitian Coast Guard be expedited because, "If you can hurry up our Coast Guard it will help as I cannot very well get over to Gonave until these vessels arrive. I still have faith in that Island."[9] Major Roosevelt proceeded to investigate agricultural and commercial possibilities on the islands of La Gonave, La Tortue, and Ile à Vache, and reported his findings to his cousin Franklin and to McIlhenny.[10] Harry also advised Franklin that "if [Willard] Straight could open a branch of the Amer-

---

* In fact, Roosevelt probably did not have much to do with drawing up the Constitution. The Constitution was chiefly the work of the Office of the Solicitor in the State Department. *NYT*, Aug. 19, 1920, p. 15. Freidel, p. 284. SD 838.011/—— series, 1917.

† Four Roosevelts served as assistant secretaries of the navy from Theodore Roosevelt in 1897 to Franklin during World War I, Theodore Roosevelt, Jr., during the Harding administration, and finally Harry Roosevelt in the 1930's.

ican International Corporation down here I think they could grab a lot of good paying properties." [11] The American entrance into World War I interrupted the plans for investment, but Harry wrote to Franklin that "After all this war business is over we can talk of Gonave which I still believe will offer a splendid field for investment." [12]

Harry Roosevelt dropped out of the picture after the war, but Franklin and John A. McIlhenny, who was by then the American financial adviser to Haiti, maintained their interest in Haitian investment possibilities. In 1919 Roosevelt's secretary Louis Howe wrote Roosevelt that one of his wealthy admirers had money to invest and that the admirer "has no more idea than a cat as to how to go about it. . . . If you are still fond of your Haiti project, this looks like easy money." [13] In 1922 Roosevelt and McIlhenny, in consultation with Roger L. Farnham, made specific plans for the founding of a trading company with a paid-in capital of $500,000, but the venture was delayed because McIlhenny apparently felt that he could not enter in a concrete business deal while he was still employed as financial adviser to the Haitian government.[14] Roosevelt had great hopes for the Haitian venture and defended his plans for a general trading company by saying:

> I cannot agree . . . that just because the Haytian native population does not use knives, forks, cups, etc. that they never will use them. As a matter of fact I feel convinced that during the next generation the Haytian population will adopt the living standards more generally in vogue.[15]

In July, 1922 McIlhenny wrote Roosevelt that "It is my intention to resign as Financial Adviser as soon as the contract of the loan is signed, and I will therefore be available to assist you in any way that you may desire," but McIlhenny was unable to resign until October, 1922, and the plan was never consummated.[16]

The interest that Roosevelt and McIlhenny had in private investment in Haiti was concurrently reflected in the two most significant developments in the Wilson administration's Haitian policy during the war years. Promotion of private investment required guarantees of security and continuing political stability, plus the legal right to own property. While the administration neglected to exercise close supervision over the marines in Haiti, the State Department, with McIlhenny as one of its principal agents, went to considerable trouble to pass the American-sponsored Constitution of 1918 and to procure a twenty-year extension of the Haitian-American treaty of 1915.

Just as the 1918 Constitution featured an alien landownership clause that was designed to open the way for an influx of American capital, the treaty extension was likewise intended to create conditions attractive to American capital investment and to lay the groundwork for refunding the Haitian external debt. In December, 1916, Lansing instructed the American financial adviser that it was necessary to exercise immediately the option for extension that had been included in the original 1915 treaty in order that American capital might be induced to invest in Haiti.[17] Client-President Dartiguenave tried to obtain a degree of political leverage by procrastinating on the proposed extension but gave in when threatened by General Cole, who reported to Washington that "if one government does not accede to the proposition, then another Government that will can be installed." [18] The twenty-year extension, signed in March, 1917, was executed for the immediate purpose of providing continuity of American control deemed necessary for the successful flotation of a new loan by which the Haitian external debt to France would be consolidated in American hands. The extension of American control until 1936 and consolidation of the Haitian debt by Americans also had commercial implications, as indicated by the fact that local French interests in Haiti were opposed to the extension and the transfer of the loans to American creditors, fearing that French commercial interests would be pushed to the wall.[19]

The treaty extension and prospective American loan, along with the encouragement of American capital investments, indicated that the United States would remain in Haiti for a prolonged period and committed the Wilson administration to continuance of the military occupation. The fact that the marines had taken over all levels of government and were maintaining American authority by martial law and military repression also tended to commit the United States to continuing the occupation. Withdrawal under these circumstances would have resulted in the immediate overthrow of the client-government and in an ugly anti-American outburst by Haitian nationalists. This was the situation when the Wilson administration reassessed the occupation in the aftermath of the European war. The threat of European incursions had passed with the defeat of Germany and the exhaustion of other European powers in the war, but the military occupation, even though it no longer had any strategic purpose, could not be practicably terminated. By the time Wilson contemplated the withdrawal of American troops in 1919, it was too late.

In earlier rhetorical statements Wilson had consistently championed the rights of small nations and, during the 1916 election when he was running as a peace candidate, he had disparaged the Monroe Doctrine and specifically renounced intervention and economic exploitation in dealing with Mexico:

The suspicion of our southern neighbors, their uneasiness as to our growing power, their jealousy that we should assume to play Big Brother to them without their invitation to do so, has constantly stood in the way of the amicable and happy relations we wished to establish with them . . . every nation, every people, has the right to order its own institutions as it will.[20]

The Wilson administration clearly did not feel that these ideals applied to the contemporaneous occupation of Haiti. Indeed, films of marines engaged in combat in Haiti were released by the Navy Department to be shown throughout the United States as part of the military preparedness campaign that was in progress at the time Wilson made the above statement.[21] Whatever the applicability of the Wilsonian right of self-determination to Haiti, Wilson did hope to limit the military involvement there after the war. Secretary of the Navy Daniels later stated that he personally had felt that "we ought to take steps to get out as soon as possible after the war was over," and that Wilson had never intended to maintain the occupation after the war and would have withdrawn the American troops had he not suffered a stroke in 1919. Wilson, however, had already tried once and failed to extricate the troops prior to his stroke. Daniels recalled that he never had a talk with Wilson about Haiti after the November, 1918, Armistice and that direction of the occupation was taken over by Lansing and by Financial Adviser McIlhenny, both of whom Daniels characterized as imperialists.[22]

The contradiction between Wilson's rhetoric about the rights of small nations and the American occupation of Haiti was dramatized at the Paris Peace Conference in March, 1919. The Dartiguenave client-government, always striving to assert itself whenever possible, instructed the Haitian minister at the Peace Conference to approach Wilson and Lansing in an attempt to capitalize on Wilson's widely publicized posture as the champion of self-determination.[23] The reminder of the potentially embarrassing presence of American marines in Haiti caused Wilson and Lansing to hastily reconsider the occupation. The American mission to the Peace Conference, headed by Wilson and Lansing, cabled the State Department that it desired the withdrawal of the marine brigade and the substitution of a small legation guard, noting that the Haitian-American treaty of 1915 did not provide for the continuance of American military occupation and martial law. In this cable the American mission observed that military occupation had been continued because it was "impossible for military and strategic reasons to make any change" after the outbreak of the war, but that with the return of peace "the same excuse for the several reasons cannot be advanced . . . it would seem impossible to continue the occupation in the present form, without subjecting the United States to much criticism, particularly, as the rights of smaller nations are being kept to the fore and in the light of the President's utterances." [24]

Wilson and Lansing hoped that the Gendarmerie, backed by the moral support engendered by the presence of a token marine legation guard, would suffice to control the situation.

The State Department relayed the message to Port-au-Prince, where the proposition was discussed by the various military and civilian figures who controlled the occupation. The consensus of all the officials directly involved, both in Washington and in Port-au-Prince, was that it would not be feasible to reduce the troop strength for some time to come.[25] In fact, the time for such a move was most inopportune because the marines were in the midst of suppressing the caco guerrilla uprisings of 1918–19. A week after Lansing and Wilson had suggested the change to a legation guard another brigade of marines was sent to Haiti as reinforcement to the beleaguered garrison. On being informed of the situation, Wilson and Lansing dropped their proposal to withdraw the marines, acknowledging that "it would appear impossible to make any change in status quo in Haiti at present." [26]

Faced with the necessity of continued military commitment, the Wilson administration turned to the problem of reorganizing the chaotic and ineffective American administration of the occupation. As provided by the 1915 treaty, American civilian officials had been sent to Haiti as overseers of the financial, commercial, and administrative functions of the client-government. These officials, headed by a financial adviser, were in continual conflict with marine commanders. Shortly after assuming the position of financial adviser in 1919, John A. McIlhenny wrote Assistant Secretary of the Navy Roosevelt that "I find that in the past there has been an extraordinary amount of friction and bad feelings between the Gendarmerie and the Treaty Officials." McIlhenny noted that this friction had begun during Butler's regime and had been "greatly intensified" by General Cole, who had "openly stated his disbelief in the possibility of sound administration under the Treaty, and frankly stated his belief in the necessity of a military or civil governorship . . . he set himself out to prove his premises, and make the change to military or civil government a necessity." [27]

Another treaty official, a navy surgeon who had been appointed sanitary engineer, reported that "I have been surprised to find since my arrival here [1917] a complete plan on the part of the Marine Corps toward the abandonment in toto of the treaty and all it inferred." Butler, for his part, alleged that the civilians had "blood in their eye for me and the Gendarmerie and are going to try to take the roads and other incidentals that we are performing, away from us," adding that, if Marine jurisdiction was curtailed, "we will certainly obey, but not cheerfully." [28]

The major point of conflict between military and civilian officials centered around the question of who was in charge. The treaty officials resented the interference and usurpation of power by the marines, and the marines felt that they had complete authority by virtue of the alleged paramount necessity of maintaining American authority. Admiral Knapp, who was absentee administrative commander in Haiti, conceded after a personal visit that "the Gendarmerie in Haiti is striving to get too much power in its hands," but stated that the main difficulty was the failure of all American officials except General Cole to understand "the powers inherent in martial law and the right of the person exercising it." The admiral, who was concurrently the United States Military Governor of Santo Domingo and resided there, later stated that martial law exercised on foreign soil was equivalent to military government, and added significantly that "There is no fundamental difference between the exercise of governmental powers in Haiti and the Dominican Republic . . . what was called Military Government in the Dominican Republic is the same thing in principle as what is called Martial Law in Haiti." [29]

With the marines asserting their authority as best they could, the Dartiguenave client-government and the American civilian officials who were sent to direct it were placed in an ambiguous position. An American businessman testifying at the 1922 Senate Inquiry stated that governmental authority in Haiti had been "undefined" and that resulting confusion had "deprived those who are in Haiti of confidence as to just what the Government of Haiti was and where the responsibility lay, a problem we all know." [30] This ambiguity was increased by the rapid turnover of American officials; during the years between 1915 and 1922 there were six marine brigade commanders and six commandants of the Gendarmerie, as well as numerous changes within the State Department.[31] With the arrival of Financial Adviser McIlhenny, the civilian treaty officials gained a larger measure of authority. McIlhenny had direct personal contact with Assistant Secretary of the Navy Roosevelt and was able to cut across the complicated official chains of command to the extent of being able to influence the selection of marine commanders.[32] Nevertheless, the basic problems of disorganization and administrative confusion remained.

The situation was always complicated by the continuing lack of positive direction from Washington. American financier Roger L. Farnham, who had been intimately acquainted with affairs in Haiti for a decade, told the 1922 Senate Inquiry that American officials had done the best they could "in the absence of any definite policy to be pursued," and noted that "They always seemed to me to be drifting and waiting for some plan to be presented to them, along which they could proceed." [33] The Wilson administration was aware of this difficulty and of the conflicts between occupation officials. A 1918 Division of Latin-American Affairs memorandum referred to "complete disorganization" in Haiti and stated that "It is not humanly possible for these separate officers to function as a whole, and cooperate satisfactorily; 'Too many cooks spoil the broth.'" In an August, 1920, memorandum entitled "The Present Situation in Haiti," Dana G. Munro of the Office of Foreign Trade Adviser noted that "treaty officials have been acting on their own personal initiative without the knowledge or support of the Department" and that the current system was a "failure" because of "the indefiniteness of the treaty and the failure of the department, through the treaty officials, to pursue a consistent, intelligent and tactful policy leading to any definite object." [34] Possible efforts by the administration to reform the occupation were dropped when Wilson's Haitian policy became the object of widespread public criticism during the 1920 presidential election campaign. Internal criticism within the administration ceased and public pronouncements emphasized the "benevolent purpose" of the occupation, the "gratitude" of the Haitian people, and the intention of the United States to withdraw shortly.[35]

The Wilson administration's activities in Haiti had become a subject of national attention in August, 1920, when Democratic vice-presidential candidate Franklin D. Roosevelt made the following campaign statement: "You know I have had something to do with the running of a couple of little republics. The facts are that I wrote Haiti's Constitution myself, and, if I do say it, I think it a pretty good Constitution." [36]

The assertion about authorship of Haiti's Constitution was dubious. Nevertheless, Republican presidential candidate Warren Harding took up the Haitian issue in a speech from his front porch in Marion, Ohio, nine days later, saying that if he were elected president he would not "empower an Assistant Secretary of the Navy to draft a constitution for helpless neighbors in the West Indies and jam it down their throats at the point of bayonets borne by U.S. Marines." In subsequent campaign speeches Harding referred to the "rape of Haiti" and charged that "thousands of native Haitians have been killed by American marines." [37] James Weldon Johnson, a prominent black Republican and a member of the Republican National Advisory Committee who was active in opposing the occupation, discussed the Haitian situation with Harding in Marion and observed that "I could see that he looked upon the Haitian matter as a gift right off the Christmas tree. He could not conceal his delight." After the election President Harding told Johnson, "We certainly made a good shot with that Haitian material." [38]

Public criticism of the occupation intensified after the Navy Department released Marine Commandant Barnett's report alluding to "indiscriminate killing of natives" in the closing weeks of the 1920 election campaign.[39] Newspapers decried "slavery in Haiti," "slaughter," "shameful abuse of power," and Wilson's hypocrisy, but statements were also made in defense of the president. The *Literary Digest* pointed out that the same charges had been made against the Republicans with reference to the Philippine insurrection during the 1900 election campaign.[40] One of the more sensational atrocity stories appeared in the *New York Times* two days after the release of the Barnett statement:

How American marines, largely made up of and officered by Southerners, opened fire with machine guns from airplanes upon defenseless Haitian villages, killing men, women, and children in the open market places; how natives were slain for "sport" by a hoodlum element among these same Southerners; and how the ancient corvee system of enforced labor was revived and ruthlessly executed, increasing, through retaliation, the banditry in Haiti and Santo Domingo, was told yesterday by Henry A. Franck, the noted traveler and authority on the West Indies.[41]

Occupation officials were sensitive to the wave of criticism, and Financial Adviser McIlhenny requested permission to place George Marvin, who had previously written the laudatory article "Healthy Haiti" for *World's Work* magazine, on the Haitian government payroll "to prepare articles for American magazines and papers truthfully showing the work of American occupation in Haiti." McIlhenny assured the department that he would censor all articles, but Secretary of State Bainbridge Colby disapproved, saying that Marvin could be hired to make commercial propaganda but not to write propaganda solely for the American occupation.[42]

Opposition to the occupation within the United States had predated the Republican attack launched during the 1920 election campaign, but most journalistic coverage had been favorable. In a

1969 study of press reaction to the occupation in Haiti and the Dominican Republic, American scholar John W. Blassingame determined that forty-nine out of sixty-nine journals included in the study endorsed the policy of intervention from 1904 to 1919, while only twenty "strenuously objected." Blassingame pointed out that few journals, excepting the *Nation*, consistently fought against the interventions.[43] Several magazines active in promoting American colonial interests, notably *World's Work* and *National Geographic*, published roseate articles praising the occupation in Haiti. In mid-1920, just prior to the denunciations attendant to the election campaign, the *Nation* published a series of articles by Herbert J. Seligmann and James Weldon Johnson, both of whom attacked the occupation for racism, brutality, and economic exploitation.[44] Johnson, who was Secretary of the National Association for the Advancement of Colored People (NAACP), and Ernest Gruening of the *Nation* organized American anti-imperialist efforts to terminate the occupation. Both men also played leading roles in the formation of a Haitian resistance movement, while Gruening, as managing editor of the *Nation*, continued to direct attacks against the occupation through the early 1930s. In 1920, with the exposés engendered by the election campaign and the impact of the Seligmann and Johnson articles, most American periodicals were critical of the occupation.[45]

James Weldon Johnson visited Haiti in February, 1920, and met with prominent members of the Haitian elite, urging them to set up an organization similar to the NAACP in Haiti. Georges Sylvain, who had opposed the occupation since its inception, and other disaffected Haitians followed Johnson's advice and founded the Union Patriotique, which undertook propaganda work in Haiti and the United States.[46] The activities of the Union Patriotique in Haiti were severely limited because of American martial law and rigid press censorship, but it did manage to organize public demonstrations that took place during the visit of the 1922 Senate Inquiry. Sylvain kept in close touch with Ernest Gruening in New York, where Gruening coordinated anti-occupation activities in the United States and helped raise money for the presentation of the Union Patriotique's case before the Senate Inquiry.[47]

The fight against the occupation in the United States centered around the *Nation*, where Gruening and Oswald Garrison Villard publicized the argument for Haitian independence, arranged for presentation of the Haitian case before the 1922 Senate Inquiry, and promoted the activities of the Haiti-Santo Domingo Independence Society, which held several public meetings. In 1921 the *Nation* printed the lengthy memoir that the Union Patriotique prepared for submission to the State Department and the Senate Foreign Relations Committee.[48] The Union Patriotique's memoir could not be reprinted in Haiti on orders from the brigade commander, nor could comments on the memoir from the American press.[49] Because of repression within Haiti, the assistance of anti-imperialists in the United States was all the more valuable, especially when it came to making an effective presentation before the Senate Inquiry.[50] During the early 1920s the Union Patriotique was marginally effective at best, but few alternatives were open to Haitian nationalists under American military rule. Some, including exiled former presidential candidate Dr. Rosalvo Bobo, persisted in plotting futile secret political alliances that were to go into effect if and when the American troops were withdrawn.[51] After 1921 the Gendarmerie intelligence section kept records on the reputation, influence, and attitude of all prominent Haitians toward the occupation.[52]

The Republican denunciations of the occupation during the 1920 election campaign and associated agitation in the press culminated in a full-scale Senate Inquiry in late 1921 and early 1922. The inquiry was made by a special Select Committee on Haiti and Santo Domingo consisting of three senators and chaired by Republican Senator Medill McCormick of Illinois.* McCormick had advocated reforming the occupation since 1920 and was in close correspondence with Ernest Gruening, whom he sent to Haiti in advance of the committee to arrange contacts with the Haitians. Gruening, corresponding with McCormick by code because of marine censorship, managed to schedule a social affair with the Haitian elite for one of the committee's three nights in Port-au-Prince. The Occupation had previously arranged for the committee to be entertained exclusively by the Occupation. Gruening also contacted his friends in the Union Patriotique and personally suggested many of the

---

* The committee nominally consisted of five senators: Philander C. Knox (R-Pa.); Tasker L. Oddie (R-Nev.); Atlee Pomerene (D-Ohio); William H. King (D-Utah); and McCormick; but Knox and King did not participate.

slogans, such as "Don't Make Haiti America's Congo," that were carried on placards by Haitian demonstrators who greeted the arrival of the senators in November, 1921.[53] While in Haiti the committee heard testimony from elite representatives of the Union Patriotique and from peasants in the interior who related numerous atrocity stories, but the committee was unimpressed by the more sensational statements and in its final report pointed to contradictions in Haitian testimony which suggested subornation.[54]

The committee conducted an elaborate and thorough investigation of the occupation in Haiti and also expended a lesser effort on the occupation in the Dominican Republic. The printed record of the hearings came to several thousand pages. Yet the whole elaborate exercise was largely redundant, since the decisions to reorganize and rationalize the occupation had been made in advance of the inquiry and were mainly unaffected by it. The hearings were a consequence of the impulse to reform the occupation generated during the 1920 election campaign and served more as a public expiation and official peroration on the confused, mismanaged first phase of the occupation than as an impetus to new decisions. The conclusions reached by the committee coincided almost exactly with the opinions Chairman McCormick had previously expressed in 1920. In a magazine article entitled "Our Failure in Haiti," McCormick had stressed the need for administrative reorganization rather than withdrawal, and stated, "We are there, and in my judgment we ought to stay there for twenty years." [55] The committee criticized "blunders" made by the Wilson administration in failing to centralize authority in Haiti, in enforcing the corvée, and in failing to select occupation personnel who were "sympathetic to the Haitians and able to maintain cordial personal and official relations with them." On the other hand, it praised sanitation work, road building, currency reform, governmental administrative reforms, alleged increases in trade, and the maintenance of peace and security, concluding that "In brief, under the treaty, the peace of the republic, the solvency of its Government, and the security of its people have been established for the first time in many years." [56] The committee hearings provided a forum for the various divergent views on the occupation, ranging from a statement by the Right Reverend Charles Blayney Colmore, Episcopal Bishop of Puerto Rico and Haiti, that "The reconstruction work of the United States marines in Haiti provides one of the most thrilling and gratifying chapters in contemporaneous American history," to stories of water torture and brandings indulged in by marines.[57]

In its final report the McCormick Committee recommended that the marine garrison be maintained in Haiti because "drastic reduction of the marine force, or its early withdrawal, would certainly be followed by a recurrence of brigandage and by the organization of revolutionary bands." Instead of relinquishing control, the senators recommended that the United States undertake a program of industrial and agricultural education, abolish martial law, and coordinate the administration of the occupation.[58] In an informal preliminary report to Secretary of State Hughes, McCormick and his colleagues recommended that an American "High Commissioner" with powers of "Minister Extraordinary and Envoy Plenipotentiary" should be appointed by the State Department to supervise the Gendarmerie, the marine brigade, and the several civilian treaty officials, all of whom would be relegated to subordinate positions.[59] Hughes had come to a similar conclusion even before the inquiry, and, in October, 1921, had asked Secretary of the Navy Edwin Denby to recommend a marine officer to be put in charge of Haiti as "Representative of the President" with duties similar to those currently exercised by General Enoch H. Crowder in Cuba, but with more power and greater initiative. Hughes suggested General Smedley Butler for the position, noting that Butler had already served in Haiti and had been "exceedingly successful." [60]

The selection of a military officer to be high commissioner, rather than a civilian as had been hoped by many observers, indicated that the major concern of the United States remained that of exercising American authority. American troops could not be gracefully withdrawn, as they were from the neighboring Dominican Republic, so the Occupation was left with the primary function of sitting on Haiti until circumstances permitted the relinquishment of military control. Under military leadership the Occupation did not make systematic preparations for American withdrawal, and most departments were reluctant to promote Haitians to positions of responsibility. The key factors in the American withdrawal from the Dominican Republic in 1924 involved transferring control of the Guardia Nacional to trusted Dominican protégés and the working out of a contingent political solution.* In Haiti, the Haitianization of the Gendarmerie officer corps made relatively little progress until after the strikes and riots of 1929.

The selection of General Butler as high commissioner was averted by the intercession of Dana G. Munro of the Division of Latin American Affairs, who, along with several members of the McCormick Committee, pointed out to Secretary of State Hughes that Butler was temperamentally unsuited for the job.[61] The eventual selection, General John H. Russell, had been brigade commander through most of the period since late 1917, and ultimately spent thirteen years as the top marine in Haiti, finally retiring as high commissioner in late 1930. Russell later recalled that his first introduction to Haiti had been on an 1893 midshipman's cruise while he was attending the United States Naval Academy:

In my midshipman's journal, under remarks covering this visit I speak of Port-au-Prince as the dirtiest city I had ever seen and I express the hope that I will never have to visit the country again. However, inexorable Fate decreed otherwise and some twenty-four years later, again, I arrived in Haiti and lived for approximately thirteen years in Port-au-Prince.[62]

In 1921 Russell clarified his own attitude toward sharing authority with Haitian collaborators in a memorandum to the State Department entitled "Regarding a Constructive Policy for Haiti":

The absurdity of dual control, or of two nations administering the affairs of a country is too obvious to need comment. Two men can ride a horse but one must ride behind. If the United States is to ride behind in its conduct of Haitian Affairs it had better withdraw entirely and let the country revert to a condition of chaos when, after a time, the United States would be forced to again occupy Haiti or permit some foreign nation to do so.[63]

Russell, serving as high commissioner from 1922 until 1930, expended considerable personal effort in supporting progressive poli-

---

* The most notable American protégé was Colonel Rafael Trujillo, who assumed command of the Guardia less than a year after American departure and began, with American support, a thirty-one-year dictatorship in 1930.

cies in educational and economic uplift, but he did not hold the Haitians in high regard. In 1919 he expressed the opinion that they had "the characteristics of both the negro and the Latin races" and that "The uneducated Haitien who lives in the country is more or less of an animal, who will do whatever he is told." In 1925 he observed that the peasants had been held in a backward state by the elite and had "the mentality of a child of not more than seven years of age reared under advantageous conditions." Russell felt that "a large proportion" of the Haitian population was "bordering on a state of savagery, if not actually existing in such a state," and apparently believed spurious stories about voodoo priests practicing human sacrifice.[64]

Unlike some of his marine predecessors whom the McCormick Committee had criticized as "unsympathetic," Russell made a point of maintaining polite and cordial relations with members of the Haitian elite, and his wife, who spoke French perfectly, associated with elite ladies.[65] At various times during his command of the marine brigade and tenure as high commissioner, Russell was accused of being a racist, but he appears to have been a racial moderate who was subjected to attack because of his position as commander of the Occupation and figurehead of the American presence, which was pervasively racist. Russell, a Georgian, supported Jim Crow racial segregation, as when he was chairman of the board of the all-white American Club and vetoed the membership application of a white Swiss who was about to marry a Haitian mulatto, but he was scrupulously courteous in his personal relations with Haitians. He avowed to the chairman of the 1930 Presidential Commission that he had made determined efforts to personally "cultivate Haitian society regardless of color."[66] That relations were never particularly warm or enthusiastic can be attributed more to generally operative social conventions of racial and cultural segregation and to Russell's personal aloofness as commander in chief, rather than to exceptional prejudice on Russell's part.

General Russell was appointed high commissioner in February, 1922, with orders to supervise and coordinate all American activities in Haiti and report directly to the State Department as the personal representative of the president in Haiti.[67] The position of high commissioner involved a fusing of diplomatic and administrative authority, and, as Financial Adviser Arthur C. Millspaugh noted, bore "an interesting resemblance to Great Britain's position in Egypt from 1882 to 1914." [68] Russell himself recognized the analogy between his role and that of the British high commissioners and had read Lord Cromer's "interesting and instructive" book on Egypt, but when he requested special reports on Egypt the State Department demurred, replying: "The Department has read with interest your despatch . . . in which you compare the relations between the United States and Haiti to the relations between Great Britain and Egypt. You will doubtless realize that critics of this Government's policy toward Haiti have sometimes made this same comparison a basis for attacks upon the Department." [69]

Client-President Louis Borno, whose term of office coincided with Russell's tenure as high commissioner, was also attracted by the Egyptian analogy, and stated, according to Russell, that "unquestionably" United States control over Haiti was essential to the security of the Panama Canal just as British control in Egypt was necessary to protect the Suez Canal. [70] Gendarmerie Commandant Butler, referred to "a deadline drawn between me and the Haitiens, the same as there is in Egypt—between the British agents and the Egyptians." The comparison with Lord Cromer's rule as high commissioner in Egypt was apt. Cromer, in his history of the British occupation, observed that "one alien race, the English, have had to control and guide a second alien race, the Turks, by whom they are disliked, in the government of a third race, the Egyptians." The Egyptians, in turn, were "unsympathetic" to the dominant "races." [71] A similar tripartite system existed in Haiti, with the Americans, the mulatto Haitian elite, and the black rural masses.

Russell's authority in Haiti was no less than that of his British counterpart; he supervised all civilian treaty officials, controlled the marine brigade and the Gendarmerie by virtue of his military rank, and dominated the Haitian client-government. All correspondence between treaty officials and both the United States and Haitian governments was forwarded through his office. In early 1923 Russell instructed his subordinates that "Treaty Officials whose functions are purely of an administrative character will in no case comment on matters of policy unless specifically requested to do so by me." Throughout his tenure as high commissioner, Russell remained extremely jealous of his authority, complaining to the Secretary of State about division of authority when treaty officials were consulted directly by the department, insisting that he be consulted on nomination of marine personnel for Haitian commands, procuring the dismissal of recalcitrant marines and civilians, and feuding with civilian officials who challenged or questioned his policies.[72]

The Occupation bureaucracy over which Russell presided consisted of about 250 American civilians who served in departments headed by the several treaty officials. The most powerful treaty official, the financial adviser, had the prerogative of drawing up the Haitian government budget and authorizing the expenditure of all governmental funds, but even this official was subject to dismissal in case of conflict with Russell. Financial Adviser Arthur C. Millspaugh, who was dismissed following a controversy with Russell, described the high commissioner's authority as follows:

Nominally, the treaty officials are responsible to the President of Haiti or to their respective [Haitian] Ministers; in practice, they are directed by the High Commissioner. . . . He not only vetoes but also drafts Haitian legislation. He negotiates contracts with American companies, determines the administrative attitude to be assumed toward them by the American treaty officials, and interests himself in the details of claims, the collection of revenue, road construction and in agricultural, educational, and sanitary matters. American treaty officers have little official contact with the Haitian executive and their relations with the Ministers have necessarily become perfunctory or formal.[73]

Colonel J. S. Turrill, commandant of the Gendarmerie, wrote Marine Corps Commandant Lejeune that "Nothing of importance can be done in the Gendarmerie without General Russell's sanction," and that when the Gendarmerie received orders from its nominal chief, the Haitian client-president, Turrill always had to get Russell's approval before carrying them out.[74]

The appointment of High Commissioner Russell and the administrative reorganization of 1922 were intended to centralize authority and increase the internal efficiency of the Occupation. A corresponding change was made in the leadership of the Haitian client-government. Dartiguenave, who had again become recalcitrant and obstructive, this time over the questions of contracting the proposed

American loan consolidation and the granting of a monopoly on the importation of currency to the Banque Nationale, was replaced by Louis Borno.[75] Borno was a man of stature and refinement who was accomplished as both a poet and a statesman.[76] Although he had opposed General Waller's regime as Dartiguenave's minister of foreign affairs in 1916, and Russell himself (as a colonel in 1918) had insisted on his dismissal from the Cabinet, Borno was temperamentally and ideologically sympathetic to the purposes and methods of the occupation.[77] As an avowed admirer of Mussolini, he welcomed the suppression of political dissent in Haiti and defended the occupation as a period of great progress; the people of Haiti, who were "illiterate, ignorant and poor," were "incapable of exercising the right to vote" and had to be governed by progressive, authoritarian leaders.[78] Borno's inclinations toward authoritarian uplift and adoption of American technical proficiency were comparable to the advanced, sophisticated program of fascism in Italy, but Borno and other Haitian collaborators sorely lacked the popular, nationalistic appeal of Mussolini. Any effective appeal to nationalism or ethnic, racial assertiveness in Haiti would have had to, and eventually did, begin with the demand to rid the country of foreign domination. In contrast to the charisma of contemporary fascist leadership elsewhere, Borno was stolid and distant. For the occupation to have excited popular political awareness would have been self-destructive. At the same time the occupation's total lack of popular appeal and indifference to public relations helped precipitate anti-American resistance.

Borno cooperated closely with High Commissioner Russell in an arrangement which Financial Adviser Millspaugh termed a "Joint Dictatorship," and was retained as client-president until the strikes and riots of 1929.[79] Despite the apparent outward harmony between Borno and his sponsors, the Americans always retained effective control of the occupation as demonstrated by the action of Financial Adviser Dr. W. W. Cumberland, who withheld Borno's pay check the first time the president failed to cooperate with him. Cumberland remarked that "He respected me from that day forward" and that after this incident he and Borno became "very close friends." [80]

The close and sympathetic relations between Borno and the Americans were in marked contrast to the turmoil and conflict characteristic of the last years of the Dartiguenave government. Dartiguenave had alternated between pliant cooperation and recalcitrance according to shifting political circumstances, trying to please the Americans, on the one hand, while playing the part of a Haitian patriot, on the other. In the end he was rejected by both sides; the Union Patriotique refused his offer of a large donation and the Americans cast him off.[81] In 1919 Brigade Commander Russell described Dartiguenave as follows: "At heart he is anti-American, a man of no integrity, a schemer, a Vaudou believer, and he will only work for the good of Haiti when it is to his own personal interests or he is forced to do so by the Occupation." [82]

Most Americans involved in the occupation concurred in disparaging Dartiguenave. Butler, for instance, referred to Dartiguenave's government as "despised and distrusted by a vast majority of the people at large, not on the official pay rolls, and as far as I have personally observed to my own humiliation, with justice." [83]

Financial Adviser John A. McIlhenny had made a favorable impression on his arrival in Haiti in 1919 and had, in turn, been taken in by the Dartiguenave client-government. At the time, he described Dartiguenave as "fully imbued with the belief in the absolute necessity for American Occupation, and in accord with all that the Occupation is seeking to do." McIlhenny felt that various objections raised by Dartiguenave and his Cabinet were "all due to their effort to have it appear to the people of Haiti that they are in fact the Government of Haiti . . . but when it comes to the last show-down, they are perfectly willing, upon proper show of firmness by the Occupation, to do that thing which is deemed necessary by the Occupation." [84]

A year later McIlhenny reported to the State Department that the Dartiguenave government was "definitely and strongly anti-American" and that it would be necessary to reorganize the Cabinet and take measures to force the government to cooperate with the Occupation.[85] The final estrangement between the Dartiguenave government and the Americans came about as the result of conflicts involving the transfer of the 1910 Banque charter to the National City Bank and the flotation of a new loan by which American creditors were to consolidate Haiti's external debt.

The United States had hoped to transfer control of the Banque

Nationale and the Haitian external debt to American financial interests from the outset. In January, 1918, F. L. Mayer of the Division of
Latin American Affairs noted:

Political influence by one country in the affairs of another is, it would
seem, in direct ratio with economic control therein, especially in the
case of a small state such as Haiti . . . outright progressive American
banking methods would result in increased good feelings toward the
United States in Haiti and added American influence in Haitian life and
politics.[86]

A few weeks later the American minister and the financial adviser
reported to the State Department that they were "of the opinion
that the transfer of the control of the Banque Nationale to American
banking interests would be highly desirable from the standpoint of
advancement of American influence and interests in Haiti." [87] With
the support of the State Department, National City Bank purchased
the shares held by the other American participants in the Banque
in April, 1916, and bought out the French stockholders for $1,412,-
000 in June, 1920.[88] In order to complete the transfer of the Banque
to American interests it was necessary to revise the 1910 Banque
charter.

The State Department, National City Bank, and the Dartiguenave
government began three-way negotiations for transfer of the Banque
charter in 1920. McIlhenny, representing the Haitian government,
reached tentative agreement with National City Bank on charter
modifications, but the bank then proceeded to insist on additional
concessions which the Dartiguenave government, backed by American and other foreign business houses who feared monopoly of
foreign currency by the Banque Nationale refused to approve.[89] Dartiguenave's refusal to accept the new modifications of the Banque
charter coincided with an already exacerbated dispute over laws
restricting the right of foreigners to own property and returning
sequestered property to Germans which the Dartiguenave government had attempted to pass without American approval. In response
to this obstinacy, McIlhenny refused to consider the new governmental budget for the coming year and suspended the salaries of
President Dartiguenave and his Cabinet.[90] Secretary of State Colby
expressed displeasure at the stopping of salaries, informing Mc-

Ilhenny that the department had not authorized the move, and another State Department official noted that "arbitrary and radical steps taken by treaty officials without authorization from the Department have committed the Department to an extreme position." [91] This confusion was apparently caused by the change of leadership in the State Department following the dismissal of Secretary of State Lansing early in 1920. When McIlhenny was about to appear before the 1922 Senate Inquiry, Sumner Welles of the Division of Latin American Affairs informed Secretary of State Hughes that McIlhenny's stoppage of Haitian salaries in 1920 had been "based upon certain confidential and oral instructions given to him by the then Secretary of State, Mr. Lansing" and that, since "the publication of these instructions would be harmful at this time," it would be best if Hughes persuaded McIlhenny not to disclose the conflict in orders.[92]

McIlhenny later attributed the failure of the Banque charter negotiations to the obstinacy of National City Bank, and Sumner Welles accused National City Bank of having "deliberately disregarded an agreement which they entered into with the Department of State." Welles, in 1922, argued that "I do not feel that we should permit the City Bank people to exact conditions from the Haitian Government which this Department regards as too onerous and which the City Bank formally agreed to renounce in the understanding reached in 1920." [93] The State Department persisted in trying to procure modifications in the Banque charter favoring Haiti, and National City Bank abandoned its demands for monopoly of the importation of foreign currency, but the final Contract of Transfer, signed after the departure of the obstructive Dartiguenave government, was little different from the original 1910 charter that Secretary of State Knox had considered unduly exploitative.[94]

The most binding facet of the 1921–22 reorganization of the occupation was the consolidation of the Haitian external debt in the hands of American creditors. This had long been a major objective of United States policy and had prompted the 1917 treaty extension. The Wilson administration had tried to procure a Haitian loan during the war, but Wilson, who realized the importance of refunding the debt to ensure complete American control, observed that "this Administration has not access to banking assistance that some previous administrations have had, and I do not feel at all sure that we could make the refunding here proposed look attractive to The Street." [95]

In 1917 Roger L. Farnham informed the State Department that National City Bank, J. P. Morgan, Guaranty Trust Company, and First National Bank would make a loan offer as "a patriotic duty," but only on condition that the loan be regarded by the Treasury Department in the same light as a Liberty Loan, that the Treasury Department accept Haitian bonds as security for public bank deposits, that the controversial Haitian Railway bonds be liquidated, and that the United States guarantee to supervise Haiti during the life of the bonds. [96] Shortly after this the second Liberty Loan and other circumstances attendant to financing the European war forced the abandonment of the Haitian refunding operation.

The Dartiguenave client-government, which had originally been eager to procure a new loan as a means of alleviating its desperate financial condition, vigorously opposed refunding negotiations after it became clear that Haitians would in no case be allowed to participate in allocation of new funds or in determining occupation policies. Frustrated in all his many intrigues to achieve some influence in the management of the occupation, Dartiguenave became increasingly recalcitrant after 1920 and, according to Acting Financial Adviser A. J. Maumus, was intent on allowing his client-government to drift into bankruptcy as a means of discrediting the Americans, feeling that his own salary as president was safe in any case. Maumus, supported by Financial Adviser McIlhenny, who was absent in the United States negotiating the new loan, threatened to stop payment of all Haitian government salaries until Dartiguenave agreed to cooperate with the refunding operation, but Dartiguenave remained hostile and the loan could not be officially concluded until the advent of Louis Borno as president. [97] In changing his position on the desirability of a loan in 1920, Dartiguenave argued that a refunding loan was no longer necessary because increased revenues made it possible to care for the debt service, that an advantage to be gained from devaluation of the French franc had been eliminated, and that the new loan would cost 7 or 8 percent, while the old loans cost only 5 or 6 percent interest. [98] These considerations were of no great importance to the United States, which was intent on dominating Haitian finances.

Faced with Dartiguenave's obstinacy in refusing to sign the new loan, the State Department considered using an executive order issued by the "Military Government of Haiti" under the Martial Law Proclamation, but the impasse was eliminated with the inauguration of Borno as the new client-president in June, 1922. Borno had earlier promised to pass the loan contract within three or four days of assuming office.[99] The 1922 refunding loan was awarded to National City Bank, which bid 92.137 and sold $16 million of thirty-year Haitian government bonds on the American market at a price of 96½.[100] The bonds were supported by a general lien on Haitian government revenues and yielded 6.25 percent interest when held to maturity. The loan permitted the refunding of earlier debts, the settlement of pending foreign claims, and reform of the cumbersome system of revenue pledges associated with the old debt, but provided little in the way of extra funds for economic development and had no clear financial advantage over the earlier French loans, which it consolidated.[101]

The 1922 loan committed the United States government to long-term supervision of Haitian finances, since it would be called upon to protect the interests of American bondholders until the loan was fully paid. The loan effectively completed the 1921–22 reorganization and rationalization of the occupation, which now emerged as a static, efficient, and internally disciplined organization. Henceforth, so long as Haiti remained quiet, the occupation attracted little notice in Washington or in the American press. So far as United States foreign policy was concerned, no news from Haiti was good news. President Harding, who had championed the cause of Haitian independence during the 1920 election campaign, took little personal interest in the occupation beyond trying to replace competent treaty officials with his own political appointments.[102] Secretary of State Hughes repeatedly expressed a desire to withdraw from Haiti and limit the extent of martial law, and remarked to Joseph Grew in 1924 that he had no intention of intervening anywhere in Central America because the country and the Congress would not support any extension of the situation that existed in Haiti and the Dominican Republic. In 1928, Hughes wrote: "We do not wish to remain in Haiti. We wish to leave as soon as we can do so with assurance that there will not be a recurrence of bloodshed and a disregard of the obligations of international intercourse which might require renewed interposition on the part of our Government." [103] This was a stale rehash of State Department press releases issued during the Wilson administration. No practical measures were contemplated to rescind martial law, withdraw American troops, or move up the 1936 termination date stipulated in the treaty. Within Haiti the Occupation did little to broaden its political base or shift responsibilities to Haitian subordinates. President Calvin Coolidge, who thought little about Haiti, remarked:

Of course, we want to withdraw. We had some plans to withdraw. We have there a few marines—sent there for the purpose of maintaining peace and order and protecting American interests, and, incidentally, perhaps more than incidental, for protecting also the Haitians. But the Government of Haiti sent a very strong request that we continue the occupation, and that we have done. [104]

This statement was, at best, haphazard and ill-informed. Several United States senators, especially William H. King, George W. Norris, and William E. Borah, continued to make sporadic attacks on the occupation during the 1920s. King offered an amendment to a 1922 military appropriation bill providing that no money be spent to maintain marines in Haiti, the Dominican Republic, and Nicaragua, but the motion was defeated by a vote of 43 to 9. [105] In general, Haiti received little attention in the United States after the 1921–22 reorganization, and the Occupation continued to sit on Haiti without any spectacular developments until the strikes and riots of 1929.

From Faustin Wirkus and Dudley Taney, The White King of La Gonâve
(Garden City, N.Y., 1931)

The United States fleet in Port-au-Prince harbor in 1917 for a visit that featured elaborate observance of protocol and diplomatic honors for President Philippe Sudre Dartiguenave. One of the public markets is in the foreground.

The Bureau de Port at Cayes. Customshouses were of special interest to the United States government, bankers, and investors because duties collected there on exports and imports constituted the major part of the revenue of the Haitian government.

Courtesy of Mrs. Virginia A. White

Courtesy of Mrs. Virginia A. White

A street scene in Port-au-Prince about 1920. The narrow-gauge train hauled sugar cane from the fields through the city streets to the mill where it was refined for local use. The major export item was coffee, which was sold primarily to the French, with whom Haitians had long had close cultural and economic ties.

Courtesy of Mrs. Virginia A. White

The National Palace, Port-au-Prince, home of Haiti's presidents. This building was begun after the previous palace was blown up in 1912; it was completed during the occupation.

Photograph by Clifton Adams, courtesy of the National Geographic Society

The lifestyle of the elite of Haiti. The awnings, tiles, furniture, fashions, and language were French.

A peasant home and family in the interior of the island about 1917

From World's Work Magazine, *courtesy of Sojourner Truth Library*

From World's Work Magazine, *courtesy of Sojourner Truth Library*

A unit of the Haitian army prior to United States intervention

From World's Work Magazine, *courtesy of Sojourner Truth Library*

The Gendarmerie d'Haïti, developed and officered by United States marines during the occupation

From World's Work Magazine,
courtesy of Sojourner Truth Library

President Dartiguenave (right) and his minister of foreign affairs Louis Borno, who signed the treaty between Haiti and the United States. Borno succeeded Dartiguenave as president in 1922.

From World's Work Magazine,
courtesy of Sojourner Truth Library

Marine General Eli K. Cole (left) with a city official of Hinche and Assistant Secretary of the Navy Franklin D. Roosevelt during Roosevelt's 1917 visit to Haiti

Courtesy of Marine Corps Museum, Quantico

Colonel Littleton W. T. Waller, Commander Marine Expeditionary Forces in Haiti (front right), negotiating with Haitian leaders in October, 1915. Charlemagne Peralte, who was to lead a caco revolt in 1919, is in the front row, third from the right.

Brigadier General John H. Russell, American High Commissioner to Haiti

Courtesy of Marine Corps Museum, Quantico

Courtesy of Marine Corps Museum, Quantico

Prisoners at the national penitentiary, Port-au-Prince, making footgear for the military under the supervision of marine officers of the Gendarmerie d'Haïti

From Literary Digest, *courtesy of Rutgers University Library*

In 1921 tales of Marine Corps atrocities in Haiti and Santo Domingo resulted in a senatorial investigation. When the committee reached Port-au-Prince in November, it was met by demonstrators carrying banners bearing such inscriptions as "Shall Haiti Be Your Congo?" "Shall Haiti Be Your Belgium?" "The American People Have Been Betrayed in Haiti." The committee reported in favor of continuing the occupation.

A cartoon by Private Paul Woyshner which appeared in the *Marines Magazine* for April, 1917

THE MISSIONARY

Courtesy of Historical Division, U.S. Marine Corps, Washington

Courtesy of Princeton University Library

National Headquarters, Garde d'Haïti, Port-au-Prince, built in 1926, one of many government buildings erected by the Occupation's Department of Public Works

Courtesy of U.S. Marine Corps Combat Pictorial Section, Washington

Marine patrol with Haitian guide about 1919

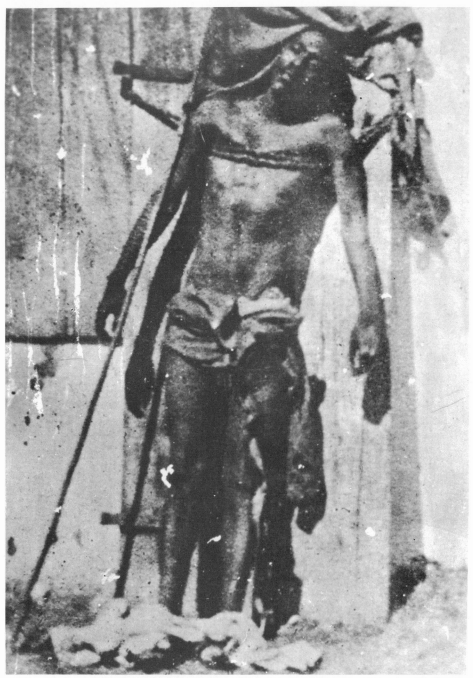

Courtesy of U.S. Marine Corps Combat Pictorial Section, Washington

Charlemagne Peralte, caco leader, after his assassination by two marines disguised as Haitians in 1919. This photograph was circulated in an attempt to undermine anti-American resistance; but to Haitians the posture of the corpse suggested Christ crucified, and the photograph enhanced the legend of Peralte's martyrdom.

Courtesy of Princeton University Library

Students at work in the shop of the Service Technique's industrial school at Jacmel

Courtesy of Princeton University Library

Rural school at Carefour Ségur, one of many school buildings erected by the Occupation

Courtesy of
Princeton University Library

The wharf at Petit-Goâve before
and after improvements by the Occupation's Department of Public
Works in 1928

Courtesy of
Princeton University Library

The River Grise irrigation system
before and after improvement by
the Occupation. The original system, built by the French in colonial
St. Domingue, fell into disrepair
after independence.

Courtesy of U.S. Marine Corps Combat Pictorial Section, Washington

Presidents Sténio Vincent and Franklin D. Roosevelt during Roosevelt's goodwill visit to Cap-Haïtien in 1934

Courtesy of U.S. Marine Corps Combat Pictorial Section, Washington

The President's Commission for Study and Review of Conditions in the Republic of Haiti upon its arrival at Port-au-Prince on February 28, 1930. The Forbes Commission, appointed by President Hoover to try to determine when and how the United States should withdraw from Haiti, arranged the removal of the American High Commissioner and for control-free elections which were won decisively by Haitian nationalists. But United States withdrawal did not take place until four years later.

7

Racial and
Cultural Tensions

The period from the 1922 financial and administrative reorganization to the 1929 strikes and riots was a time of peace, political stability, and relative economic prosperity in Haiti. There was strong
continuity in the administration of the occupation, with General
Russell and client-President Borno serving throughout the period,
and Haiti produced a series of good coffee crops in years when prices
on the international coffee market were high. During this period
the United States made a determined effort to indoctrinate Haitians
with American concepts of political morality, pragmatism, and efficiency, and to teach Haitians modern agricultural and industrial
skills through manual-technical education programs. These efforts
were largely unsuccessful because of racial and cultural prejudices
which tended to undermine the development of effective master-
disciple relationships. Instead of modeling after the Americans,
many Haitians came to despise them.

Racism and awareness of black racial origins had been important
factors in Haitian social, intellectual, and political life before the
American intervention. White somatic norms, especially lightness
of skin pigmentation, had remained significant criteria in determining social and economic status after the departure of the white
French colonial population in the early nineteenth century, and the
elite of independent Haiti persisted in copying French styles and

social mannerisms as means of justifying its assertions of cultural sophistication and refinement. The self-conscious efforts to win respect by achieving a high level of white-European cultural refinement and the concomitant repudiation of any black or African heritage were complemented by a strong pride in Haitian independence and national sovereignty. The few white foreigners in Haiti were not treated with especial deference, and white travelers noted a prevailing attitude of racial equality and even superiority that contrasted sharply with the servility of blacks in the United States.[1]

When American marines landed in 1915 they brought concepts of racial discrimination that had not held sway in Haiti since the white French colonials were driven out a hundred years before. At first there was some contact between the occupying forces and the Haitian elite. American officers attended social functions at elite clubs, danced with Haitian women, and were received in elite homes. Gendarmerie Commandant Smedley Butler later recalled how American reluctance to mingle with Haitians had been readily overcome at a 1916 Gendarmerie ball given at the National Palace: "When the American officers came in, they shied a little from the dusky belles; but, as the evening wore on, their shyness entirely wore off."[2]

American racial mores did not prohibit mixing of white males with either blacks or mulattoes, and in this case interracial conviviality was apparently furthered by heavy drinking. Butler, in his flamboyant autobiography, claimed that he counted fifteen American officers in full-dress uniform sprawled out on the grass of the palace courtyard the morning following the ball.[3]

Whatever racial harmony existed during the early days of the occupation came to an end with the arrival of American wives and families in 1916.[4] An American businessman testifying at the 1922 Senate Hearings stated:

Up to that time the American officers had free and complete social intercourse with the Haitians, both in their families and in their clubs. . . . With the coming of the women of the occupation this peaceful state of affairs was completely upset, the women having a natural aversion, due to their former training and method of thinking, to dancing

and general social intercourse with the Haitians, men or women; the
husbands of these women also strongly objecting for the same reason.[5]

The taboo against social intercourse between white women and
anyone with black blood was a long-standing axiom of American
racism. In his classic study *An American Dilemma* (1944), Gunnar
Myrdal ranked "the bar against intermarriage and sexual intercourse
involving white women" as the cardinal tenet of American racial
discrimination.[6] This tenet was supported by a comprehensive system of interracial barriers which isolated white women from contact
with blacks and, in its broadest aspects, resulted in the general social
segregation of the races.

Following the arrival of the white women, Americans instituted
Jim Crow racial segregation in Haiti. In polite American society,
this racial segregation was justified by the explanation that with the
arrival of the women the American colony became socially self-
sufficient and that segregation did not indicate "snobbishness" but
was a reflection of different cultural and linguistic backgrounds. One
American officer remarked to a traveler that "I can't see why they
wouldn't have a better time with *their* crowd, just as I do with
mine."[7] Segregation was, however, much too systematic to be explained simply as the result of casually accepted, mutually agree-
able divergences in cultural and social interests. The American
Club, which was the social center of the American colony, was
closed to all Haitians, even the client-president; the only blacks
allowed to participate in club functions were the Haitian waiters.[8]

After the closing of the American social clubs to Haitians, elite
clubs continued for a time to receive those Americans, chiefly civilians, who chose to continue their associations with Haitians, but
this courtesy was largely withdrawn as racial hostility intensified.
An American traveler observed that military personnel insisted on
strict racial segregation, while American businessmen tended to be
more gracious toward the Haitians:

By chance or design the great majority of our officers in Haiti are
Southerners, and they naturally shun any but the most unavoidable intercourse with the natives. This is one of the chief bones of contention
between the forces of occupation and the American civilians engaged in
business. The latter, while still keeping a color-line, contend that the

natives of education should be treated more like human beings. They deplore the narrow viewpoint, the indifference to industrial advancement, the occasional schoolboy priggishness of the officers, and the latter retaliate by considering the term business man as synonymous with money-grabbing and willingness to cater to the natives for the sake of trade.[9]

Irrespective of differences between the marines and the small number of American businessmen in Haiti, effective racial segregation became firmly established as an important facet of the occupation. The American colony in Port-au-Prince concentrated around its own neighborhood, special Catholic masses were created for Americans, and local hotels that catered to American guests adopted Jim Crow standards.[10]

Overt incidents of racial hostility, especially those involving white women, reinforced the tendency toward segregation and mutual resentment. At a reception attended by all official Port-au-Prince during the visit of Assistant Secretary of the Navy Roosevelt in January, 1917, American men danced with Haitian women but American women refused to dance with Haitian men. One of Roosevelt's traveling companions noted that "very few American women were inside of the house after the dancing began, most of them walking or sitting in the large gardens outside. Many of them had been forbidden by their husbands to come into the dancing rooms until the Haitians had gone." [11] This and other awkward incidents involving contact between Haitian men and American women, such as Haitian gentlemen offering their arms to American lady guests and being rejected, hastened the breakdown of social relations during the early years of the occupation.[12] Edna Taft, an American white woman whose remarkable book *A Puritan in Voodoo-Land* (1938) illustrates the pervasiveness of racism at the time of American withdrawal in 1934, broke the color line by mixing socially with Haitian men and experienced personal trauma and guilt. Miss Taft recalled warnings that her father would turn over in his grave and remembered "trembling all over, and the palms of my hands were wet with cold perspiration" on first dancing and shaking hands with Haitian men.[13]

White female contacts with Haitians were severely limited by the implementation of racial segregation in 1916 and 1917. Subsequent transgressions of the color line, such as the annual stag New Year's party given by the client-president for Americans, rarely involved white women.[14] Despite the social isolation of American women, possible breaches of racial etiquette by Haitians remained a threat to the peace and tranquillity of the occupation, especially with the intensification of hatred that accompanied the strikes and riots of 1929. In August, 1930, the brigade commander and American chargé sent alarming reports to the State Department describing a grave and "unprecedented" incident involving an "insult to a white woman" that occurred when a Haitian returning from a political meeting grabbed the daughter of a marine sergeant by the arm and was, in turn, manhandled by a marine corporal. This potentially explosive incident was carefully hushed up by American authorities, who considered it a serious threat to the safety and morale of the occupation.[15] Extreme American sensitivity about shielding their women from contact with Haitians was all the more offensive to the Haitians because American men showed no compunction about living openly with Haitian mistresses.[16]

In addition to difficulties over the sanctity of American women, another source of open clashes between Haitians and Americans was drunkenness by marines, especially enlisted men on liberty. Drinking and whoring had been problems since the early years of the occupation, and marine rowdiness inspired some Haitians to render the initials U.S.M.C. into "Use Sans Moindre Contrôle" (use without the least control) and "Un Salaud Mal Costumé" (a sloppy bum).[17] A number of American civilian observers noted that marines under the influence of alcohol bragged about their cavalier treatment of Haitians, disparaged them as "niggers" and "gooks," and otherwise behaved in a manner offensive to Haitian pride.[18] Financial Adviser W. W. Cumberland ascribed the breakdown of social relations with the Haitian elite to boisterousness and improprieties by marine officers: ". . . when there were efforts to have joint social activities some ebullient officer would drink a little too much and then would say or do something which would offend the Haitians. Then we were all in trouble." Cumberland recalled that after these unfortunate incidents social contacts were "largely confined . . . to formal and official functions . . . where you might say only a select group of officers who knew how to behave themselves would be in attendance and incidents were reduced to a minimum." [19] A visiting American author noted that the elite Club Bellevue had a standing rule forbidding Americans in military uniform to enter its doors which dated back to a "socially objectionable" incident involving Gendarmerie Commandant Butler early in the occupation.*

Overt altercations between Americans and Haitians, which usually involved marines and the hypersensitive Haitian elite, became less frequent with effective racial segregation and measures taken by marine commanders to seclude the marine garrison and enforce standards of courtesy and tact. In 1927 Marine Corps Commandant Lejeune wrote the State Department that there were "very few, if any, points of contact with the Haitiens" by officers of the Marine Brigade, who were following the policy established by High Commissioner Russell "to keep the military occupation as much in the background as possible." [20] The marine garrison was concentrated in the two major cities of Port-au-Prince and Cap Haïtien and served exclusively as a reserve force to back up the Gendarmerie in times of trouble. Marines were instructed to avoid incidents with the local population, and those who mistreated Haitians were subject to severe penalties. [21]

The establishment of Jim Crow segregation led to the isolation of those individuals who crossed the color line and to an anti-American reaction by the Haitian elite. Americans who associated with Haitians were subjected to ostracism and ridicule by the American colony. Edna Taft related that "My social contacts with conservative, upper-class natives shocked my American friends. . . . The Americans who entertained me and whom I entertained felt keenly ashamed of my interest in the dusky elite." [22] The few American men who married Haitian women were treated as outcasts by their fellow countrymen. A marine officer who married the niece of client-President Borno was denounced by his former fellows for having "disgraced the service." [23] Because of the perverse workings of racial prejudice in Haiti, Madame Placide, an American white woman who married a Haitian, was not only ostracized by the American colony

---

* Colonel Robert D. Heinl, Jr., head of the American military mission to the Duvalier government in 1959, was the first marine to be elected to the Club Bellevue since the Butler incident. Seabrook, 139. Heinl letter to me, July 20, 1970.

but also lost caste with the Haitians for having lowered herself, while her husband enjoyed increased social prestige by virtue of his marriage to a white woman.[24] Faced with American racism, the elite drew a retaliatory color line, excluding Americans from most Haitian social life while still maintaining social relations with other white foreigners. The elite set up its own system of ostracism, excluding members of the client-government and Haitian families that fraternized with marines from elite society.[25]

The complex elite racial ideology, marked by both emulation of white characteristics and intense pride, included disdain for American blacks, who were looked down upon as being servile. The Haitian minister to Washington informed the State Department in 1924 that even poor black Haitians looked down upon American blacks. This attitude, strengthened by direct contact with American racial discrimination, prevented President Harding from rewarding black Republicans with Haitian appointments, and resulted in the posting of whites to Haitian diplomatic positions previously held by blacks.[26] Thus the American presence in Haiti was all white, since the Marine Corps at that time did not accept blacks.

While racial segregation remained in effect throughout the occupation, the problem of racial hostilities was progressively ameliorated by the appointment of tactful and sympathetic personnel to positions in the occupation. High Commissioner Russell pursued a policy designed to eliminate racial friction, and his wife was one of several American women who went out of her way to be cordial to Haitians. There were always a number of Americans who treated Haitians with respect and consideration, and some, such as Gendarmerie Commandant and later Brigade Commander Louis McCarty Little, made special efforts to observe local customs and cultivate friendly relations.[27] After the abolition of the office of high commissioner in the aftermath of the 1929 uprisings, successive State Department ministers were conspicuously tolerant, and Brigade Commander Little was specifically retained for Haitian duty because he was liked by the Haitians. In 1928 an American author with egalitarian biases observed that the occupation was not characterized by Prussian swagger and the pushing of natives off sidewalks, but rather by an attitude of "kindly" racial superiority and aloofness.[28]

The American attitude of racial superiority was by no means simply a reflection of ignorance or exceptional prejudice on the part of occupation personnel. The scientific literature of the period amply supported the idea that blacks were inherently inferior to whites, as did contemporary popular literature. Lothrop Stoddard, in his book *The Rising Tide of Color Against White World-Supremacy* (1921) noted that "the negroe when left to himself, as in Haiti and Liberia, rapidly reverts to his ancestral ways," and argued that "No one except a doctrinaire liberal would be likely to assert that the Andaman Islanders had an imprescriptible right to independence, or that Haiti, which owed its independence only to a turn in European politics, should forever remain a sovereign—international nuisance." [29]

A University of California professor, writing for the scholarly *Hispanic-American Historical Review* in 1927, compared Haitian and American blacks and observed that "the Haitian lacks the thick lips and nostrils and rolling eyes of his brother in the north" but displayed the same "happy traits of the negro type." [30]

High-ranking military officers also subscribed to prevailing racial stereotypes and concepts of black inferiority. An admiral who had served as military governor of Santo Domingo and administrative commander of the occupation in Haiti compared Haitians with blacks in the American South:

> The people of Haiti have had no immediate contact with a superior cultivation and intelligence such as the negroes of the United States have had since their emancipation. . . . The same traits of negro character that are found in the United States exist in Haiti, both good and bad; but I consider that the bad traits are more in evidence in Haiti than in the United States, where they are under better control.[31]

In his reminiscences General Russell observed that "The corpulent 'mammy' of our southern states is rarely seen and the strapping 'buck' of Africa and the United States still less frequently." In assessing Haitian cultural achievements, Russell stated, "The elite came not as result of racial evolution but as a result of racial intermixture." [32] The Gendarmerie commandant from 1919 to 1921 later recalled that one of the American treaty officials had arrived with a book entitled "The Development of the Negro Mind" from which he quoted frequently, much to the annoyance of the Haitian elite.[33]

The State Department was well aware of the racial problems in Haiti. Russell reported in 1919 that "As a rule the foreigner does not mix with the Haitien and this is especially true of the American, who has little or nothing to do with them except in a business way." [34] The Forbes Commission, sent by President Hoover to investigate the occupation in the aftermath of the 1929 strikes and riots, reported that "Race antipathies lie behind many of the difficulties which the United States military and civil forces have met in Haiti." [35] In 1927 an officer in the Division of Latin American Affairs observed that

most of the Marine Officers, whether accidentally or not I do not know, come from the South and do not differentiate between the educated Haitian mulatto and any other gentleman of color. In general, the American Officers I found to be incapable of understanding that any necessity existed for making an impression even on the best of Haitians. Any general officer who issued an order on this subject would be very unpopular and would be considered a fool. I discussed the matter fully with Colonel John Meyers [Myers], Commander of the Brigade in Haiti.[36]

State Department officers themselves were not devoid of contemporary racial prejudices. Assistant Secretary of State Francis White refused to testify before the Senate Finance Committee in 1932 when the State Department's Haitian loan policy was attacked by a visiting Haitian nationalist; White remarked, "I had no idea of getting into an argument with a coon on the stand." [37]

After the 1929 uprisings the United States made renewed efforts to minimize racial friction. In August, 1930, the American chargé at Port-au-Prince reported that most incidents of racial intolerance were being manifested by Haitians rather than Americans, and that cordiality would prevail "given the watchfulness of the American Government to prevent any manifestation of color prejudice on the part of American officials in Haiti," except for Haitian political agitation, which was "reinforced by certain unfortunate incidents which occurred during the early months of the Intervention." [38]

The advisability of recruiting occupation officials who would be "sympathetic" to the Haitians had been pointed out by the 1922 Senate Inquiry. During the Wilson administration no special effort was made to send unprejudiced personnel to Haiti, indeed, virtually all of the leading civilian treaty officials were appointed from the Deep South where racial prejudice was especially prevalent: the head of Wilson's Customs Service was a former Louisiana parish clerk; the second-in-charge of the Customs Service had been a Mississippi customs collector; Financial Adviser McIlhenny was from Louisiana; the Superintendent of Public Instruction was a former Louisiana schoolteacher; and the State Department representative, Minister Bailly-Blanchard, was from Louisiana.[39] Irrespective of their geographic origins, which probably related to political obligations, Wilson's appointments were generally selected with a view to their professional qualifications. Unlike Harding, who had hoped to reward black Republicans with Haitian appointments, Wilson specifically stipulated that treaty appointments should involve considerations beyond politics, although the posting of McIlhenny as financial adviser was questionable in this respect.[40]

A number of observers believed that the marine contingent, both during the Wilson administration and thereafter, consisted predominantly of Southerners.[41] A United States trade commissioner, after an extremely frank conversation with an American businessman in 1922, reported:

It would appear that the bulk of the men in charge of policing, sanitation and other duties were drawn from those States where the race question has always been a matter of delicacy—Louisiana, Texas, etc.— and that the Southern attitude towards the black man was imported at the beginning and has operated to alienate many natives who might have been useful.[42]

American scholar James G. Leyburn, in his book *The Haitian People* (1941), made the unsubstantiated charge that the United States had deliberately sent marines from Southern states to Haiti in the early days of the occupation "on the theory that they would, from long acquaintance with Negroes, know how to 'handle' them." [43] This charge is dubious. While the 1922 Senate Inquiry specifically recommended that a marine officer be charged with scrutinizing the backgrounds of all men sent to Haiti,[44] thereby indicating that a deliberate selection policy might be administratively feasible, I have found no evidence of any deliberate selection policy in Marine Corps records. It is true that several prominent marines, notably General Waller and High Commissioner Russell, were Southerners, but others were not. Gendarmerie Commandant Butler, for instance, was a member of a distinguished Pennsylvania Quaker family. In a 1964 undergraduate term paper, Ann Hurst of Wellesley College investigated the proportion of marine officers serving in Haiti from 1916 to 1932 who had been born in Southern states and found that the mean percentage of Southerners in the total United States population was greater than both the percentage of Southern officers in the Marine Corps and the percentage of Southern officers serving in Haiti.[45] Hurst's study deals exclusively with officers and does not delve into the important question of enlisted men, who, as officers of the Gendarmerie, were most in contact with the Haitians. Marine recruiting statistics for periods in 1921 and 1924 show that Southern enlistments for the corps as a whole were not disproportionately large.[46] In any case, whether or not there was a disproportionately large number of Southern marines in Haiti, the fact that many observers felt that this was the case indicates that Southerners and Southern racial codes were conspicuous.

Racial prejudices, severely disruptive in themselves, were complemented by cultural prejudices. Americans tended to resent the aristocratic French cultural sophistication of the elite, and the elite looked down on the uncultured, pragmatically materialistic Americans. Technical expertise did not rank high on the scale of elite values, which were oriented toward polite learning. In 1930 American Chargé Stuart Grummon provided the State Department with the following commentary on Haitian "Latin" mentality:

In general, while the Anglo-Saxon has a deep sense of the value of social organization and of the obligation of democratic government to assume a large share of responsibility for the social welfare of the masses, and has in addition a profound conviction of the value of democratic government, the Latin mind, on the contrary, is apt to scorn democracy and neglect activities looking to the health and educational welfare of the masses. . . . The Anglo-Saxon, who excels in collective action is apt to be impatient with the Haitian characteristic of intense individualism inherited from the French regime. . . . The action of the Haitian, in common with the Latin in general, is in the main directed by emotion rather than by reason, which in the main dictates the action of the Anglo-Saxon.[47]

High Commissioner Russell expressed a similar view when he reported during the 1929 uprisings that "Haitian mentality only recognizes force, and appeal to reason and logic is unthinkable." [48]

American hostility to Latin cultural traits merged with and was sometimes indistinguishable from racial prejudice. In 1917 Brigade Commander Cole stated:

The Negroes of mixed type [mulattoes], who constitute the majority of educated people and politicians, have the general characteristics of such people the world over—vain, loving praise, excitable, changeable, beyond belief illogical, and double-faced. Many of them are highly educated and polished, but their sincerity must always be doubted.[49]

There was also a tendency on the part of many Americans to identify all Haitians with the black peasantry, who were looked down upon as ignorant and uncivilized. Cole remarked that "fully 75 percent are of a very low mentality and ignorant beyond description," and "No matter how much veneer and polish a Haitian may have, he is absolutely savage under the skin and under strain reverts to type." [50] Haitians were caught in a web of vicious American prejudices from which there was no escape. The several facets of American prejudice, specifically racist hostility to blacks, disparagement of "Latin" and Continental culture, and condescension toward illiterate peasants, were interrelated and reinforced each other to form a formidable barrier to Haitian-American communication and cooperation at all levels of the occupation.

The cultural clash between Americans and the Haitian elite was all the more exacerbated because the Americans, who subscribed to political ideologies of democracy and egalitarianism, were repulsed by the very concept of elitism that was fundamental to the social and economic position of the elite in Haiti. This revulsion, of course, ignored the paradox of American racial and cultural elitism. During the early years of the occupation American military commanders were especially trenchant in this respect, scorning the aristocratic pomposity of the elite while expressing affection for the common people. This attitude was firmly rooted in ideals of democratic egalitarianism. It also indicated an escapist tendency based on American inability to cope with blacks on a level of equality, and corresponding preference for those interracial contacts in which the Americans, by Western standards, were clearly superior in all respects. Gendarmerie Commandant Butler, for instance, expressed disdain for the "1 per cent that wears vici kid shoes with long pointed toes and celluloid collars," but was very fond of his "ape man" black servant Antoine, who was a "faithful slave" to the Butler children.[51] The American attitude toward the peasants was often extremely patronizing. A marine officer who served in the back country and, according to his own version at least, was kind and even affectionate toward the Haitians and was well liked in return, said, "A man who is born with a semi-ape's brain cannot rise in life's competition. That was the kind of brain ninety percent of the Haitian peasants seemed to have." [52]

In 1921 Brigade Commander Russell, soon to be appointed high commissioner, stated that he had a sincere concern for Haiti, but that "sympathies lie entirely, however, with the huge uneducated mass of Haitiens who have by the despicable action of an inappreciable few of their countrymen been kept for years in a bondage that is akin to slavery." [53]

American educational and economic development programs were all designed to favor the peasants and undermine the privileged position of the elite. In 1926 the chief of the Division of Latin American Affairs wrote Secretary of State Frank B. Kellogg that "The aim of our Occupation of Haiti has been to benefit the country as a whole, and especially the peasants. . . . The political class which has been debarred from the spoils of office is consequently hostile to the Occupation, whereas the great mass of the people is favorable and friendly to it." [54] Client-President Borno strongly subscribed to the American policy of breaking down the established class system and eliminating the "social crime" of elite exploitation of the impoverished masses.[55] Ironically, the occupation also enhanced the political position of the elite; under the Americans, mulattoes were installed in the presidency and major Cabinet posts for the first time in many years. Before Dartiguenave, eleven of the preceding twelve presidents had been black. The apparent contradiction was probably the result of American preference for well-educated collaborators, as opposed to the less-polished black strongmen who had been prominent in the past. American choices may also have been influenced by white somatic norms. If so, this would be further evidence pointing to the escapist element in the avowed special sympathy for the black masses. With elite nationalists replacing the collaborators after the 1929 uprisings, mulatto domination of Haitian politics continued until the "black revolution" of 1946.

The ideological disparity between the democratic, egalitarian Americans and the aristocratic elite, compounded by previously mentioned racial and cultural antagonisms, was further complicated by the different levels of sophistication that the elite and the occupation personnel exemplified within their respective cultural traditions. One American woman journalist observed that the elite were "so many layers in culture above the army or navy man and his wife that the visiting American must feel ashamed of his country's representatives,—especially when an officer after several drinks asks him, 'How do you like the big niggers?' " [56]

The marine officer corps of this period was not characterized by the higher levels of education and cultural finesse attained in later years. The cosmopolitan, culturally refined elite looked down on American lack of manners and crass materialism. In 1930 American Chargé Stuart Grummon reported that members of the elite were "contemptuous of the American practical nature and confident that their own suavity and politeness . . . placed them in a distinctly superior position to the average eminently practical-minded American." [57] Acts such as American Minister Bailly-Blanchard's appearing at the National Palace dressed in sports attire and Financial Adviser Cumberland's blatant and apparently unwitting refusal to follow the polite French custom of the visiting dignitary paying first call on the local dignitary offended the sensibilities of the proud and formal elite.[58] The elite likewise deprecated American lack of savoir-faire, as exemplified by American ignorance of foreign languages. The chairman of the 1922 Senate Inquiry wrote Secretary of State Hughes that he was "amazed to find in Haiti not a single officer of the United States Navy or Marine Corps who spoke French with perfect accent and fluency." [59] American rowdiness also offended the elite, as when guests sitting in the garden at an elite piano recital given by a graduate of the Paris Conservatory were bombarded by rocks thrown from the neighboring dwelling by a drunken marine officer.[60] Such incidents, given the various other animosities, were magnified out of proportion. The abundant availability of alcohol in Haiti at a time when Prohibition was in force in the United States tended to aggravate the problem of marine rowdiness. Despite numerous indignities which Haitians suffered during the occupation, many of them maintained their pride and haughtiness; one elite lady remarked to a 1934 French visitor that the Americans had copied Haitian fashions, imported from France, rather than the other way around.[61]

The overall Haitian reaction to the occupation was complex and far reaching in its consequences. At the outset, some Haitians welcomed the American intervention as a means of ending political and economic chaos, and a small minority of the elite were always willing to collaborate with the Americans by participating in successive client-governments.[62] The majority, however, were hostile. The shock of American intervention was cataclysmic for the elite. Prior to the coming of the Americans, their commanding economic and social position had been unchallenged; the elite constituted an aristocracy which arrogantly dominated the masses in terms of education, political advantages, wealth, and economic privilege. The elite were all the more complacent in their exercise of aristocratic privilege because Haiti was isolated from the outside world, making the elite, for local purposes, the masters of all creation. The dominance of black political strongmen qualified but did not fundamentally alter the social and economic hierarchy. This idyllic world of privilege was rudely shattered by the Americans, who, practicing American patterns of racial discrimination, did not differentiate between mulattoes and blacks or between educated and illiterate, but looked down upon all Haitians, irrespective of admixture of white blood and degree of achievement, as simply "Negroes" or "niggers." [63] Under American rule, the elite was not only subjected to humiliating Jim Crow racial discrimination by white Americans but also lost their privileged position as the dominant group in Haiti to the resident American colony. The elite were confronted with the realization of their own ineptitude in the face of American power and their proved inability to manage national affairs in such a way as to have prevented the occupation in the first place.

The forced realization of their own failings and limitations and the pressures of daily exposure to American culture left educated Haitians in a state of intellectual crisis. Suave Continental values were clearly irrelevant in the new situation. All the old bases of elite pride and self-respect, most notably identification with white French culture and condescension toward black culture, were undermined by the occupation. Haitian intellectuals began to attack elite cultural values and social attitudes shortly after the American intervention, the most incisive effort being Jean Price-Mars's *La Vocation de l'élite* (1919), which described how and why the irresponsible, self-centered elite had failed to provide effective national leadership. The failure was especially apparent because the intervention had taken place in the midst of an impressive period of elite intellectual accomplishments. Some Haitians now sought to replace discredited Continental idealism with American pragmatism, materialism, and technical efficiency. Client-President Borno was an advocate of this approach. Adaptation of American values was, however, repulsive to most Haitian intellectuals because of American racial and cultural bigotry.

A more common reaction to the occupation, especially among younger Haitian intellectuals, was to reject both the effete emulation of French culture and the new pragmatic culture of the Americans in favor of seeking national identity in black and African origins. Educated Haitians who had based their pride and self-respect on careful emulation of white culture, only to be scorned and humiliated as "Negroes" by the white American invaders, now began to search for an indigenous black cultural heritage. New intellectual movements, known variously as *l'indigénisme, l'haitianisme,* and *l'africanisme,* emphasized Haitian ethnography and glorified black folk culture. Ethnographic studies, notably Price-Mars's pioneer work *Ainsi parla l'oncle* (1928), investigated and romanticized Haitian folklore, religion, and language and, by tracing Haitian origins to advanced civilizations in Africa, demonstrated that blacks had a history of their own. Many of these studies by Haitian intellectuals of the *génération de l'occupation* recognized that Haiti was a mixed culture with European facets but emphasized that African characteristics predominated in determining basic attitudes and ways of thinking.[64]

Interest in ethnography and folk culture was also manifest in the reaction of Haitian poets and novelists to the occupation. Prior to the American intervention Haitian writers had imitated French literary styles and dealt mainly with romantic and idealistic topics. The literary reaction to the occupation, often called "la littérature engagée," had a strong social orientation, featuring the Haitian peasant and his African and black heritage. This problack literature was one of the earliest manifestations of the world revolutionary phenomenon which the Martinican poet Aimé Césaire and Jean-Paul Sartre labeled "négritude."[65] In his article "The French West Indian Background of 'Négritude'" (1961), G. R. Coulthard traces the roots of négritude to the American occupation of Haiti: ". . . in Haiti is to be found the first awareness, the first *prise de conscience*, of the Negro in the white world, and it is the unbroken continuity of the theme in Haitian literature that forces the conclusion that to a very large extent, historically, the concept of négritude grew out of the Haitian situation."[66]

Haitian novels written about the occupation stressed American racism and vulgarity. The villain of Stephen Alexis' *Le Nègre Masqué* (1933), Major Smedley Seaton, is probably a take-off on Marine Major Smedley Butler; the fictional character Smedley Seaton is pictured as a crude racist who despises Haitians and drives a dazzling Cadillac automobile.[67] Virgile Valcin's *La Blanche Négresse* (1934) describes a Haitian girl who passes for white, marries an American, and then has a baby daughter, but is abandoned along with the baby when the American husband finds out that she is really a mulatto; the husband, who is still attracted to the girl offers to set her up as his mistress after the divorce.[68] "Engagée" literature of the period also expressed sentiments of international black solidarity against white oppression and a Marxist-oriented sympathy for the Haitian lower classes.[69] The leading Haitian novelist of the period, Jacques Roumain, founded a fledgling Communist party in 1934.

The Haitian reaction to the occupation also included a certain amount of active political resistance, such as that undertaken by the

Union Patriotique, but overt resistance was effectively suppressed by the Occupation until the 1929 uprisings. During the 1920s Haitian political opposition to the occupation centered around local newspapers, whose editors were promptly and frequently jailed, and also included several attempts to bring complaints about the occupation before international bodies such as the League of Nations.[70]

There were some Haitian political activists who neither collaborated with the occupation nor opposed it, but simply expressed frustration and contempt. A marine officer reported a 1929 desecration of the Dessalines statue in Port-au-Prince as follows:

The investigation into the Dessaline's [sic] statue affair has brought out another side of Haitien politics which involves the younger class of Haitien. These people, mostly aged up to 22 years, are ANTI-EVERYTHING, even Dessalines [a national hero]. Their attitude is strictly anti all that might have caused the present condition of Haitien politics. Their claim is that their fathers and forefathers done wrong, because, had they not done wrong, the Republic would not be in the condition it is today. They are against their parents, the Government, the opposition and the Occupation. . . . Such is the sentiment of the Younger people's leagues of Haiti.[71]

Subsequent information raised the possibility that marines on liberty might have desecrated the statue rather than nihilistic Haitian youths, but the attitude described above indicates the serious disaffection of some Haitian young people after fifteen years of American occupation. The above report was written just four months before the 1929 student strikes.

The various racial and cultural antagonisms which acted as barriers to Haitian-American cooperation were augmented by mundane hostilities attendant to most foreign military occupations. Haitians resented being ruled by foreigners, and resistance to the occupation rallied around the central theme of nationalism and patriotism. Haitians also resented the fact that Americans took over the most expensive houses and neighborhoods for themselves. The American colony in Port-au-Prince was located in the best part of town, and the street on which Americans lived at Cayes * was known locally as "millionaires' row."[72] Americans enjoyed pleasant social lives

* Also known as Les Cayes and Aux Cayes.

and could afford high standards of living. A 1927 Department of Commerce pamphlet stated that the "average" American family in Haiti employed four servants.[73] Marines and their families, especially enlisted men who would have been relatively poor in the context of contemporary United States society, were the most affluent social stratum in Haiti. Americans who worked for the civilian branches of the occupation were paid higher salaries than were Haitian employees who did comparable work; an American office worker in the Service Technique was paid $150 per month, while a Haitian doing the same work was paid $35 per month.[74] All these factors contributed to and helped sustain the racial and cultural impasse.

8

Uplift—The Prospects

The basic American policy decisions that resulted in the original intervention, the continuation of the occupation after World War I, and the establishment of an authoritarian government under an American military high commissioner were determined by broad international considerations. The United States intervened to strengthen its strategic position in the Caribbean, and it retained military control after the war mainly because it could not gracefully terminate the occupation and because self-imposed commitments to maintain political and economic control could not be fulfilled without military force. The strategic buildup, the installation of and commitments to National City Bank of New York, the insistence on consolidation of the Haitian debt in American hands, the elimination of European influence, and the imposition of effective political and economic control were all part of a larger effort to achieve American hegemony in the Caribbean. Compared with the economic potential of other Caribbean countries, especially Mexico, Cuba, and Venezuela, Haiti itself was relatively inconsequential. By 1920 most of the major American objectives in Haiti, with the exception of the pending loan consolidation, had been either achieved or obviated. American military domination of the Caribbean was no longer threatened by Germany or anyone else, American interests controlled the Banque Nationale, and continued financial and political control was assured by the 1917 treaty extension. The way was open for an influx of American capital by virtue of the alien landownership clause in the 1918 Constitution; conversely, prospects for lucrative capital investment had been dampened by the frustrating experiences of American entrepreneurs who had invested in Haiti and by the realization that Haiti had limited potential for economic development.

The Wilson administration, recognizing that there was no longer any vital purpose in maintaining military control, attempted to withdraw American troops in 1919 but found that it could not. American withdrawal would have resulted in victory for guerrilla forces, an embarrassing overthrow of the client-government, and vociferous denunciations of American imperialism by Haitian nationalists that would have clearly discredited the United States. So long as Haitians refused to accept the minimal American control deemed necessary by the State Department and threatened instead to obliterate the American presence, it was deemed necessary to maintain a garrison in Haiti. In terms of the vital purposes of United States Caribbean policy, the occupation became a stagnant holding operation designed to sit on Haiti until American troops could be gracefully withdrawn without the prospect of a violent anti-American reaction and without abandoning long-term commitments to American investors. With respect to American plans for the Caribbean, the occupation remained an awkward anachronism, reminiscent of an earlier type of colonial conquest already in disrepute.

Quite apart from the international policy considerations that had led to the intervention and were to determine the duration of the occupation, most Americans involved with Haiti felt that the occupation would and should benefit the Haitians. Gendarmerie Commandant Butler stated that his ambition was to "make Haiti a first class black man's country" and another marine officer observed that "in a sense our task formed a civil counterpart to the work of Christian missionaries who were devoting their lives to these people." [1] Americans, as representatives of an advanced, modern, industrialized nation, felt that they could transform backward, underdeveloped Haiti with American technology and practical ingenuity. They expected to pull Haiti up by its bootstraps if only Haitians would follow the formula of the American success story.

In keeping with its numerous ulterior motives and the imperious style of the occupation, the United States applied only select ingredients of the American success formula to the uplift of Haiti. While American concepts of civil service reform, pragmatism, and efficiency were systematically introduced into Haiti, political democracy definitely was not. Americans felt that the Haitians were too ignorant to know what was good for them. The United States disbanded the Haitian legislature, eliminated popular control over the presidency, and even canceled communal elections. In the rare instances when popular elections were permitted at the local level results were subject to the approval of the occupation. High Commissioner Russell reported that experimental 1926 communal elections "were not altogether satisfactory" and that the client-government had rescinded them, dissolved the elected councils, and appointed its own communal commissions instead.[2] In 1925 the chief of the Division of Latin American Affairs recorded that he and General Russell felt "that congressional elections under present conditions would be little more than a farce" because most Haitians were "so ignorant that they would have no conception of the meaning of an election."[3]

Misgivings about the capacity of the electorate did not prevent the Occupation from using national plebiscites to pass the pro-American Constitution of 1918 and constitutional amendments in 1928, but these were the only instances when Haitians were encouraged to participate in democratic processes. In both cases there was no possibility of an anti-American outcome.[4] Democratic institutions were suppressed because popular elections would have resulted in victory for anti-American candidates and would have thus weakened the authority of the Occupation. This, according to the Occupation view, would have hindered programs of material and moral uplift.

In applying the American success formula to Haiti, Occupation officials placed special emphasis on concepts of pragmatism and technical efficiency. Indeed, pragmatism and efficiency were basic in the formulation of Occupation policies to the extent that abstract American ideals and principles, such as national self-determination and the rights of individual citizens, were blatantly violated in order to achieve practical results. The practical approach dominated American efforts to reform Haiti just as it dominated the international aspects of America's Haiti policy. In a 1926 article entitled "Haiti: An Experiment in Pragmatism," Ulysses B. Weatherly argued:

Before the people can be really free there must be an elaborate process of building; there must be constructed the material equipment through which society may function, and there must be developed the intelligence and the civic spirit which are absolutely essential in a democracy. The impossibilists argue that it is better that a nation be allowed to work out these results for itself, even at the expense of waste, muddling and violence. The pragmatists insist that intelligent guidance from without may sometimes accelerate the process of national growth and save much waste.[5]

These sentiments were clichés of European white-man's-burden colonialism. In Haiti American pragmatists, with fresh confidence, expected that intelligent guidance, which had so recently made the United States a great world power, could not help but bear fruit.

This American fixation on pragmatism and efficiency, with the implied corollary that progress is effected mainly through material achievements, had been popular among a small number of Haitians on the eve of the intervention, but most Haitians had been traditionally hostile to these concepts and became more so in reaction to contact with American racism and cultural prejudices. In 1927 Financial Adviser W. W. Cumberland noted that Haitians were particularly resistant to American-style progress: "Human psychology is a strange complex of tradition, heritage and experience. A more unsatisfactory background for present-day enlightenment and progress could hardly be devised than in the case of Haiti." [6]

Given the wide divergence of cultural backgrounds, there were few common points of sympathy from which a viable synthesis of Haitian and American ideals could be created. Many of the elite retained their idealistic orientation toward French cultural sophistication, the masses had an esoteric culture of their own and remained skeptical of American ways, and younger intellectuals and political activists vigorously opposed everything American. The Americans, for their part, had little respect for Haitian cultural traditions; the director of the American School in Port-au-Prince observed that "The daily life and performances of the Haitian is hopelessly old-fashioned or even ludicrous to the proverbially untactful American." [7]

The Occupation attempted to indoctrinate Haitians in the advantages of modern technology and efficiency through the example of American genius in constructing roads, bridges, and government buildings, and by direct tutelage of Haitian subordinates who worked under American supervisors in the Department of Public Works, the Customs Service, the Gendarmerie, and the several other departments of the client-government. The American-sponsored Service Technique provided formal schooling in modern agricultural and industrial technology. While Haitians were already reluctant to assimilate American methods and attitudes because of American racial and cultural prejudices, the problem of introducing American pragmatism and efficiency involved confrontation with basic Haitian values and ambitions regarding work and material rewards for work. The elite traditionally held that manual labor was demeaning, while the peasants were enmeshed in subsistence farming and were reluctant to risk an already tenuous existence in outlandish experiments that were fundamental to American technological progress. Financial Adviser Arthur C. Millspaugh stated: "The peasants, living lives which to us seem indolent and shiftless, are enviably carefree and contented; but, if they are to be citizens of an independent self-governing nation, they must acquire, or at least a larger number of them must acquire, a new set of wants." [8]

After the occupation, anthropologists and sociologists doing fieldwork in Haiti found that peasants had to work hard to scratch a living from poor soil and were extremely competitive in merchandising what little they produced beyond their immediate needs. [9] In 1952 a field ethnologist for the Smithsonian's Institute of Social Anthropology described the resistance of Haitian peasants to technological innovations as follows:

Subject to innumerable vagaries of chance, multiplied by the primitiveness of his hoe technology, the very livelihood of the Haitian farmer is at the mercy of a great many unpredictable factors over which he has little or no control. He is not prone, therefore, to risk even greater insecurity by accepting new practices as long as he retains any doubt as to the certainty of their immediate profit to him. [10]

During the occupation very little effort was made to fathom the intricacies of peasant culture. When peasants failed to react enthusiastically to American technology, they were dismissed as ignorant and lazy. Here, again, racial and cultural prejudices played an important role.

Americans tried to stimulate Haitian participation by offering incentives for increased production and efficient performance and by trying to create a competitive spirit among government employees. The Customs Service graded the several customs posts on an elaborate point system which reflected accuracy and promptness of returns and other criteria of excellence, and awarded the winning post with a suitably engraved loving cup plus a 10 percent salary bonus. An individual grading system penalized customs employees with a 10 percent salary reduction when their performance fell below a specified numerical scale.[11] A marine officer once stimulated a local house-building boom by awarding eighteen Ingersoll watches as prizes to otherwise skeptical peasants.[12] In general, however, Haitians were not excited by American promises, and efforts to encourage economic development by offering incentives failed miserably.

Aside from the formal schooling offered by the Service Technique, the several branches of the client-government constituted the major area of direct American tutelage of Haitian subordinates. Haitian government employees, from Cabinet officers to local justices of the peace, were subjected to close supervision and were forced to conform to American standards of competence and efficiency. The Department of Public Works and the Public Health Service assigned Haitians as apprentices to American engineers and doctors in the expectation that they would eventually take over by themselves. American supervisors made efforts to imbue their Haitian subordinates with the concept, implicit in American ideals of pragmatism and efficiency, that government should perform effective public services and that government employees were public servants who necessarily must be honest and conscientious. This concept of political morality contrasted sharply with the traditional Haitian political ethic which recognized graft as a perquisite of public office. American Chargé Stuart Grummon observed that "Haitian politicians, in common with those of the other backward Latin American countries, have no conception of the Anglo-Saxon ideal of government for the benefit of the governed, looking upon government solely as a means of enriching themselves at the expense of the governed." [13]

Immediately after the intervention American officials scrutinized the government payroll and eliminated employees who were deceased, not working, or grossly incompetent. The Occupation virtually eliminated wholesale graft by instituting rigorous accounting and auditing procedures and by placing Americans in charge of government expenditures. Occupation officials demanded honesty and efficiency from Haitian subordinates and in most cases lived up to high standards of honesty and public service themselves.[14]

American efforts to reform Haiti were inextricably tied to American administration of Haitian finances. Not only did the creation of an efficient government bureaucracy hinge upon systematic fiscal reorganization, but the client-government and all Occupation uplift programs were financed exclusively from Haitian government revenues and were therefore dependent on the state of the Haitian treasury and on the fiscal priorities established by the United States. American financial policy placed first priority on the repayment of Haiti's external debt to American bondholders. During the prosperous years between the 1922 loan consolidation and the advent of the World Depression in 1929 American financial advisers used budgetary surpluses to pay off the debt owed to American investors far in advance of required payment schedules. Funds available for development programs, such as education and public works, were correspondingly limited.

The United States exercised virtually complete control over Haitian finances. Financial control had always been the key tactical objective of American intervention policy. The Wilson administration had pressed for a customs receivership prior to the intervention, and the 1915 treaty featured American control of customs and government finances while making scant mention of other uplift possibilities with the notable exception of provisions for developing a native police force. The treaty provided that an American financial adviser be attached to the Haitian government to coordinate Haitian finances and recommend suitable policies, and an additional accord in 1918 gave the financial adviser exclusive control over drafting

the Haitian budget, which was then submitted to the client-government for approval.[15] In the years between 1922 and 1930, the United
States extended its financial control beyond stipulated concessions
under the presidency of Louis Borno. In 1929 General Russell stated:

The financial control now existing in Haiti has been one of gradual
growth. It goes far beyond the provisions of the Treaty. . . . The present system of financial control has been built up by the High Commissioner largely through a spirit of cooperation, intelligence, and good
judgement on the part of President Borno. It does not rest on the provisions of the Treaty but is beyond the Treaty, an extension brought about
through the honest desire of President Borno to rehabilitate and develop
Haiti.[16]

Financial control was facilitated by the 1922 debt consolidation,
which entailed a pivotal reorganization of Haitian finances in American hands and the acceptance by the client-government of long-
term accountability to American financial interests.[17]

The debt consolidation involved a series of three loans consummated between 1922 and 1925, the largest of which was the initial
1922 Series A loan totaling $16 million floated for the purpose of
refunding Haiti's external debt. A subsequent $5 million Series B
loan was used to refund the internal debt from the 1912–14 period
and to pay the awards made by an international Claims Commission; and a separate Series C loan of $1.7 million refunded National
Railway bonds. Of the $15 million proceeds from the Series A loan,
$6 million was used to refund the external debt to French bond-
holders, which had been worth $21.5 million prior to the devaluation
of the franc during and after World War I, and sums of $4.1 million
and $2.2 million were paid to the Banque Nationale and the National
Railway, respectively.[18] Claims held against the Haitian government
by the American-owned Banque and Railway had been specifically
exempted from the scrutiny of the international Claims Commission
established by a 1919 Haitian-American protocol.[19] The Series B
loan covered $3.5 million awarded by the Claims Commission. These
awards amounted to less than 9 percent of foreign claims which
Financial Adviser Millspaugh later referred to as "a long-festering
mass of pecuniary exaggeration." [20]

The Series C loan was used to refund National Railway bonds, the amortization and interest of which had been paid by the Series A loan. The exchange of Series C bonds for National Railway bonds at 75 percent of par value and an attendant reorganization plan greatly reduced the government's liabilities to the Railway and practically ended its financial involvement in what had been a disastrously expensive and economically worthless enterprise. The P.C.S. Railway continued to operate under government subsidy, and Roger L. Farnham drew a lucrative salary as absentee receiver of the National Railway by virtue of a 1920 New York court decision; but the Railway no longer enjoyed the staunch support of the State Department, and the American financial advisers tended to back the Haitian government in subsequent contract disputes, even to the extent of authorizing stoppage of the subsidy.[21]

Compared to the exorbitant loan flotations undertaken before the intervention, Haiti received a relatively high rate of return for the 1922–25 loans. The State Department had originally committed itself to an offer for a $16 million loan by Lee, Higginson, and Company that would have netted the Haitian government 85 percent of face value. Lee, Higginson made the bid, according to a State Department memorandum, "upon the understanding that the competitive features would be held confidential and would not be used as trading points for playing one banker off against the other," but a change in market conditions and pressure from the Haitian government and National City Bank forced Financial Adviser McIlhenny to reopen negotiations and ask for competitive bids.[22] Informed of this, Lee, Higginson offered to make a substantial increase in its earlier bid, but the loan was finally awarded to National City Bank, which made a low offer of a $16 million loan that would yield the Haitian government 92.137 percent.[23] Despite the presence of American marines and complete American financial control, this rate was no better than the average for Latin-American loans of the period, which were much more expensive than either internal American corporate bonds or the worldwide average for foreign bonds. In 1922 sixty representative American corporate bonds yielded investors 4.9 percent while the average for new Latin-American bonds was 7.5 percent.[24] The 7.9 percent yield of the $16 million Haitian Series A loan and the $5 million Series B loan included, as was typical of Latin-American loans of the period, a 4 percent bankers' commission payable to National City Bank, which handled the loans.*

At the 1932 Senate Finance Committee investigation of foreign bond transactions, National City Bank submitted a statement of its loan flotations that listed the Series C $1.7 million Haitian loan of 1925 as having been sold to Haiti for 81.3 percent of face value resulting in a phenomenal profit spread of 14.7 percent to National City Bank, which stated that it had sold the bonds to the public at 96 percent of face value.[25] This information is spurious inasmuch as the bonds were never actually sold by the Haitian government but were simply exchanged for National Railway bonds. The 14.7 percent profit registered by National City Bank, which was the bank's largest spread on any Latin-American transaction of the 1920s, represented, according to Financial Adviser Cumberland, a speculative venture in which National City Bank had its Paris branch gradually and inconspicuously buy up National Railway bonds at low prices on the assumption that they would eventually be redeemed by the Haitian government. Cumberland noted that "the railroad itself had no value and that neither from the point of view of assets or earnings was it capable of supporting any bonded indebtedness," and that National City Bank profits represented the rewards of speculative risk rather than an excessive underwriting commission.[26] Redemption of the dubious Railway bonds had, of course, been contingent on United States control of the Haitian government and the specific exemption of Railway claims from investigation by the 1919 international claims commission.

All in all, National City Bank enjoyed a high but not outrageously exorbitant rate of profit on its various Haitian operations. Its Haitian subsidiary, the Banque Nationale, averaged, according to a high-ranking Haitian employee, $160,000 total profit per year from 1924 to 1930 for its services as the government treasury and its commercial banking activities.[27] The treasury service was basic to the Banque's consistent profit returns on into the Depression years, with government funds averaging 60 percent of total Banque deposits for

* The National City Bank purchased Series A and B bonds from the Haitian government at 92.137 percent of nominal value and then sold the bonds to the American public at 96.5 percent of nominal value. United Nations, Department of Economic and Social Affairs, *Foreign Capital in Latin America*, pp. 7–8.

the years 1922–35.[28] Haitian government funds deposited with National City Bank in New York earned either no interest or less than could be obtained from other competitive banks, but the American financial adviser and the State Department consistently applied pressure on National City Bank and partially succeeded in ameliorating blatantly exploitative practices which derived from the 1910 and 1922 Banque charters.[29]

In negotiating the 1922 loans with the State Department, National City Bank insisted that the United States government give public assurances of its intention to retain control over Haiti. An October, 1919, Haitian-American $40 million loan protocol had stipulated that "the control by an officer or officers duly appointed by the President of Haiti, upon nomination by the President of the United States, of the collection and allocation of the hypothetical revenues, will be provided during the life of the loan after the expiration of the aforesaid [1915] Treaty," but the protocol also stated that "It is clearly understood that this Protocol does not in fact or by implication extend the provisions of the Treaty of September 16, 1915," and that the authorized loan would have to be consummated within two years of the date of signature of the protocol.[30] In 1921, National City Bank President Charles E. Mitchell wrote Secretary of State Hughes that "it will be necessary to include a strong and definite assurance by the United States Government that this control over Haitian finances will continue throughout the life of the loan until all the bonds have been paid."[31] The presence of American troops and commitments to long-term control were, of course, crucial to the successful flotation of Haitian bonds on the American market and to the procurement of relatively favorable terms for Haiti. Distributors of securities that competed with Haitian bonds on the stock market spread rumors that the United States was getting out.[32] Referring to National City Bank's request for a firm official statement on continuation of the occupation for publication on bond flyers, President Harding stated: "I doubt if we ought to convey the impression that we mean to maintain American supervision until the maturity of these obligations. I assume, however, that we will maintain such supervision until conditions are established which will warrant the confidence of American investors that Haiti has reached a stable order where her pledges are wholly acceptable."[33]

The expectation that the bondholders would accept reversion to Haitian control, no matter how stable, at the time of United States withdrawal in 1934 proved unrealistic. In 1922 the State Department demurred from making a direct commitment, but instead had American Financial Adviser McIlhenny make a public statement emphasizing the firm financial grip that the United States then had over Haiti. Three pages of the four-page flyer issued by National City Bank as advertisement for the $16 million 1922 bonds consisted of a letter from McIlhenny to the bank pointing out, with appropriate paragraphs underlined, the various guarantees of American financial control that were included in the 1915 treaty.[34] No mention was made of what would happen when the treaty expired in 1936. Since the bonds ran until 1952, the extent of United States government obligations to the bondholders was ambiguous, being moral rather than legal, and would become a major source of difficulty when the United States attempted to terminate the occupation in the aftermath of the 1929 uprisings. In the end, despite the absence of any explicit or legal commitments, the United States government stood by the bondholders even at the expense of complicating the new Good Neighbor policy. The United States retained financial control after the 1934 troop withdrawal through a resident fiscal representative who remained in Haiti until 1941, when his functions were transferred to the Banque Nationale, which remained under United States supervision until the bonds were completely paid in 1947.

Repayment of the bonded indebtedness to American investors remained the focal point of United States administration of Haitian finances from the 1922 debt consolidation through the 1929 depression. By the terms of the loan agreements and the 1915 treaty, service of the external debt and payment of customs receivership expenses constituted a first lien on all Haitian revenues. American financial policy went further than this by consistently making debt payments far in excess of contractual requirements and by building up large cash reserves in anticipation of lean years. Financial Adviser Cumberland, who held office for a four-year period ending in December, 1927, acknowledged that Haitian revenues were "entirely inadequate" for necessary development programs and that "To remedy all of these defects large expenditures, both for capital improvements and for maintenance, will be necessary." [35] Neverthe-less, Cumberland formulated a plan whereby only one-third of surplus revenues were used for public works projects, while two-thirds were applied to the retirement of the debt in advance of requirements and to building a cash reserve.[36] Cumberland's avowed purpose in conducting Haiti's finances "upon the most conservative basis" was to safeguard the interests of American bondholders and strengthen Haiti's credit standing.[37] This policy also saved interest costs and shortened the period of financial obligation to American bondholders.

Debt reductions in excess of actual requirements totaled $2.4 million for the years 1924–29, and in several years debt payments were more than double the contractual obligations.[38] The Haitian public debt was reduced from $24.2 million in 1924 to $16.5 million in 1930 and further application of 1930 cash reserves would have reduced the debt to $12.6 million.[39] The policy of emphasizing rapid debt retirement and buildup of large cash reserves was later criti-cized by the 1930 Forbes Commission, which reported to President Hoover that "it might have been better to have reduced taxation, especially the export tax, and left the debt to work itself out during its normal term, thus keeping more money in the country where experience has shown it was badly needed." [40] In response to this argument, Cumberland stated that one of his principal motives for proceeding with rapid debt retirement had been to give "ample protection to the bondholders" in view of the uncertainty of Amer-ican financial control after 1936 and that "if these gentlemen [the Forbes Commission] had been holders of Haitian bonds . . . their conclusions might have been different." [41] In reviewing his four-year tour, at the time of his resignation, Cumberland noted that his "conservative policies" had "placed the treasury in an admirable position, but this had not been accompanied by proportionate progress on the part of the population." [42] Whatever the extent of lost opportunities for development, the Occupation's financial pro-gram certainly resulted in the establishment of Haitian finances on a firm and solid basis, as had been promised in the 1915 treaty.*

---

* Cumberland's efficiency as a tight fiscal manipulator has been incorporated into Haitian popular culture. Wiring devices for by-passing electric meters, estimated as bleeding half the American-owned power company's output, are known today as "the Cumberland" in Haiti; Bernard Diederich and Al Burt, *Papa Doc: The Truth About Haiti Today* (New York: McGraw-Hill Book Co., 1969), 270–71.

Financial Adviser Sidney de la Rue, who took over in March, 1929, sharply reversed the policy of supplemental debt retirement, but by this time the change in fiscal priorities was irrelevant because there were no more revenue surpluses after the advent of the 1929 depression, and cash reserves were needed to keep up payments on the debt, which was serviced throughout the 1930s, when all other Latin-American countries went into default. Commenting on the previous policy of rapid debt retirement, de la Rue observed:

Throughout the period we have the anomalous situation of an administration expressing the intention of carrying on a development program which would make necessary the flotation of one or more new loans at rates which could hardly have been more favorable than the original issue, and at the same time using surplus cash for retirement of a loan which it had been fortunate enough in 1922 to secure on comparatively favorable terms.[43]

Without commenting on the fact that previous policy had deliberately favored American interests at the expense of Haitian uplift, de la Rue argued that the payment in excess of requirements suggested that "money recently borrowed is being used to pay off the debt without having been put to the productive use for which it was originally obtained" and that this policy was "an admission that under normal conditions the administration is unable to use borrowed funds for productive use."[44] Where Cumberland pointed with pride to savings in interest costs and improved Haitian credit standing that had been achieved by rapid debt retirement, de la Rue contended that prospective creditors would have been more impressed with productive use of excess funds. As it turned out, the question of credit standing became irrelevant after 1929, when Haiti's relatively high credit standing was of interest only to American bondholders, since new funds for development were unavailable in any case.

The development programs of the Occupation had been hampered by lack of funds from the outset. Only $2.4 million of the $16 million 1922 loan had been allocated for public works, and Occupation officials were at a loss as to how to spend even this sum since adequate programs had not yet been developed.[45] A substantial part of the sum, $600,000 set aside for irrigation projects, was kept intact until the contemplated projects were abandoned in 1929.[46] The priority given to debt retirement and creation of cash reserves during the relatively prosperous period from 1922 to 1929 obviously left the other facets of the Occupation's uplift program with proportionately less money. In 1927, when external debt reduction exceeded requirements by $1 million, the leading budgetary expenditures broke down as follows: [47]

Public debt	$2.68 million
Public works	1.44 million
Gendarmerie	1.28 million
Public health	.68 million
Agricultural service	.50 million
Public instruction	.40 million

The fact that Haitian government funds for the development programs were limited by American financial policy was all the more significant because hoped-for economic development through private American capital investment did not materialize.

American hopes for uplifting Haiti had been based largely on the expectation that American private investors would finance and direct economic development. This expectation, involving as it did the ideology of free-enterprise capitalism, assumed that investors would be drawn to Haiti by the prospect of extracting greater profits than could be obtained elsewhere and that their activities would engender residual economic benefits for Haiti. Americans would bring economic progress to Haiti as an attendant feature of United States economic imperialism, since American entrepreneurs would coincidentally help build up Haiti while they were exploiting investment opportunities.[48] In 1921 a State Department officer prophesied that the fantastic prosperity of French-colonial Saint Domingue could be re-created under American auspices through an influx of capital, "properly safeguarded to prevent its monopolizing the land and driving the peasant class," and abetted by a program of agricultural education.[49] In practice, however, Occupation officials were constantly faced with the dilemma of trying to encourage American investments while simultaneously protecting Haiti against blatant despoliation. Since possibilities for investment projects that would be both equitable and lucrative proved to be severely limited and American officials conscientiously barred what Financial Adviser Cumberland referred to as "unconscionable concessions," the influx of capital never amounted to much.[50]

Prior to the intervention American investments in Haiti had been based on exploitation of government concessions and special privileges rather than upon productive enterprise. The Occupation, by ending graft, incurred the enmity of most American and other foreign businessmen who frequently complained about being discriminated against by treaty officials. The largest American enterprise, the Haitian-American Sugar Company (HASCO), engaged in a running controversy with Occupation officials and the State Department over the honoring of special privileges and concessions which predated the intervention. The chief of the Division of Latin American Affairs noted:

After the American intervention the treaty officials properly regarded many of these special privileges as unfair to the Haitian Government and detrimental to the welfare of the country, and attempted to restrict their operation so far as possible with due respect for existing contractual rights. . . . The officials of the Department who have gone into the matter have no sympathy whatever for the corporation in its efforts to retain and make the most of the onerous concessions obtained by its predecessors from earlier Haitian governments . . . new companies which have gone in on fair terms and without seeking to profit by old concessions obtained before 1915 have not made complaints.[51]

State Department reluctance to sanction unfair concessions resulted in the abortion of a proposed 1923 concession that would have granted exclusive rights for petroleum exploration to the Sinclair Oil Company. A similar monopolistic concession had been denied to a British firm in 1916, and State Department officials felt that under the circumstances they could not turn around and grant the same concession to an American company.[52] Commenting on the department's objections to the Sinclair concession, A. N. Young of the Office of Economic Adviser stated that he did not think that the United States could "do things in the region of our own 'sphere of influence' to which we would object if done by others in regions in which they claim to be specially interested." [53] President Harding, whose administration was then being rocked by a series of graft scandals, wrote Secretary of State Hughes in June, 1923, that "If there are to be any private monopolies sanctioned in Haiti I would prefer that the sanction be made after our surrender of sponsorship there." [54]

Prospects for replacing the old pattern of exploitative concessions with viable, self-supporting development projects quickly dimmed. At the outset of the occupation, Haitian potential for economic development had been an unknown factor. Initial estimates by Americans indicated that Haiti was "a land of almost unexampled fertility" with "luxuriant" vegetation and that "nothing but sheer lack of initiative and industry keeps them [the Haitians] from becoming rich." [55] In 1915 former Governor W. A. MacCorkle of West Virginia declared eloquently:

This island has within its shores more natural wealth than any other territory of similar size in the world. By reason of its rich valleys and splendid mountains it has every temperature known to man. All tropical plants and trees, as well as the vegetables and fruits of the temperate climes, grow there in perfection. The best coffee known to commerce grows wild, without planting or cultivation . . . in the earth are silver, gold, copper, lead, iron . . . this island is more capable of supporting life in all its phases, more able to create wealth and diffuse happiness to its people, than any other land of its size on the face of the earth.[56]

An investment consulting firm reported that the rural work codes were "all in favor of the employer" and that labor was "ridiculously cheap at present and will be a great factor toward the success of any agricultural enterprise." An American journalist, noting that this was "no place for American women and children," stated that Haiti was rich in resources and that there were great opportunities for "a soldier of fortune who wishes to go there with a little capital." [57]

The cheapness and abundance of Haitian labor was indeed a real and continuing attraction to foreign investment: Haitian laborers were paid at the rate of 20 cents per day for twelve hours of work.[58] Financial Adviser de la Rue argued against passing laws to raise wages in 1930, stating: "The greatest asset Haiti has is cheap labor— labor whose daily cost to an employer does not exceed the labor of other lands whose products are similar. Should labor costs here be increased artificially, that capital will go where conditions are more favorable." [59]

Wages were so low in Haiti that recruiting agents representing most notably the American-owned United Fruit and General Sugar companies annually induced about 20,000 Haitian laborers to migrate to Cuba during the mid-1920s for seasonal work at $1 to $1.50 per day.[60] Cheap labor was, however, about all Haiti had to offer, and this by itself was not enough to compensate for basic lack of natural resources.

Original high expectations for economic exploitation and development in Haiti diminished as American business ventures encountered frustrating experiences. American businessmen testifying at the 1922 Senate Inquiry told stories of crop failures, tariff problems, insufficiency of natural resources, disruptive racism and lack of cooperation on the part of treaty officials, and failure of the Occupation to create conditions favorable to capital investment.[61] The only two major American development projects of the pre-1922 period were floundering or defunct: a $1 million cotton-growing enterprise had failed completely when its crops died, and the American sugar company, HASCO, was forced into receivership in 1921.[62] In subsequent years HASCO developed into a profitable operation which tripled its initial 1918 sugar production by 1928, and promising American sisal plantations were begun in the mid-1920s; but otherwise there was little in the way of successful American private development ventures.[63] While American sugar investments increased from $7 million in 1919 to $8.7 million in 1929 and HASCO was employing over 1,000 men by the mid-1930s, other ventures, such as cotton and pineapple plantations, closed with heavy losses.[64] Progress in mining and manufacturing was disappointing: by 1930 there were no mining operations of commercial value and the few new factories employed only several hundred men.[65] At the time of American withdrawal, when American capital investments consisted of the National Railway, HASCO, and a sisal plantation, an American businessman stated that the "roseate predictions" of American officials regarding the "benefits the Haitians would derive from economic developments" resulting from American control had "failed to materialize." [66] The problem was the relative lack of natural resources. Haiti simply was not a rich country and had little to offer that could draw American investors from more lucrative opportunities elsewhere.

American illusions regarding Haitian economic potential, partially dispelled by early business failures, were destroyed by systematic governmental surveys of Haitian resources undertaken in the early 1920s. American agricultural and geological experts lent to Haiti by the State Department concluded that resources were extremely limited. A 1922 "Agricultural Survey of Haiti" reported light rainfall, poor soil, poor variety of crops, little hope for mineral exports, and a negative outlook for pasturage.[67] A comprehensive six-month survey by three technical experts lent by the United States Geological Survey resulted in a thorough 631-page report which was generally pessimistic about agricultural development and disclosed no commercially exploitable mineral resources.[68] A 1924 United States Department of Commerce pamphlet entitled *Haiti: An Economic Survey* noted that possibilities for agricultural development were limited by the chaotic system of small-scale agriculture and "squatter sovereignty," which made it difficult for investors to obtain clear title to large tracts of land.[69]

By the mid-1920s the original optimism about potential for economic development was being replaced by an increasing awareness that Haiti was headed for economic disaster rather than for American-sponsored prosperity. In his 1925 *Annual Report,* High Commissioner Russell made ominous reference to overpopulation, noting that "The laws of Malthus show that a population tends to increase in geometric progression while the food supply increases only in arithmetic progression." [70] Financial Adviser Cumberland, whose conservative fiscal policies favored rapid debt retirement at the expense of development programs, later recalled that the navy captain who headed the Public Health Service had once told him:

Do you realize that you and I are largely responsible for this enormous crop of pickaninnies that has come since we've been here—you, because you have financed it, and I because I have reduced the death rate somewhat. Now, what's going to happen? Why these poor innocent infants are going to grow up, and they will have just the same starvation life that their parents had.[71]

In 1929 Financial Adviser Millspaugh observed that "Haiti is already overpopulated even relative to its potential production," and that rising birth rates and falling death rates tended to "keep the masses near the level of primitive living." [72] The doubling of the population in subsequent years coupled with continuing lack of economic development bore out these morbid predictions.

With limited potential for economic development and consequent absence of American investment capital, hopes for economic progress devolved mainly on the Occupation itself. Government action was circumscribed both by budgetary limitations and by free-enterprise ideology with its narrow definition of the role of government in economic matters.

9

Uplift–Success
and Failure

Even with the limitations imposed by free-enterprise economic ideology and fiscal priorities based on rapid debt retirement, the Occupation initiated a number of impressive measures designed to promote economic well-being. These ranged from informal personal efforts, such as a plan by Mrs. Russell, wife of the high commissioner, to relieve hard times among the elite by selling in the United States embroideries knitted by Haitian ladies, to the comprehensive technical education program of the Service Technique. During the economic dislocation caused by World War I, the Occupation even went to the lengths of directly engaging in commercial transactions. Colonel Russell, then Brigade Commander, intervened to relieve a wartime food shortage caused by the curtailment of shipping by arranging for the client-government to purchase flour and other commodities from the Navy Department at contract prices; the flour was then sold to local wholesalers and retailers, who were allowed only small profit percentages.[1] This, however, was an emergency measure and most economic activities were more conventional.

The main contribution of the Occupation to Haitian economic progress was the establishment of law and order. During the years following complete pacification in 1920 merchants were able to conduct their businesses in peace and, moreover, profited from the expenditure of an average of one thousand marine salaries. In marked contrast to the turmoil and incessant revolutions of the pre-1915 period, peace and governmental stability under the Americans permitted the development of effective and productive public works and public health programs. Construction of roads and pubic buildings proceeded at an unprecedented rate. Likewise, continuity in government administration achieved by ending revolutions was prerequisite to a whole series of administrative reforms which greatly improved governmental services in general and services to the business community in particular.

The Occupation made persistent efforts to attract American capital investments beginning with the passage of the 1918 Constitution, which legalized alien landownership and later included the 1928 reform of Haitian courts, which had been hostile to American businessmen.[2] Public works projects, most of which were undertaken after the 1922 reorganization, helped develop necessary communications and public services; indeed, a German *Geopolitik* theoretician, writing in 1938, pointed to American-sponsored roads and government services as having been expertly conceived as requisites of economic penetration.[3] Americans reorganized and rationalized Haitian customs duties and provided for standardization of grades of coffee which facilitated commerce. The Service Technique, which encompassed a technical education program, conducted agricultural experiments, imported new breeds of livestock, and was helpful in developing sisal cultivation. In addition to the various formal uplift programs promoted by the Occupation, individual Gendarmerie officers did what they could, according to personal inclinations, to help peasants at the local level and were required to include information on crops and commerce in their monthly reports.[4] All of this, however, did not produce significant economic development since most Occupation uplift programs remained oriented toward creation of circumstances that would attract American capital investment and this investment never materialized.

In trying to attract capital investments, Occupation officials were always faced with the dilemma of offering profitable opportunities, on the one hand, while simultaneously fulfilling their moral responsibility to protect Haiti from spoliation, on the other.[5] Protracted efforts to induce the Sinclair Oil and United Fruit companies to invest in Haiti failed because neither company would agree to terms deemed conscionable by the State Department.[6] The requirement that capital investment be advantageous to both Haiti and the United States complicated all development plans, and the problem of conflict of interests involved Occupation officials even at the personal level. Financial Adviser Cumberland personally drew up plans for a sisal plantation and then induced an American firm to develop sisal production into what eventually turned out to be a major economic achievement of the Occupation. He scrupulously remained officially detached from the enterprise while in the employ of the Haitian government but was taken in as a part owner shortly after his return to the United States.[7] There was no apparent conspiracy to obtain undue concessions from the client-government in this case, but the question of where Cumberland's primary interests as financial adviser lay remains ambiguous. Cumberland also invested heavily in Haitian government bonds in the names of his wife and mother, and, since he determined the exact times when surplus government revenues would be used to purchase bonds on the open market, he was accused of having taken improper advantage of his position as financial adviser.[8] High Commissioner Russell reported to Secretary of State Kellogg that he had approved of Cumberland's private bond dealings, but Russell had previously expressed surprise and disbelief when confronted with an American businessmen's plot, led by Roger L. Farnham, to expose the incident.[9] Cumberland stated that he deliberately sold the bonds early to avoid implications that he was exploiting his position.* Occupation personnel were subsequently forbidden to invest in Haitian securities. The ambiguity of Cumberland's role illustrates the larger ambiguity of the entire occupation, charged as it was with responsibility for the interests of both the United States and Haiti.

The balance between emphasizing Haiti's interests and United States interests was clearly resolved in favor of the United States with respect to the Haitian import trade. The Occupation abrogated a 1907 Franco-Haitian commercial convention which had granted preferential tariff concessions to French imports as compensation for

---

* Cumberland said that he had purchased $12,000 face value Series B bonds at 57 and then sold them a year later at 80; he then purchased $10,000 face value Series B bonds at 77 and sold these at 88. SD 838.51A/76, Cumberland to Kellogg, Jan. 8, 1928.

the fact that France annually purchased upward of 50 percent of Haitian exports while French products amounted to only about 5 percent of Haitian imports.[10] Prior to the abrogation of this convention, Secretary of State Hughes had defended the State Department against a charge that it was allowing Latin-American countries to give special tariff concessions to France by asserting that ". . . the state of our commerce with Haiti is sufficiently indicated by the fact that in 1923, imports from the United States into Haiti amounted to 84 percent of the total, whereas the imports from France into Haiti constituted but 4 percent." [11] American domination of the Haitian import trade, which dated back to before the intervention, was further strengthened by the 1926 tariff reform which, although basically a revenue measure, increased duties on wines and perfumes, traditionally imported from France, while reducing duties on certain products imported from the United States.[12] Haitian imports from the United States averaged about 75 percent of total imports during the 1920s, while exports to the United States amounted to less than 10 percent of total exports.[13]

The primary factor in determining the weakness of the Haitian export economy and its reliance on French purchases was the predominance of coffee as the single major export crop. When bad weather limited coffee production or when the international market deteriorated, such as it did during World War I and again when Brazilian coffee valorization collapsed in 1929, the Haitian economy was ruined. Occupation officials attempted to correct this weakness by encouraging diversification of agriculture. The Service Technique, headed by American agricultural expert Dr. George F. Freeman, who had recently returned from a job in Indochina, experimented with pineapples, bananas, cotton, and various other products. Freeman even tried to interest the United States government in selecting Haiti as a site for developing "a rubber supply in its own sphere of influence." [14] These efforts were largely unsuccessful because most diversification opportunities were not sufficiently attractive to bring in American capital, and Haitians were either too unsophisticated in agricultural techniques or indifferent. The Service Technique, moreover, was poorly managed and overambitious in attempting too broad a program for its capabilities.[15] A series of prosperous years in the mid-1920s, based on good coffee crops and high prices on the international coffee market, were correctly described by Financial Adviser Cumberland as "fortuitous" and not indicative of any permanent economic improvement; in fact, coffee exports during the period 1925–29 were only 9 percent greater than for the four-year period immediately preceding the intervention.[16] By the end of the occupation, coffee remained the basic export crop although sisal production was growing in importance and bananas, originally encouraged by the Service Technique, were to become a major crop after 1935 subsequent to the granting of an export monopoly to the Standard Fruit Company.[17]

In attempting to promote American capital investment and Haitian economic progress American officials realized that agriculture would have to be the basis of any significant advancement. Plans to introduce American capital, modern technology, and efficient organization of production all presupposed the establishment of large-scale plantations, which were common features of foreign investment enterprises in other countries in the Caribbean region. Financial Adviser Millspaugh noted that "Individualistic small farming precludes the use of capital, of irrigation, of skilled management, and of efficient marketing," and High Commissioner Russell advocated abolishing the Haitian system whereby each peasant owned and farmed his little plot of land in favor of establishing large plantations controlled by foreigners.[18] This, however, involved the unpleasant likelihood that Haitian peasant freeholders would be reduced to peonage. An American journalist observed that "The condition of the native workers on big American plantations elsewhere in Latin America has not impressed me as appreciably better than that of the small landholding peasants of Haiti." [19] American officials, including President Coolidge, expressed concern about the possibility of unfair exploitation of Haitian peasants; indeed, the few American plantations actually in operation maintained wage levels at the abysmally low rate of 20 cents per day and the largest firm, HASCO, absolved itself of all responsibility for its workers by subhiring through native gang bosses.[20]

Despite the dismal agricultural forecasts and misgivings about undesirable effects of plantations, the Occupation continually looked to plantation agriculture as the primary means for promoting economic development and luring American capital investment and did all it could to remove barriers to large-scale agricultural investments. One barrier to the latifundia solution was the Haitian courts, some of which remained free from control by the Occupation by virtue of judicial tenure. These had been a constant source of grief to American businessmen. A State Department officer remarked in 1927 that it was "primarily and almost solely because foreigners and local business interests cannot secure a square deal in Haitian courts that foreign capital has been slow in going to Haiti." [21] The Occupation eliminated this problem by abolishing life tenure for judges through the 1928 constitutional amendment which allowed the client-government to revamp the courts.

A related and much more substantial impediment to plantation development was the long-standing division of land into minuscule plots held by peasant freeholders. American companies experienced great difficulty in buying up large plots of land and in gaining clear titles. The United States tried to solve this problem by court reform and by instituting a massive cadastral survey which would have permitted land consolidation since few peasants had legal documents to prove their ownership, which dated back to the division of former French colonial plantations in the early nineteenth century.[22] Marines took aerial photographs of a large part of the country in 1925 and 1926 in preparation for the contemplated cadastral survey, but all negatives were destroyed when the building in which they were stored burned down at night in an unexplained fire. The survey, which would have involved fantastically complicated legal proceedings given the almost complete absence of legal titles even for government land, was still in the planning stages at the time of the 1929 uprisings.[23] The reluctance of American officials to permit exploitation of peasants, as indicated by the refusal of treaty officials to force peasants to sell their lands to American companies, and fear of arousing the masses against the occupation prevented any summary solution of the land redistribution problem.[24] In early 1929 a State Department officer cautioned against pushing the cadastral survey too hard and thereby alienating "the mass of the Haitian people" who presumably had "been hitherto either friendly or indifferent to our policies in Haiti." [25] Plantation development was, in any case, inherently limited by natural factors. Financial Adviser Millspaugh remarked that "Those who are fearful of the future may take assurance from the fact that topographically and economically Haitian conditions set rather definite limits to plantation development." [26]

With all the other problems of deficient resources, contradictory financial priorities, fragmentary land distribution, and conflicts of interest, a major impediment to economic uplift programs remained the Haitian peasantry itself. While the elite was ideologically hostile to American pragmatism and efficiency, the peasants lived in an altogether different world in which they had had few points of contact with modern American technology. In one case Haitian laborers unloading a shipment of American wheelbarrows were reported to have carried them off balanced on the tops of their heads.[27] Prevailing agricultural techniques consisted of cultivation by hoe and machete rather than by plow. In 1952 an American field ethnologist reported that, while technical aid programs had failed to successfully introduce the plow, Haitian farmers in several areas had on their own eventually adopted plows left behind in the late 1920s by defunct American companies.[28] During the occupation Americans did not appreciate or understand how to adapt their uplift programs to peasant cultural traditions. Financial Adviser Cumberland expressed dismay and frustration on finding the peasants impervious to what seemed to him compelling profit incentives:

attractive prices have failed to stimulate the peasants of Haiti to increase their production of coffee. . . . Evidence is plentiful that the Haitian peasants merely pick such coffee as nature provides when the price is low and do the same thing when prices are above average. In the former case there is no abandonment of such minimum cultivation of coffee as has traditionally been in vogue, and in the latter case there is little impetus to improve the yield or quality of coffee already in production.[29]

In later years field research among the peasantry disclosed strong profit motives and quite reasonable bases for reservations about modern technology. The Occupation never effectively grappled with the problem of how to draw upon or stimulate peasant interest or cooperation.

Americans did make, through the Service Technique, a systematic effort to introduce modern agricultural techniques. This was extraordinarily difficult because of the tremendous gap between peasant technology and American technology. Peasants were basically skeptical about new machines and methods and about foreign white civilization in general. The experiences of their ancestors with French colonists and the more recent American forced-labor corvée of 1918–19 did not encourage confidence in the white foreigners' methods and motives. Americans, for their part, had little respect for peasant technology and failed to adapt modern innovations to existing local skills and traditions. Ironically, this weakness cost the Americans dearly in their own private agricultural enterprises. In 1929 Dr. Freeman, the chief American agricultural expert, reported to the State Department that many American agricultural ventures had failed because promoters had been unwilling to study the techniques employed by local people who had, through generations of practical experience, developed locally viable methods. Paraphrasing Freeman's oral remarks, a State Department officer recorded one aspect of the 1929 postmortem: ". . . today the natives were raising cotton more successfully than the plantations which were scientifically cultivated, as when land around the trees was too consistently plowed and kept clean from weeds, etc. the cotton trees [sic] had a tendency to develop large branches, leaves, etc., but gave very meager results in bolls." [30]

Here, as in other instances, Americans were partly defeated by their own sense of racial and cultural superiority. Confident of their own superiority in contrast to "ignorant" and "uncivilized" blacks, Americans were frequently obtuse in adapting to local conditions.

In pointing to this failure on the part of American promoters to appreciate peasant ways, Freeman touched upon a basic weakness of his own Service Technique, which experimented with a wide variety of sophisticated techniques, equipment, and new crops that were of little practical use to the peasants. As was recognized by some American observers, elaborate and expensive agricultural experimentation stations that emphasized the most modern technology were of doubtful value when the peasants needed cheap, primitive devices that they could work themselves.[31] Here, again, the emphasis on modern plantation agriculture proved to be largely irrelevant since capital investment did not materialize. Peasant skepticism and indifference to American-style progress was in part vindicated when the 1929 depression, a function of modern economic interactions, effectively ended all hopes for economic development in Haiti by ruining the international coffee market, forcing the peasants to dispense with cash crops and revert to subsistence farming.

The Service Technique also conducted a program of vocational education designed to provide trained manpower necessary for agricultural and industrial development. This was the major contribution made by the United States to Haitian education during the occupation and was conceived primarily as a facet of the economic development program rather than as an attempt to increase literacy or promote general education.

General education was one of the few areas of government responsibility left to the Haitians. The 1930 Forbes Commission reported to President Hoover: "Under the treaty of 1915 the assistance of the United States was not provided for in the matter of education, and it has been only recently and indirectly that the American Occupation has interested itself in this field." [32]

The Occupation did nothing to further education prior to the 1922 reorganization, and by the late 1920s, total expenditures for education amounted to only 10 percent of the Haitian budget compared to 28 percent in Puerto Rico.[33] By 1930 approximately 15 percent of Haitian children were enrolled in some kind of school, while approximately 95 percent of the population remained illiterate, the same percentage as before the intervention.[34] On several occasions Financial Adviser Cumberland expressed concern about insufficiency of funds for education but the American budgetary priorities precluded larger expenditures.[35]

The Occupation promoted the technical education program of the American-controlled Service Technique at the expense of traditional Haitian classical education. The Haitian-controlled Department of Public Instruction, which directed general education along traditional French classical lines, had ten times as many students but received less than 40 percent of the money allocated to the Service Technique for manual/technical education.[36] In 1930 the student-teacher ratio in Haitian-controlled public schools was 70 to 1 and rural schoolteachers were usually paid from $4 to $6 per month. The Service Technique, in contrast, was adequately financed for the scope of its activities; salaries for beginning Haitian instructors started at $30 per month.[37] American emphasis on vocational education was the embodiment of American concepts of technical elitism and efficiency, while corresponding disparagement of Haitian classical education reflected American aversion to the idealism and refinement of the Haitian elite. The technical-vocational orientation also exactly paralleled the Tuskegee Institute model for vocational as opposed to general education for blacks in the United States. High Commissioner Russell observed that as a result of classical Haitian education the "young men of Haiti have been guided *from*, rather than *toward*, productive industry" and that classical studies led to training for careers in the professions, when what Haiti really needed was agriculturists and skilled workers.[38] According to the American view, Haiti already had an overabundance of doctors, lawyers, and civil servants, who, in any case, constituted a revolutionary class, while the country desperately needed skilled workers to increase production and national wealth.[39]

The Haitian elite, which traditionally prided itself on educational refinement and sophistication in French belles lettres, abhorred American vocational education and, moreover, resented the implications of racial inferiority associated with manual training programs for blacks in the Southern United States under Booker T. Washington's Tuskegee Institute system.[40] His exhortation to blacks to strive for success at menial trades and forgo intellectual pursuits fitted in with the premises of the Occupation's educational policies, and Tuskegee faculty predominated on the several American commissions which the State Department sent to investigate education in Haiti.

Dr. Freeman reported that Haitian peasants resisted vocational training too; they claimed that they already knew all about agriculture, and those peasants who were interested in education for their children wanted them to learn to read and write so they could go into the city and get jobs.[41] Since the Service Technique began its technical education program at an advanced level in the hope of training Haitian teachers, the illiterate peasants, who were supposed to be the eventual beneficiaries, were excluded from participation, and initial drafts of agricultural students had to be procured from the educated city elite. Elite hostility to manual work was overcome by offering students sufficient monetary incentives in the form of scholarships. The director of the American School in Port-au-Prince remarked that elite students were "virtually hired to go by means of scholarships, at five or six times the wages earned by the fathers of many of them and equal to, for example, the salary paid to surgeons in the hospitals." [42]

Elite students attending vocational schools were instructed in a variety of technical subjects, such as chemistry and agronomy, and were required to perform manual farm labor and shopwork. Dr. Freeman, who was well aware of elite hostility to manual labor, exhorted students to repudiate their prejudices and partake in the glory of manual labor:

> We therefor, have no place in the Service Technique for a man who is afraid or ashamed to work with his hands. The strong, steady, and skilled hand is the first and primary requisite of all industry. . . . Give us men who know labor. Give us men who are not ashamed of honest toil . . . when I first travelled over your country and studied your natural resources, I found valleys, rich in fertility, capable of loading thousands of steamers with cargoes of sugar, cotton, bananas, pineapples, and other fruits. . . . How appropriately there sprung to my thought that expression of our Holy Master "The harvest is ripe but the reapers are few." [43]

Students were to care for cows, clean stables, learn carpentry in Service Technique shops, and then go off into the interior as teachers in rural farm schools. On the eve of the 1929 student strikes, after five years of operation, the Service Technique had developed a network of 68 schools with 256 teachers and 8,848 students; but student hostility had still not been overcome, and the project was vociferously denounced by almost all observers, both Haitian and American. [44]

Originally conceived as a broad, comprehensive agency for agricultural and industrial uplift, the Service Technique had engaged in all manner of agricultural experiments as well as the ambitious vocational education program. The Occupation had provided it with ample funds and complete political support; but Freeman, who was a poor administrator,[45] failed to concentrate his activities on feasible projects, and most ventures ended in failure. In 1931 a State Department officer recorded a conversation in which Roger L. Farnham criticized the Service Technique as having been "so woefully mismanaged, so extravagantly conceived and executed, and with such negligible practical results that anything associated with it was detested by the Haitians without exception." [46] An American treaty administrator who had recently returned from Haiti stopped off at the State Department in 1929 and, according to W. R. Scott of the Division of Latin American Affairs, "dwelt at some length and with some bitterness" on the Service Technique, which he described as having spent much with meager results, spread its activities over a wide range of unimportant items, and otherwise discredited itself; he characterized Dr. Freeman as incompetent and stated that American agricultural experts were considered a joke by both Haitians and Americans. [47] Other criticisms of the program were that American instructors did not know French and had to lecture through student interpreters, and that these teachers were overpaid in relation to their value to Haiti. [48]

American educational efforts, like most of the uplift programs, were hampered by basic contradictions in policy objectives and by racial and cultural difficulties. The perplexity of the United States attitude was dramatically illustrated when President Hoover's distinguished commission to investigate Haitian education, headed by President Robert R. Moton of Tuskegee Institute, could not obtain passage to Haiti on Navy ships because the educators on the commission were black. This incident served as an ironic capstone to the Occupation's systematic sponsorship of Tuskegee-type vocational education, which, according to Haitian critics, was rooted in racial discrimination. In arranging for commercial transportation for the Moton Commission, which had originally been promised passage on a United States warship, Dana G. Munro of the Division of Latin American Affairs referred to "the embarrassment and complications which would ensue if we asked the Navy to provide accommodations." [49] When the commission was stranded in Haiti for lack of return transportation, the navy evasively offered a minesweeping tug with two berths that was obviously inadequate for the ten-man party. Moton complained that "I feel that the people of Haiti as well as the colored people of the United States will regard this as a humiliation." [50] The commission eventually returned on a commercial ship.

The moribund Service Technique, which played a major role in generating hostilities that led directly to the 1929 strikes and riots, continued to be a center of antagonism and frustration. As an agency for reorienting Haitian society on a modern technical basis, it certainly proved to be a major disappointment. In terms of the American purpose of uplifting Haiti through technocratic efficiency, the material accomplishments of the Occupation were much more impressive than the efforts at human persuasion. Material progress was the ultimate criterion for American success in any case, and the Occupation found it much easier and more comfortable to build new construction projects and rationalize administrative hierarchies than to cope with people in subtle areas of human interaction. The list of physical accomplishments, including roads, public works, health improvements, efficient government agencies and such, was quite formidable despite persistent budgetary limitations.

In 1929, which was a watershed year followed by rapid disintegration of the Occupation's programs, the *Eighth Annual Report of the American High Commissioner* [51] listed these substantial accomplishments:

(1) The maintenance of order for fourteen years, except for the pre-1920 caco uprisings and the 1929 riots, through the establishment of an efficient police force. The Garde d'Haïti was a soundly administered organization devoid of graft, which had characterized the pre-1915 Haitian army. According to the high commissioner, this achievement had been "accomplished in the face of the handicaps of the mentality and tradition of the people . . ."

(2) Haitian finances had been systematized, bonded indebtedness reduced, and the currency had been permanently stabilized at the rate of five gourdes to the dollar.

(3) The Occupation had created a strong Public Works Department with proper accounting procedures and efficient personnel. Prior to 1915 there had been no definite public works organization, no passable roads connecting cities and towns, poor port facilities, and only rudimentary telegraph service. The telephone system had failed in 1911. The Occupation built 1,000 miles of roads * utilizable

---

* By 1931, when the Public Works Department was turned over to the Haitians, 1,075 miles of roads had been completed. All but five miles were, however, unpaved. These roads deteriorated quickly in later years. Republic of Haiti, Public Works Administration, *Annual Report, 1930–1931* (English trans.), pp. 57, 62.

by motor vehicles and 210 bridges totaling 5,870 feet in length. In 1929 there were nearly 3,000 automobiles in Haiti. The Occupation had installed a modern telephone system with 1,250 miles of long-distance service, a telegraph system, and a radio station. All these were judged significant aids to commerce. In addition, the Public Works Department had improved and beautified many public buildings, squares, and parks, built new schools, hospitals, and Garde d'Haïti buildings, and constructed twelve of Haiti's sixteen lighthouses plus nine wharfs. Irrigation, which had been nonexistent since French colonial times, was revived with the development of over 100 miles of functioning ditches. Municipal water systems also were overhauled. While emphasizing the considerable accomplishments in the field of public works, the High Commissioner added that "The work has been retarded due to the insufficiency of these revenues. An enormous task still faces the department . . ."

(4) The Public Health Service set up and operated eleven modern, fully equipped hospitals, a medical and hospital training school, and rural plus traveling clinics. Important advances had been made in the reduction of diseases, such as malaria. Of 159 physicians practicing in Haiti, 42 percent were employed by the Public Health Service. In 1929 the Service administered 1,341,000 treatments. Under the auspices of the Occupation, private American organizations contributed significantly to this humanitarian effort. In 1929 the Rockefeller Foundation and the American Red Cross contributed $52,000 to augment the $916,000 provided out of Haitian government revenues. Nevertheless, here again there were difficulties with budgetary limitations. The high commissioner observed that Public Health work had been "limited and handicapped" by "insufficient funds."

(5) The Service Technique had, in addition to operating schools, maintained five experiment stations, an agricultural extension with 35 agents, and veterinary clinics which, in the past five years, had healed 315,267 animals. The Service Technique had also completed soil surveys of 107,000 acres and sent 10 students to the United States for university study.

These material achievements, which looked so attractive in statistical reports and on progress charts, created the impression that the Occupation was doing well, while the failures in many areas of political and cultural interaction were largely unnoticed in Washington and by the Occupation Command in Port-au-Prince. The substantial and ongoing progress in material construction and rationalization of government agencies, along with the aforementioned economic and educational programs, were rudely disrupted by the 1929 strikes and riots.

10

Strikes and Riots

In the years following the 1922 reorganization, High Commissioner Russell, assisted by the collaboration of client-President Borno, exercised rigid authoritarian control over the occupation and implemented the various American programs with little regard for opposition from Haitians or from dissident American subordinates. Russell's reports to the State Department indicated continued progress in debt retirement, public works projects, development of the Service Technique, and training of the Gendarmerie.[1] Russell and other leading American officials attributed the continuing hostility of the Haitian elite to resentment at having been cut off from the spoils of public office rather than to any compelling patriotic motives.

While ostensibly making preparations for American withdrawal at the expiration of the treaty in 1936, most Occupation departments did not promote Haitians to positions of responsibility and no effort was made to broaden the political base of the client-government. Financial Adviser W. W. Cumberland later stated that he had tried to work with Haitians but that this was a waste of time because Haitians had nothing to contribute: "in my four years experience in Haiti not a single Minister of Finance made *one single* constructive suggestion on any economic, commercial or financial subject."[2]

The Occupation, while making the most of President Borno's wholehearted cooperation and submissiveness, concurrently sought to promote the illusion that the client-government possessed a degree of independent authority. The most notable assertion of client-government independence involved a widely publicized 1927 incident during which Borno dramatically barred a visit to Haiti by United States Senator William H. King of Utah, a long-time opponent of the occupation. Both Russell and the State Department insisted that they had urged Borno not to exclude Senator King but that they were powerless to interfere, and the incident appeared in the Haitian and American press as a bold assertion of Haitian sovereignty.[3] Years later Financial Adviser Cumberland disclosed that he had initiated the whole affair by suggesting the King exclusion to Borno as a ploy to prove Haitian independence.[4] Borno was far from being independent of American control, and was completely dependent upon American protection for his personal safety and continuance in office. In a popular joke among both Haitians and Americans in Port-au-Prince Borno was rumored to have said, "Gentlemen, if you move the marine barracks from the rear of my palace out to the aviation field, I move the palace along with you." [5] The marine barracks, named Caserne Dartiguenave after the first client-president, were located on the grounds directly back of the President's palace.

Although the years following the installation of Russell as high commissioner were peaceful and orderly, this did not indicate any marked increase in American popularity. Martial law remained in effect, mainly as a reminder of American authority rather than as a day-to-day governing instrument. The use of American military provost courts for trying Haitian civilians declined from a high of 911 cases in 1920 to no cases at all from 1926 to 1929.[6] Manifestations against the occupation and the client-government were limited to journalistic attacks in the opposition press, for which editors were frequently jailed without trial, and to infrequent public demonstrations, as when Borno was publicly booed on his departure for a visit to the United States in 1926.* Except for keeping the marine garrison in the background and instructing marines to avoid overt clashes with Haitians, the Occupation did little to make itself popular. Deference to popular opinion was minimal. During the 1926 communal elections, which were subsequently rescinded, Borno did request that American warships using Gonaïves Bay for target practice be temporarily pulled back because their presence tended

* Borno's arrival in New York also was marred by a hostile demonstration.

to hurt the client-government's chances, but few positive measures were taken to win popular support.[7] The goodwill visit of Colonel Charles Lindbergh to Port-au-Prince in 1928, a rare American gesture of friendship and respect, was partly counteracted by the closing of the elite Cercle Bellevue Club for political opposition to the occupation a week before.

Instead of seeking to win popular support and widen participation in the occupation by making concessions, Russell maintained the rigidly authoritarian and exclusive character of his administration, even with respect to divergent viewpoints among American treaty officials. Financial Adviser Arthur C. Millspaugh, who was dismissed for having disagreed with Russell's policies, wrote: "The High Commissioner's relationship with him [Borno] has been so intimate as to exclude practically all other salutary contacts between Americans and Haitians. Moreover, the Occupation has functioned in such a manner as to set itself apart, not only from the people but also from the body of the government."[8]

Millspaugh's successor, Sidney de la Rue, found bitter animosity among Occupation officials and their wives in the wake of the Millspaugh-Russell feud and noted that "all the people who had been in the fight including all the soreheads who hate the General [Russell], are still here."[9]

The unwillingness of the Occupation to take steps leading to increased Haitian participation in politics and eventual self-government was most clearly demonstrated by Russell's continued suppression of democratic institutions and his determination to retain Borno as client-president despite the growing apprehension of the State Department. The department, which hoped eventually to reconvene the popularly elected legislature, became vaguely uneasy as Russell persisted in emphasizing military force and authoritarian rule. Russell's steadfast dependence on force rather than persuasion became unpleasantly apparent when he requested that 350 marines embarked for Nicaraguan duty in early 1927 be returned in time for "constructive work contemplated for next winter, including, perhaps, the modifying of the present constitution and drastic, but much needed reforms in the judiciary system of Haiti."[10] A State Department officer expressed alarm at this "unfortunately worded" message and stressed that the important thing was to avoid violence, noting that Russell, in a personal conversation, "seemed totally oblivious" of the violent methods implicit in his dispatch.[11] The "constructive work" proposed by Russell for the winter of 1927–28 involved revisions of the Haitian Constitution that would further strengthen the authority of the Occupation and ensure Borno's continuance in office.

Borno had been reelected to a second four-year term in 1926 under the provisions of the American-sponsored Constitution of 1918. The 1918 Constitution suspended legislative elections until "an even-numbered year" to be designated by the client-president, and it delegated legislative functions, which included election of the president, to a Council of State appointed by the president. Borno was thus reelected by a group of his own political allies whom he had personally appointed to the Council of State. The 1928 constitutional amendments included an extension of the presidential term to six years, which would safeguard Borno's continuance in office against the likelihood that the Occupation would be forced to call popular elections in 1930. Other provisions stipulated that freedom of the press and jury trials would be regulated by laws passed by Borno's Council of State, and that "Within a period of twelve months from the publication of the present amendments the Executive Power is authorized to proceed to make all changes in the present personnel of the Courts that he deems necessary."[12] A further amendment proposed by Russell and Borno that would have permitted Borno to seek still another term was forbidden by the State Department.[13]

Russell advocated having Borno's Council of State adopt the constitutional amendments, but the State Department insisted that the amendments be passed by a national plebiscite, as had been done in the case of the 1918 Constitution when the Haitian legislature, the only body legally competent to tamper with the Constitution, proved hostile to American purposes.[14] The department also objected to the extension of Borno's term to six years and eliminated the clause providing for his reelection, but severe restraining action was out of the question since this would have compromised both Borno and Russell, who had proceeded on the assumption that the department approved of the amendments. Even the limited action of forbidding Borno's reelection was described in a Division of Latin American Affairs memorandum as "extremely unfortunate, for the prestige of President Borno or General Russell must suffer by the action of the Department." [15] Despite misgivings in Washington, the amendments, including the provision for extension of Borno's term, were submitted to a plebiscite in 1928 and passed by a vote of 177,436 affirmative as against 3,799 negative.[16] The department subsequently persisted in favoring early legislative elections and procured assurances from Russell, who continued to oppose elections, that Borno would call for elections in 1930 and that he would not be a candidate for reelection under any circumstances.[17]

The State Department felt that some beginnings had to be made in popular participation in the government in preparation for the scheduled withdrawal of American troops in 1936 and disapproved of "the anomalous character of the present arrangement under which the President appoints the legislature and the latter elects the President," but as the time for the 1930 elections drew closer department officials found that they could not reconcile the long-range plan for popular elections with the imminent certainty of a disastrous defeat for the Occupation at the polls, and the elections were postponed.[18] In rationalizing the postponement of the elections the chief of the Division of Latin American Affairs reiterated the familiar argument that Haitians were too ignorant to vote, that elections would only provide opportunities for anti-American propaganda, and that elections would be feasible after just a few more years of American uplift:

It is very doubtful, furthermore, whether an election held at present would have any appreciable value in training the Haitian people for self-government. The masses of voters are still too ignorant and too much out of touch with the world. A continuance for a relatively short time of the development work now in progress, including the opening of roads and trails and the education of the peasants in the new rural schools, will work a great change in this respect.[19]

While the United States persisted in rationalizing authoritarian control by claiming that Haitians were "ignorant" and "out of touch," there was still no inclination to undertake remedial or palliative measures. Instead of trying to reduce illiteracy and educate voters in democratic procedures and responsibilities, the Occupation's educational program remained focused on manual and technical training. Likewise, the Occupation remained grossly insensitive to public relations. It had the means to reach the Haitian public, as with radios which later proved so effective in rallying popular enthusiasm during the Algerian Revolution, but the Americans in Haiti failed to use them imaginatively.* After fifteen years the Occupation remained an authoritarian monolith; there had been no officially sponsored or even sanctioned movement toward democracy or self-determination.

Within six months the United States was forced to a dramatic reversal of its decision to postpone elections in the face of the 1929 strikes and riots. Indeed, President Borno's October, 1929, pronouncement canceling the elections was an important factor in fomenting the uprisings. Borno publicly justified the cancellation by stating:

In the groups of the opposing parties, blindfolded politicians, condemned to remain slaves of their passions, have persisted in disguising the most laudable enterprises of the Government, and have created, through their plottings in the midsts of people easily moved and credulous, a dangerous state of mind, propitious to the worst impulsions of disorder.[20]

Popular dissatisfaction over the cancellation of elections was compounded by the widespread fear that Borno would be retained by the Occupation for another term as client-president.

Distrust of the Occupation had long been engendered by its high-handedness in dealing with political problems. General Russell, annoyed by continuing opposition from the Haitian elite and American anti-imperialists throughout the 1920s, often responded cantankerously. In a 1927 letter to the *Nation,* suppressed by the State Department because it displayed "too much petulance and temper," Russell attacked an article criticizing the Service Technique as being "so childishly foolish that an intelligent reader could hardly fail to be amused and wonder at the underlying motive for its publication," and angrily charged that "The purpose of the article is obviously to discredit the United States Government."[21] Dissident

* The Occupation used its radio network, which included receivers set up in peasant marketplaces, to disseminate agricultural and public health information.

journalists writing for the opposition press in Haiti were in no way shielded from the wrath of the Occupation and were frequently arrested by the Gendarmerie on orders from President Borno. Since Borno's orders to the Gendarmerie were not carried out without the prior approval of General Russell, these arrests were, in effect, ordered by Russell.* Despite rigid press censorship under martial law, about a dozen journals kept up a constant agitation against the Occupation and sometimes as many as seven editors were in jail at the same time. Charles Moravia, a former minister to Washington and editor of *Le Temps,* told an American traveler in 1928 that he had been jailed four times without trial and had spent 120 days in jail in the previous year.[22] Some editors were made into literary martyrs by frequent jailings and later capitalized on their resulting popularity during the elections that followed the 1929 uprisings.

The opposition newspapers, which raised a feeble dissenting voice in an otherwise closed society, were persecuted far more than their importance warranted. The Occupation even went to the trouble of censoring incoming news reports from the wire services so that foreign news unfavorable to the Occupation would not reach the opposition press. In 1927 American Chargé Christian Gross reported the Occupation's censorship of both incoming and outgoing telegrams in addition to the wire service censorship:

In an endeavor to confine agitators of a local press to a semblance of truth local telegraph companies have been requested to use their discretion about receiving messages of an absurd and politically defamatory nature and if in doubt to request approval of Department of the Interior before sending. Local companies sending without question all business messages also all news items which approach the truth.[23]

While the opposition press tended to be irresponsible in spreading rumors, most editorials considered offensive by the Occupation were fairly innocuous, with criticism tending toward veiled sarcasm, such as printing the American Declaration of Independence with

* One chief of the Gendarmerie, a marine colonel, wrote the commandant of the Marine Corps in 1927: "When I get any instructions from the President I always have to get General Russell's approval on such orders before carrying them out." J. S. Turrill, COL, USMC, to John A. Lejeune, Mar. 14, 1927; Lejeune MSS, Container 4.

appropriate passages underlined as a protest against alleged Occupation tyranny.[24] Prior to 1920 all criticism of the Occupation had been strictly forbidden but later, with denunciations of press censorship from within the United States and the State Department's inclination toward liberalizing the occupation, restrictions were somewhat eased.[25] In any case, Haitian editors continued to be arrested since they pressed the limits of Russell's tolerance, whatever these happened to be. With the exception of the few journalists who constituted a minor nuisance and whose jailings made Russell and Borno appear despotic in both Haiti and the United States, the Occupation effectively suppressed all dissent. Vociferous Haitian nationalist agitators, such as Joseph Jolibois fils, who toured Latin America denouncing the United States in the wake of President-elect Hoover's 1928 goodwill trip, had to operate from abroad.

The stolid domination of the Occupation, which had for so long effectively controlled Haiti with so little overt resistance, was broken by explosive political and economic forces which converged in the fall of 1929. Economic distress caused by falling coffee prices and increases in government taxes were coupled with discontent over the postponement of the 1930 legislative elections and the apparent continuance of Borno as client-president. These factors exacerbated the latent hatred of the Occupation inspired by American racial condescension and boorish military dictation. A poor coffee crop in 1928, the collapse of the coffee market in 1929, and the restriction of migrant labor emigration to Cuba were compounded by the Occupation's policy of pressing new tax collections. By the fall of 1929, unbeknown to complacent officials and the State Department, popular discontent in Haiti needed only a rallying point to develop into a major uprising against the Occupation. This rallying point was provided by a series of student strikes against the Service Technique.

The student strikes began in late October, 1929, when the students at the Service Technique's central agricultural college at Damien walked out in a body protesting a reduction in incentive scholarships for city students and corresponding increases in scholarships for field work. Students in the medical college and law college followed in a sympathy strike, and the strike quickly spread throughout the nation to both public and private schools. Idle students milled about in the streets for a period of five weeks while General Russell tried unsuccessfully to meliorate the situation by conceding a substantial raise in student scholarship rates. Student demonstrators focused their hostility on Dr. Freeman, the widely despised head of the Service Technique, and stoned his home in Port-au-Prince as part of an unauthorized parade dispersed by the Garde, while elsewhere striking students rallied around the cry "A bas Freeman!" (Down with Freeman!) and paraded Freeman's effigy in the streets.[26] Freeman himself was surprised and distressed by the strikes and recalled to President Hoover's 1930 Forbes Commission that he had misjudged the extent of student disaffection: "There was one young man especially in whom I had great trust, in fact, it hurt me so badly at the time I almost cried, he swore he would go down and restrain the boys in their action and then became a leader." [27]

High Commissioner Russell later expressed the opinion that "the striking students were acting according to Latin and European tradition which prescribes that students take a prominent part in radical political action." He described the strikes as "a petty students' affair" which was being used by disgruntled politicians, the "outs," to undermine the Occupation.[28] In fact, Haitian nationalists of all ages were already much exercised over the cancellation of elections and the prospect of Borno's being foisted upon them for a third term. Opposition agitators and newspapers, of course, made the most of the situation.[29]

By the end of November the student strikes, supported by French Catholic brothers and sisters in Catholic schools, was widening to include the threat of a general strike.[30] In mid-November Borno issued a declaration that he would not seek a third term and on December 2 Russell requested that the State Department publicly confirm Borno's noncandidacy in order to quiet popular unrest, but these moves were inadequate. On December 3 Russell reported to the State Department that politicians and businessmen were aligning themselves with the strikers, that the loyalty of the Garde was "very questionable," and that an additional force of 500 marines would be immediately required to protect American lives.[31]

The following morning the expected general uprising began with a strike by customs employees in Port-au-Prince. A large, angry mob gathered at the site of the customs strike and by the end of the day the streets of Port-au-Prince were crowded with excited people who stoned marine patrols which had been called out to reinforce the Garde.[32] Financial Adviser de la Rue noted that the marines had been called out just in time:

the Garde had stood silently by or had walked around shaking hands with leaders and tipping their hats politely to lady agitators, etc. It seemed that they were not disloyal to the Americans so much as they were just dumb, low-class nigger boys who had no idea of what to do to handle an angry crowd . . . the minute the marines got busy, the Garde stiffened up. . . .[33]

The general uprising spread quickly throughout the country. In Cap Haïtien, the Garde was unable to handle 1,000 demonstrators without the support of marine patrols and several towns in the Cayes district reported thousands of peasants gathering around American outposts shouting "A bas Borno! A bas Freeman!"[34] On December 4, Brigade Commander R. M. Cutts reported to the commandant of the Marine Corps that the loyalty of the Garde was "becoming more doubtful" and envisioned the possibility of "re-occupation of outlying important towns by Marine forces, heavily supplied with automatic shoulder weapons."[35]

High Commissioner Russell reacted to the uprisings by reinvoking curfew and martial law, by interdicting the opposition press, which suspended publication from December 5 to 16, by canceling the independent status of the Garde d'Haïti and incorporating it as a regiment of the Marine Brigade, and by dispatching Garde reinforcements to Jacmel, Petit Goâve, and Leogane, where their timely arrival thwarted attempted uprisings.[36] The Hoover administration, which was trying to develop a Good Neighbor policy toward Latin America, was appalled by all these developments and ordered Russell to exercise utmost restraint in suppressing the uprisings. Secretary of State Stimson cabled Russell on December 4 that the department did not consider that the situation warranted a declaration of martial law unless "absolutely necessary for the protection of lives," and on December 5, after Russell had already reinstituted martial law, Stimson urged him to have faith in the loyalty of the black troops and to keep cool, adding: "I seriously question the wisdom of the ['your' deleted] proclamation yesterday as to martial law. To me it seems that the benefit of such a proclamation in an illiterate population like Haiti is outweighed by the unfortunate effect produced in the United States, particularly as you state that martial law was already in force." [37]

Stimson advised Russell to rescind the proclamation and to withdraw Americans from exposed places rather than send out reinforcements. As a precautionary measure, five hundred marines were embarked at Norfolk for possible Haitian duty, but these men would be used only in dire emergency, since Stimson was "extremely reluctant to increase the strength of the Marine Brigade" and felt that "the sending of additional forces would give rise to sensational reports regarding the Haitian situation." [38]

All this was before the disastrous Cayes massacre of December 6. Fifteen hundred angry peasants, armed with stones, machetes, and clubs, surrounded a detachment of twenty marines armed with rifles and automatic weapons.[39] The marines had gone out to meet the peasants, who were advancing on the town intent on securing the release of prisoners arrested the day before and on airing various grievances against the Occupation, including complaints about alcohol, tobacco, and other taxes. Marine airplanes had dropped bombs in Cayes harbor in an attempt to awe the local population into submissiveness, but this demonstration apparently had the undesired effect of creating terror and frenetic excitement.[40] A district marine officer unsuccessfully attempted to persuade the mob to retire, but then, according to an account given by two marine participants, a Haitian leader instigated a scuffle:

The leader made a suspicious move and Gillaspey countered with a blow with the stock of his Browning gun, breaking the stock. The belligerent fell, tackling Gillaspey around the right leg and biting him. William T. Meyers, private, first class, bayoneted the man without seriously hurting him, but forcing him to release Gillaspey. The clash with the natives followed.[41]

The State Department announced that the Haitians first threw stones and then rushed the marines.[42] In any case, the marines opened fire at point-blank range and dispersed the mob.

Initial marine reports and State Department press releases indicated that 5 Haitians were killed and 20 wounded, but Russell later informed the department that the final hospital list totaled 12 dead and 23 wounded, and that "It is possible that other wounded were not brought in and other deaths occurred in the hills from contaminated wounds. Reports are current that this is the case, but verification cannot be secured." [43] Casualty lists published in the Haitian press in January, 1930, totaled 24 dead and 51 wounded.[44] In response to pointed questions from Under Secretary of State Joseph P. Cotton, who referred to the marine detachment as a "firing squad," Russell explained the curious fact that both the officer in charge of the detachment and his second-in-command had arrived in Haiti only two days before the massacre by saying that they "were selected for this duty as they would operate on a military basis, having no bias or preconceived ideas of the Haitian situation." [45] Russell reported that 600 rounds had been fired by rifles, automatic rifles, and one machine gun, but that most firing had been deliberately over the natives' heads and that "Had punitive effect been desired, it is reported that from three hundred to four hundred, perhaps more, could easily have been killed." [46] A State Department press release indicated that one marine was hurt in hand-to-hand encounter with a mob leader. The marines were later officially vindicated of any taint of brutality or indiscretion when the Navy Department awarded the Navy Cross to the Cayes detachment commander for "commendable courage and forbearance." [47]

Military decorations notwithstanding, the Cayes massacre was exactly what the Hoover administration wanted most to avoid. President Hoover had stated in his first annual message to Congress on December 3 that he did not want the United States represented abroad by marines on foreign soil and that he was anxious to find a solution to the Haitian problem.[48] On December 7, after learning of the masacre, Hoover sent a special message to Congress requesting a $50,000 appropriation to send a commission of investigation to Haiti. Meanwhile, he urgently sought to prevent further calamity in Haiti by trying to get General Russell to make do without the five hundred marine reinforcements who were waiting off Port-au-Prince aboard the U.S.S. *Wright*. Stimson cabled Russell on December 9: "The President feels that it would immensely help the situation so far as public opinion in this country is concerned if the

Marines now on the *Wright* could be diverted. . . . This would not only diminish criticism here but would reflect credit on the efficacy of the steps you have already taken." [49] In a separate message, Stimson added that landing additional troops would "very adversely affect our relations with all Latin America." [50]

Russell managed without the reinforcements. Women and children from American colonies at outlying posts were brought into Port-au-Prince and marines and Garde detachments in the interior kept within the bounds of their regular stations so as not to arouse further hostility. Striking government employees either returned to work on the day following the December 4 walkout or were fired. Reinvigoration of martial law and arrests of demonstrators quashed the uprisings in Port-au-Prince and Cap Haïtien. By December 12 only 33 of 145 Haitians arrested during the strike at Port-au-Prince were still in jail.[51] An official State Department reaffirmation that Borno would not be a candidate for reelection helped calm popular unrest; in fact, the American commander at Cap Haïtien credited the department's declaration with having averted bloodshed,[52] and President Hoover's announced intention of sending a special presidential commission further placated the opposition. After order was restored, the State Department exonerated Russell of previous allegations that he had been unnecessarily severe in reacting to the uprisings. Chief of the Division of Latin American Affairs Munro noted: "When the situation became acute in Haiti we were inclined to feel that General Russell had been precipitate in declaring martial law. More complete information, however, makes it very clear, in my opinion, that he did not take this action until it was absolutely necessary to prevent an outbreak which would have cost many lives." [53] At the end of December Secretary of State Stimson sent Russell a congratulatory message praising him for having handled the uprisings well.[54]

In explaining the uprisings, which tended to disprove the long-standing assertion that opposition to the Occupation was confined to a small number of disgruntled elite politicians, General Russell argued that a few agitators had caused all the trouble. Less than a year earlier Russell had reported to the State Department that it was "particularly worthy of note that the ignorant peasant no longer looks upon the intervention with distrust, but now rather regards it as a friend." [55] The 1929 uprisings, according to Russell, were not caused by widespread popular discontent but rather by a few elite politicians who cared nothing for the peasants. Russell asserted:

The students' strike disorders were utterly unsupported, almost unknown and completely uninteresting to the passive, politically inarticulate peasants. . . . Only in the vicinity of Cayes were agitators able to play upon the ignorance of a mob containing some peasants; and among the causes of that outbreak were liquor, hatred of the town, and the expectation of loot. [56]

With respect to the mass uprisings in Port-au-Prince and Cap Haïtien, Russell noted that, following the declaration of martial law and curfew, "Almost immediately these two chief cities became calm, showing the lack of real popular interest in the affair." [57] In subsequent reports Russell made vague allusions to international Red conspiracy and blamed the Cayes massacre on "dishonest, paid agitators." [58] However, writing a personal memorial several years later, he alleged that the Cayes peasants had been "liberally incited by rum." [59] Russell's later minimizing the extent of unrest was, of course, belied by the many urgent and dire communiqués he had sent to Washington during the uprisings.

The placing of all blame on agitators and the attendant implication that most Haitians were not really hostile to the Occupation, although unsupported by concrete intelligence information, was in keeping with the familiar Russell-Borno argument that popular elections were not feasible because the masses were ignorant and could be manipulated into voting against the Occupation by unscrupulous and selfish politicians. While the "subversive agitator" theory served as a neat justification for paternal authoritarian rule in the interest of the masses and excused the Occupation of failings otherwise implicit in the uprisings, the basic weakness of Russell's assessment of Haitian opposition was clearly demonstrated by the fact that he was caught completely by surprise when the roof fell in in 1929.* The marines' elaborate intelligence surveillance of virtually all Haitian political activity had provided no advance indication of the

---

* American surprise at the 1929 uprisings was similar to the slave revolt syndrome in colonial Saint Domingue, where repression yielded superficial acquiescence that was comforting to the masters but proved illusory.

uprisings. The Garde's cumbersome intelligence network included ongoing personal files on hundreds of individuals, from Cabinet officers to small-town barbers, yet there was no material to substantiate allusions to any serious conspiracy to overthrow the Occupation.[60]

The only indications of any international Communist conspiracy to foil American plans for Haiti were several mass demonstrations against the Occupation staged in Washington and New York. The *New York Times* reported that five hundred Communist party members battled New York City police at City Hall Plaza following a call for demonstrations against the Occupation issued in the party's newspaper, the *Daily Worker*.[61] These demonstrations, however, took place after the uprisings in Haiti were over, and coincided with widespread American and worldwide public attacks on United States policy following the Cayes massacre. In the United States Congress, long-dormant opposition to the Occupation suddenly revived as critics pointed to American hypocrisy in championing democracy and freedom while gunning down natives and noted that the American position in Haiti was strikingly similar to that of Great Britain in India and Japan in Korea.[62] As had been typical of anti-imperialist agitation throughout the occupation, the major concern was not with Haiti but with the alleged decline of American political idealism. One congressman stated that

those who finally suffer most from despotism are those who practice it upon others. I sympathize with the Haitian people, but I regard our disregard of the right of self-government by the Haitians as more harmful to our own institutions than to the Haitians, because we disregard the great principles announced in the Declaration of Independence. When we cease to practice justice, the moral fiber of the people will begin to decay.[63]

Another congressman, admitting that he was "not especially interested in the Haitians," echoed the familiar anti-imperialist chiché that "An imperialism abroad can not remain a democracy at home." [64] The congressional debate over the occupation also reflected political divisions within the United States, with Northern and Southern congressmen accusing each other of hypocrisy with respect to the denial of the ballot to Negroes in the Southern United States and Haiti, respectively.[65]

The 1929 uprisings attracted worldwide attention. Prior to the uprisings very little had been heard from Haiti since telegraph services were censored by the Occupation, and the only two news agencies with reporters in Haiti, the Associated Press (AP) and the United Press (UP), were both represented by marine corps officers. The AP representative at the time of the uprisings was also the commandant of the Garde; and a previous marine reporter, who had simultaneously represented the AP and the UP, was a former publicity officer for the Marine Corps in Washington.[66] During the strikes and riots both AP and UP sent special correspondents to Haiti, as did several American and other foreign newspapers, and press coverage increased correspondingly. Press reaction in the United States was not especially hostile to the Occupation, but it was not favorable either; and criticisms of the Occupation, such as those made by Senators Borah and King, were given a great deal of publicity.[67] The foreign reaction to the uprisings was decidedly hostile to the United States. As one congressman remarked while criticizing the United States for playing the role of "praying pirates" in Haiti, "Our smugness irritates the world and does not blind it. The White House often fools the country, but seldom fools the world." [68]

Foreign attitudes toward the occupation, insofar as the occupation was a subject of attention, had always been unfavorable. British members of Parliament had created a minor fuss over the 1920 Marine Corps report that alluded to indiscriminate killings of Haitians, pointing out that the United States was quick to criticize British activities in Ireland but paid little notice to its own ruthless repression of resistance in Haiti.[69] In 1924 American scholar Samuel Guy Inman noted that the occupation was being attacked in France, Britain, and Spain, and that "In no country has the military occupation of Santo Domingo and Haiti been more discussed than in Japan, where the Government has formed now its own Monroe Doctrine of the Orient, by which it justified its recent Twenty-one demands on China, and its imperialism in Korea." [70]

The French press was especially critical of American racism, which was seen as a dominant feature of the occupation.[71] The 1929 uprisings and the Cayes incident spurred a dramatic increase in unfavorable foreign newspaper reports. The Paris press followed the uprisings closely and was characteristically critical, with some papers calling for a League of Nations investigation.[72] The *Manchester Guardian* published the following dispatch from a British reporter in Haiti three days after the Cayes massacre:

The situation in Haiti, where almost the entire population is in revolt against American control . . . comes as no surprise to those in close touch with the affairs of the negro republic. Resentment against the American occupation has long been smouldering and needed only some minor dispute to cause it to burst into flame.[73]

The *Guardian* later referred to the occupation as "America's least successful experiment in imperialism." [74]

The State Department was especially concerned about the possible adverse affect of the Haitian uprisings in Latin-American countries and issued a circular instructing all Latin-American diplomatic posts to report on local reactions. The resulting reports described frequent instances of hostile press reports, such as in Lima newspapers, all of which quoted critical statements by United States Senator William Borah, but relations with Latin-American governments were not directly affected.[75] The Argentine newspaper *La Prensa* continued to campaign against the occupation through early 1930. During the mid-1920s the marines managed to keep Haiti out of the international spotlight, but now the occupation was turning into a definite embarrassment to United States efforts to develop friendly relations with Latin America. The concern about unfavorable publicity at home and abroad that Hoover and Stimson had expressed during the uprisings was justified.

The 1929 strikes and riots made the occupation untenable. Continued American rule and denial of elections would have necessitated military repression and additional international embarrassment. It was largely because the United States could not gracefully extricate itself that the marines had continued to sit on Haiti after World War I. With the 1929 uprisings, American hopes for gradual and unobtrusive extrication from the Haitian entanglement were shattered. The uprisings, especially the sensational Cayes massacre, were as disastrous as Hoover and Stimson cared to face. President Hoover, in dispatching a special commission to Haiti in February, 1930, stated: "The primary question which is to be investigated is when and how we are to withdraw from Haiti. The second question is what we shall do in the meantime. . . . As I have stated before, I have no desire for representation of the American Government abroad through our military forces." [76]

Subsequent American policy was to avoid further popular demonstrations at all costs and to get out of Haiti as quickly as could be done in an orderly fashion.

11

Withdrawal

The 1929 uprisings resulted in the abandonment of repressive, authoritarian policies and complementary uplift programs in favor of rapid transferal of political control back to the Haitians. The United States objective was to get out of Haiti as quickly as possible even though this meant an overwhelming victory for anti-American forces in popular elections and a seemingly inevitable reversion to pre-1915 political and social conditions. All allusions to uplift and progress were forsaken as officials of the occupation frankly predicted that disaster would follow in the aftermath of American withdrawal. The major barrier to early American withdrawal was not concern over having adequate time to transfer treaty services and uplift programs to competent Haitians but rather the problem of satisfying commitments to American bondholders, who insisted on continued American financial control. After a crash program of Haitianizing the government departments and laborious negotiations for transfer of the Banque Nationale and continuation of American financial control, the last marines were finally withdrawn in mid-1934, two years in advance of the 1936 date stipulated in the treaty.

Prior to the 1929 strikes and riots the State Department had been generally satisfied with progress in Haiti as reported by High Commissioner Russell. No basic change in Haitian policy had been contemplated; the occupation was expected to continue until 1936, at which time the government would be turned over to the Haitians.[1] President Hoover had planned to send a commission of investigation to Haiti before the uprisings, but this was in response to complaints by American business firms rather than to agitation for Haitian independence.[2] The uprisings came as a big surprise, and when Hoover actually got around to sending a commission to Haiti in February, 1930, the purpose was to dump the Russell-Borno regime and accommodate Haitian nationalists in order to avoid further bloodshed and embarrassment to the United States. The Forbes Commission consisted of Chairman W. Cameron Forbes, a former governor of the Philippines and leading expert on American colonial matters; Henry P. Fletcher, a former Rough Rider, diplomat, and adviser to Hoover on his 1928 goodwill tour of Latin America; Democratic newspaper editor James Kerney of New Jersey; Elie Vezina, a French-speaking Catholic; and William Allen White, liberal Republican journalist whose presence, according to White, was calculated to guarantee to the public that the investigation would not be a whitewashing affair.[3] Fletcher, Kerney, and White were predisposed toward withdrawal of the marines at the earliest possible moment, while Forbes, who had been invited by Stimson to undertake what the secretary of state referred to as "a very disagreeable and thankless job," was by temperament and training a conciliator and compromiser.[4]

Popular hostility to the occupation and to the Borno client-government was still very much in evidence when the Forbes Commission reached Haiti in February, 1930. Rumors that Borno would choose his own successor had caused a crowd of several thousand to gather in Port-au-Prince on the eve of the commission's arrival, and arrests by marines and the Garde, which also dispersed the crowd by hitting people with billies, created a tense atmosphere. On the day of arrival 6,000 Haitian demonstrators greeted the commission carrying placards denouncing the occupation; and Forbes and his colleagues reported that, although they felt that this and other demonstrations were rigged by the opposition, it was "fair to assume that public sentiment in Haiti was more responsive to the opposition than to the government."[5] No one ever demonstrated in favor of the occupation. Despite initial Haitian apprehensiveness, the commission managed to ingratiate itself with the Haitian public largely thanks to William Allen White's personal charm. Forbes had intervened to procure permission for a patriotic parade of Haitian women which had been forbidden by the Occupation, and White, who witnessed the parade, blew a kiss to a withered old black woman, which caused the demonstrators to cheer and helped create confidence in the commission's good intentions. The opposition press subsequently referred to White in glowing terms: "How well the name corresponds to and fits the character, White of soul and of heart . . . full of wise counsels and generous fervor, gay, lovable in his person." [6]

Members of the Forbes Commission made a special effort to cultivate the Haitian elite by mingling socially and by listening mainly to elite testimony during the formal phases of the investigation. General Russell, on the other hand, antagonized the opposition by inviting members of the elite to a social reception given in honor of the commission. Russell went to great lengths to convince the commission that he and Mrs. Russell had always personally extended themselves in being socially gracious toward the Haitians, but invitations to the mixed reception for the commission resulted in a series of embarrassing refusals from Haitians, some of whom were apparently being invited to the Russell residence for the first time and took the opportunity to express their hostility by publishing letters of refusal in the local press.[7] The reception was integrated, and the commission was impressed by Russell's professions of racial tolerance, but, as Forbes observed, "The large social question of the treatment of the colored people by officers in the Marine brigade was not approached." [8]

In presenting the Occupation's side of the story to the commission Russell called together all the treaty officials and, as he put it, "impressed upon them the necessity of refuting in every particular, the charges set forth by the Opposition," but the Occupation's case was publicly compromised when Dr. Freeman of the Service Technique insisted on testifying in private sessions. Russell remarked that it "looked very much as if he had something to conceal." [9] In fact, Freeman's testimony was not compromising to the Occupation, and Freeman released the commission from its pledge of secrecy after explaining that "I did not know whether or not you might ask me certain questions of a delicate nature which the dictates of diplomacy should require to be kept confidential . . . no such questions arose," [10] Freeman's candor came too late to counteract the unfavorable impression made by his initial reticence, and the testimony of other officials did not particularly impress either the commission or the Haitian public. When the commission received a detailed defense of the occupation prepared by General Russell, it refused to make the document public for fear of creating disorders in what had become an extremely delicate situation.

The immediate and pressing mission of the Forbes Commission was not so much to investigate and recommend future policies as it was to solve the political impasse between the Russell-Borno regime and the opposition and to avert the threat of further violence. In a special report entitled "Confidential Memorandum, Steps taken to solve acute political situation in Haiti," Forbes noted that "the situation was difficult at best and really required that the Haitians be permitted to elect their president . . . any alternative seemed to be out of the question, as there was no chance of a president's being elected by the Council of State resulting in anything but revolution." [11]

In a memorandum to Forbes, Russell described the situation as tense and observed that "the opposition intends to force the issue of national elections, even at the sacrifice of lives, and it is therefore of utmost importance to endeavor to effect a compromise." [12]

The problem was how to remove Borno and transfer political power to the most moderate faction within the opposition. Borno made a very unfavorable impression on the commission, and Forbes commented that he seemed to be "living in a world of illusion or delusion in regard to the depth of the feeling which had been engendered against him by the Haitian populace." [13] William Allen White described Borno as follows: "He is thin, tall, toothy and most disagreeable, and lives entirely apart from reality. . . . He has a little sneering laugh . . . I kept pinching myself—and Kerney said he did also—to realize that I was not listening to a stage melodrama. It just did not seem possible than any man should be so patent a stage villain." [14]

Borno had apparently expected that the Americans would ultimately retain him as client-president and was now becoming recalcitrant at the prospect of being thrown out of office.

Despite repeated messages from the State Department since 1928 that Borno would not be permitted a third term and frequent assurances from Russell and Borno that he would not run again, Borno had begun to hedge in the fall of 1929.[15] The Forbes Commission reaffirmed the department's decision and informed Borno that "the United States would not longer tolerate the perpetuation of a government kept in power against the desires of the Haitian people by means of the guns of the Marines." [16] The commission proceeded to negotiate with the political opposition while Russell continued to deal with Borno in an effort to work out a plan for selecting a temporary neutral president who would hold office for several months until legislative elections could be held. A satisfactory compromise involving the selection of Eugene Roy as temporary president was worked out with the help of the commandant of the Garde, Marine Colonel Frank E. Evans, who was highly thought of by the opposition and by Haitians in general. According to Garde intelligence reports, Borno had earlier stated privately that Evans was the sole cause of his not being selected for a third term, while Russell remained loyal.[17] Although it involved surrendering his office, Borno finally agreed to the compromise plan, and he and Russell played a large part in drawing up the details. Forbes later wrote the State Department that the opposition groups would never have accepted the compromise plan had they known how much of it emanated from "the initiative of General Russell and President Borno." [18] The Forbes plan provided that Borno's Council of State would elect Roy, who would then call for the legislative elections insisted upon by the opposition. The popularly elected legislature would then choose a new president other than Roy.

Borno, however, had not yet reconciled himself to defeat, and proceeded to intrigue against the Forbes plan by going back on his agreement and thereby aggravating popular unrest. Popular demonstrations, such as a clash between a hundred youths and the Garde in Jacmel, all featured demands for legislative elections as provided by the Forbes plan. While the Forbes Commission was touring the interior of the country, Borno renounced his agreement to the compromise plan by sending a telegram to local prefects declaring that his Council of State would elect the new president. Forbes referred to this telegram as "provocative of unrest and misunderstanding," and the commission informed Borno that the marines would no longer protect him if he persisted in fomenting trouble.[19] Borno, clinging desperately to what little power he had, continued to make public statements implying that the elections would not be held until 1932 and that his Council of State would select someone other than Roy as provisional president, but his various intrigues failed to create enough unrest to force the United States to retrench in the old Russell-Borno system of authoritarian rule. The State Department warned Borno that the United States would not "afford him or his adherents any support or protection in a course of action contrary to the plan" and informed Russell that the department would "take such steps as may prove necessary to have Eugene Roy installed as temporary President . . . and is prepared, therefore, to disregard any action of the Council of State which is in violation of the provisions of the plan." [20] A little more than a month after the departure of the Forbes Commission the Council of State elected Roy, according to the compromise plan, and a few weeks later Borno was publicly jeered as the new provisional president was inaugurated. Borno retired to his home in Pétionville, where he was protected by a small detachment of the Garde, and shortly afterward left the country for an extended vacation in Europe.

The Forbes Commission, in assessing the achievements and failures of the Occupation, criticized American racism, the advance payment of the debt when excess revenues could have been used for development, the dismal performance in education, the failure to train Haitians to take over the government and the Garde as rapidly as might have been done, and the attitude of independent self-sufficiency taken by officials of the Occupation. In its final report to President Hoover, the commission noted:

The acts and attitude of the treaty officials gave our commission the impression that they had been based upon the assumption that the Occupation would continue indefinitely. In other words, their plans and projects did not seem to take into account that their work would be completed by 1936, and the commission was disappointed to find that the preparation for the political and administrative training of Haitians in the responsibilities of government had been inadequate.[21]

In private talks with Hoover, Forbes said that the Russell-Borno team had pushed through reforms "without the propaganda . . . which is necessary to 'sell' the idea to the people," and in a letter to a friend Forbes noted that the most serious failing had been racial prejudice resulting from "the fact that the Americans sent down were not always judiciously selected from the point of view of locality of origin." [22]

In spite of all these criticisms, the commission's report was mainly laudatory. Forbes later remarked that the commission had made "careful and guarded criticisms" so as to avoid giving the hostile press in the United States and Latin America an opportunity to attack Russell and the marines. Forbes felt that Russell and Borno got a "dirty deal" out of the commission's report, which recommended that Russell be recalled, and the commission went out of its way to praise Russell and recommended his promotion by way of compensation.[23] Indeed, Russell's demise as high commissioner was caused by the reversal of American policy rather than by any personal shortcomings. He had served faithfully as the chosen instrument of State Department policy from 1922 on and was now being made a scapegoat to facilitate transition to the new policy of gracious disengagement. Those few instances when department officials indulged in hand-wringing reproachments over Russell's arbitrary methods, as with his handling of press censorship and the 1928 constitutional reform, can be ascribed more to the department's own foibles than to failings on Russell's part. The department had set up the occupation as a military undertaking and could not reasonably blame the marines for running it as such. Moreover, Russell's eight years' service as the State Department's representative in Haiti had cost him stature within the Marine Corps. In 1930 Assistant Secretary of State Francis White wrote to Stimson recommending that Russell, despite his not being liked in the Navy and Marine Corps because of past close associations with the State Department, be promoted to major general commandant of the Marine Corps precisely because he worked well with the State Department and understood its point of view. Other candidates, among them Major General Smedley Butler, all had combat experience in the European war and were known as hard-line marines. White pointed out that they, because of their military orientation, would not fit in with the department's new Caribbean policy.[24] Russell was appointed major general commandant in 1934.*

The White House, in a palliative statement released on the return of the Forbes Commission, announced that "The commission was particularly impressed with the splendid results accomplished under the sincere and efficient direction of General Russell," who, along with Borno, would be given "full credit" for substantial progress in public health, public works, and public order.[25] The commission reported that "There is no room for doubt that Haiti, under the control of the American Occupation, has made great material progress in the past fifteen years" and cited as examples the construction of 153 rural clinics and 11 modern hospitals, the registration of 2,800 automobiles, a threefold increase in linear feet of bridges, 800 miles of roads, and new lighthouses and telephones. The commission also noted that this progress had been mainly achieved over the span of only eight years, since a constructive policy was not carried out until after the 1922 reorganization. In conclusion, however, Forbes and his colleagues observed that the positive achievements, though great, had not fulfilled original expectations: "The failure of the Occupation to understand the social problems of Haiti, its brusque attempt to plant democracy there by drill and harrow, its determination to set up a middle class—however wise and necessary it may seem to Americans—all these explain why, in part, the high hopes of our good works in this land have not been realized." [26]

The commission recommended that Russell be replaced by a nonmilitary minister, that the United States interpose no objections to reductions in customs duties and internal taxes, and, reiterating the advice of the 1922 Senate Inquiry, that "in retaining officers now in the Haitian service, or selecting new Americans for employment therein, the utmost care be taken that only those free from strong racial antipathies should be preferred." [27] Preparations for American

---

* Another factor in the jettisoning of Russell in 1930 was the Hoover administration's less than enthusiastic relationship with the Marine Corps. Major General Commandant Ben H. Fuller wrote to General Little in Haiti as Franklin D. Roosevelt was taking over the presidency in March, 1933, that "The attitude of the Administration towards us is distinctly more favorable than it was a month ago and the future doesn't look so dark as it did when the Engineer [Hoover] was hamstringing us." Fuller to Little, Mar. 14, 1933; Louis McCarty Little Papers, MARCORPS MUS.

withdrawal were to be accelerated by more rapid Haitianization of the Garde and the other treaty services.

Russell, who had been greatly distressed by the recent uprisings, which, according to one occupation official, caused him to feel "as though his life's work was crumbling under his eyes," [28] was incensed over the criticisms made by the Forbes Commission and bitterly attacked it in a long letter of defense and vindication which he submitted to Secretary of State Stimson. Russell argued that the commission had been in Haiti only fifteen days, not long enough to gain an understanding of the complicated situation, that the commission's statement that public sentiment favored the opposition was unfair because the Occupation had held back its forces so as not to create disorder, that the commission had given 90 percent of its time to hearing the "outs" make false charges while the treaty officials had been given "scant opportunity to present their side," and that the commission was wrong in praising him for devotion to the interests of Haiti "*as he conceived them,*" since he had always acted under strict orders from the State Department. Russell took personal credit for having formulated the compromise plan put into effect by the commission * and stated that he had urged the various Occupation departments to promote Haitians and that promotions had been as rapid as possible. In this connection he observed: "The reason for the present efficiency of the Garde is due in a large measure, in my opinion, to the fact that the promotion of Haitian officers has not been rapid. An officer must thoroughly learn his duties in a lower grade before being promoted to a higher grade." In response to the commission's reference to American racism, Russell replied that "No case of racial prejudice has been brought to my attention for many years and it is, therefore, difficult to understand the Commission's remarks or on what it based them." [29]

As for the wisdom of the Forbes plan, with its arrangements for free elections, Russell felt that the Haitians were "little better fitted for self-government than they were in 1915" and that "The people have recently grown more and more bold and insulting and in my mind any reduction in the military force would be a grave error."

* James Kerney of the Forbes Commission credited Frank E. Evans, COL, USMC, commandant of the Garde, with having originally proposed the compromise plan. SD 838.00/2969, Kerney to Stimson, May 12, 1931.

Russell opposed the gradual withdrawal of forces and recommended that the United States should "get in—or get out." [30] This last epigram, so often heard among military officers during the early days of the occupation, presumably alluded to the need for total military government if the occupation was ever to be really successful.

While the Forbes Commission reported favorably on the material accomplishments of the Occupation and on the beneficent effects of American rule, its prognosis for Haiti's future after American withdrawal was highly pessimistic. In its final report the commission stated that it was "under no delusions" as to what would happen after free elections and the departure of the marines, and Forbes told Hoover that the legislative election plan offered a palliative rather than a remedy for the Haitian situation, which was "fundamentally unsound." [31] Forbes wrote Lord Irwin, British viceroy of India, with whom he corresponded comparing the similarities of American problems in Haiti with British problems in India, that the Haitians were unfit for democracy and that "Their best hope is for a benevolent despot to arise who, like Porfirio Diaz in Mexico, will guide them with wisdom, firmness, and honesty through the troubled times ahead of them." [32] Forbes's reference to Díaz * was typical of the attitude of American officials who had been involved with Haiti and was quite compatible with American sponsorship of the Borno client-government. Supporters of the Occupation had long justified it as a necessary form of benevolent despotism. The crucial question was, of course, benevolent for whom? Díaz in Mexico and Borno in Haiti were benevolent to American interests and were therefore supported by the United States. In Haiti, as elsewhere, the criteria for a "good" benevolent despotism were prolonged stability coupled with pro-United States politics. In his unpublished personal memorial "A Marine Looks Back on Haiti" (about 1934), General Russell suggested, in what can be interpreted as a thinly veiled allusion to his own performance in Haiti: "A military dictatorship for a country in which the foundations of democracy do not yet

---

* Porfirio Díaz was a ruthless dictator who opened up Mexico to exploitation by foreign investors and the Porfirian oligarchy without meaningful compensations for the mass of the population and thus precipitated the bloody Mexican Revolution of 1911–24.

exist is not necessarily a bad thing. Its first requirement is that it be strong enough to give stable rule for a comparatively long time and secondly that it have some sense of obligation to the people."

On this basis there was a close affinity between Russell, Borno, Forbes, and Russell's earlier counterpart, Lord Cromer, British high commissioner in Egypt. Russell prophesied that after complete American withdrawal Haiti would "return to a system of military dictatorships," but that, thanks to the occupation, "such dictatorships should not be as cynical, cruel, and reactionary as in the past." [33] Russell's prognosis was in keeping with both the antidemocratic policies and practices of the Occupation and with the persisting American obsession concerning order and stability in the Caribbean.

Despite the new emphasis on good-neighbor conciliation which followed in the aftermath of the 1929 uprisings, the question of despotism in Haiti was by no means irrelevant. American officials realized that an important factor in Haiti's future would be the potential political domination of the Garde, and gave due considera- tion to the choice of a Haitian commander. In 1930 a marine officer recommended the eventual selection, Démosthène P. Calixte, as follows: "I believe that if he were left in supreme command he has sufficient strength of character to withstand political assaults on the Garde. I believe he is absolutely ruthless and that he will be the power behind the administration if left as Commandant of the Garde." [34]

Whatever the intentions of the United States government,* Calixte did not follow in the footsteps of dictators Rafael Trujillo (Dominican Republic) and Anastasio Somoza (Nicaragua), both of whom had risen to power as commanders of marine-nurtured constabularies. Trujillo and Somoza enjoyed dictatorships of thirty- one and twenty years, respectively, and one scholar has asserted that "The endurance of their regimes, until and after death, testifies to their hold on modern and centralized armed forces which first came into being during United States intervention." [35] In Haiti,

---

* Dana G. Munro, chief of the Division of Latin American Affairs and then minister to Haiti during the period of withdrawal, says that the State Department had no intention of setting up a military dictatorship in Haiti. My interview with Munro, Princeton, N.J., Feb. 28, 1968.

Calixte lost out in an unsuccessful coup d'état in 1938 and was forced into exile.*

Other American officials concurred in the gloomy predictions of the Forbes Commission. Garde Commandant Evans created some consternation in the State Department by publicly prophesying in 1931 that "Future events may see the United States assuming a resumption of its present activities in Haiti, following our withdrawal in 1936." [36] Financial Adviser Sidney de la Rue attributed the economic prosperity of the 1920s to the artificial stimulus of Brazilian coffee valorization, which collapsed in 1929, rather than to any fundamental progress made under the occupation and noted that there was little reason to expect future prosperity unless crop diversification could be achieved: ". . . the Haitian problem will last beyond our time. It is ugly and for the present not in any way solved . . . we face an almost impossible situation. It is one pregnant with trouble and financially a mess." Describing his work as financial adviser in the wake of the 1929 uprisings as being "merely defensive" and not constructive, de la Rue echoed the morbid prediction attributed to Louis XV: "Apres nous le deluge." [37]

Secretary of State Stimson also was pessimistic about the future of Haiti and during a 1933 visit with President-elect Franklin D. Roosevelt stated that he did not think the United States had achieved lasting stability in Haiti. Stimson recorded his conversation with Roosevelt: "He [Roosevelt] asked whether the job in Haiti was finished and would stay put. I told him I did not think it would stay permanently put and asked him whether he knew of any self-governing negro community which had stayed put, and he could not suggest any." [38] Stimson concluded his comments on Haiti by reassuring Roosevelt that the United States was rapidly pulling the marines out of Haiti and was "making very good progress in finishing our job for the present." [39]

Public disorders in Haiti continued after the departure of the Forbes Commission in March, 1930, and the selection of provisional President Roy in April. In what High Commissioner Russell referred to as an attempt to "create a reign of terror among the Americans," local arsonists burned down the homes of Marine Colonels Cutts and

---

* In exile Calixte was supported by his friend and political ally Trujillo, who eventually gave him a commission in the Dominican army.

Horton as well as a number of other homes, several stores, and a movie house.[40] Rumors of incendiary activity caused disturbances in Jacmel, and the Garde was forced to resort to rifle fire over the heads of a large hostile mob at Abricots. In mid-1930 the Garde undertook an extensive program of training in antiriot techniques. The series of disorders culminated in a general strike of longshoremen, coffee sorters, logwood workers, agricultural laborers, and public works and sanitary department employees at Cap Haïtien in December, 1930. The government proposed a 50 percent increase in wages for longshoremen, which was accepted by steamship company agents after they were informed that the Garde could not guarantee the safety of strikebreakers. Occupation officials attributed the strike variously to Port-au-Prince politicians, labor agitators, and Communist propaganda.[41]

President Roy's provisional government, which held office from May to November, 1930, scheduled the long-awaited legislative elections for October. The State Department ordered American officials to remain strictly neutral, and the marines were confined to their barracks during the balloting. American Chargé Stuart Grummon, who referred to the election as "unquestionably the fairest election that has ever been held in the history of Haiti," reported that the election had "resulted in the complete defeat of all pro-American, pro-Borno and moderate candidates." Grummon noted that "The real hero of the elections is Joseph Jolibois *fils,* whose violent anti-American sentiments and tirades against so-called American imperialism, during his three-year pilgrimage throughout Latin America, are well known to the Department." [42]

Jolibois was, according to an American intelligence report, often called the "Borno-Made man" because he had risen from obscurity thanks to the numerous prison terms he served under Borno for writing anti-occupation newspaper articles.[43] His campaign literature featured a photograph of himself in a prison uniform breaking rocks; the picture was obviously taken after his release since he is seen breaking rocks with a broom handle and wearing shiny dress shoes. Jolibois, age thirty-nine, was too young to qualify for the presidency, but his resounding election victory ensured the selection of another long-time Haitian nationalist, Sténio Vincent, as the new president when the legislature voted in November, 1930.

In conjunction with the election of Vincent, the United States appointed Dr. Dana G. Munro as civilian minister to Haiti, replacing High Commissioner Russell. The removal of Russell, following the earlier departure of Borno and Freeman, marked the end of American military dictation. Munro was instructed to assume the functions hitherto exercised by the high commissioner, but he was to avoid interfering with the freedom of action of the new Vincent government as much as possible in view of the new United States policy toward Haiti. This new policy was spelled out in Munro's instructions: "It is this Government's desire to withdraw from any participation in the internal affairs of Haiti at the earliest moment when such withdrawal can be effected with a reasonable hope that there will be no return to the conditions which compelled its intervention in 1915." [44]

In appointing Munro and in bringing back Colonel Louis McCarty Little, who was liked by the Haitians, as brigade commander, the United States hoped to develop friendlier relations with the Haitians through tact and diplomacy. Racism, however, remained a factor. In 1931 Little noted that marines misbehaving on liberty in Port-au-Prince were never, "except in grave emergency," handled by the Garde because "Blacks arresting Whites would provoke a situation which might cause a riot." [45] Minister Munro pointedly abstained from joining the racially segregated American Club and succeeded in warming relations to the extent that a 1931 George Washington's Birthday celebration was accompanied by cordial social mixing between Haitians and Americans.

The efforts at conciliation were, however, not enough to ensure a smooth and graceful American withdrawal. The functioning of the treaty services broke down rapidly in the aftermath of the 1929 uprisings. For one thing, officials of the American occupation felt that they had been unjustly criticized, and Munro referred to their "very low morale" as a principal obstacle to efficiency. [46] Half the Americans in the Service Technique resigned within a year after the 1929 uprisings and other American civilian and military personnel expressed the desire to get out as quickly as possible. A *New York Times* correspondent reported that American employees of the Occupation especially resented the fact that General Russell had been made "the goat" for policies directed from Washington and that the Forbes Commission had never made public Russell's defense, which justified his actions by stating that the State Department had ordered them, because this would have embarrassed the administration in Washington.[47] Large government deficits caused by the Depression were another factor in curtailing treaty services; Financial Adviser de la Rue reported in 1931 that the "ambitious developmental program of recent years" had largely been given up and that funds were "insufficient to strengthen the police and constabulary, or to construct many badly needed improvements." [48] De la Rue who retained firm control over Haitian finances despite the change in governments, pursued a policy of contraction when faced with reduced revenues caused by the Depression. Taxes were increased while many government employees were discharged and others had their wages cut.[49] Payments on the foreign debt to American bondholders continued, of course, to be made on schedule. In 1935 Haiti was the only one of fifteen Latin-American countries holding publicly offered dollar bonds which had not defaulted.[50]

Low morale and fiscal difficulties were compounded by political problems as Minister Munro soon found that the Vincent government was not willing to conform to State Department plans for gradual withdrawal on American terms. In November, 1931, a State Department officer noted that at the time Munro had taken over in Haiti a year earlier, the department had hoped that Haitianization of the occupation would be an "orderly and gradual process and that the minimum American control in any of the Treaty Services would continue for several years." [51] Vincent, however, kept up a constant harassment for immediate Haitianization in a series of controversies involving the Service Technique, the Public Works Service, and the Garde. Munro reported in January, 1931, that the Vincent government was being subjected to severe pressure by Haitian nationalists who accused it of "acquiescing in a policy of delay" and stated that he was "beginning to feel that real cooperation is almost out of the question. . . . Force after all is the only thing these people have any respect for." [52]

In response to pressure from the Haitians the State Department acquiesced in complete Haitianization of the Public Works Department in February, and Munro found himself fighting what amounted to a rearguard action against constant political harassment from

Haitian nationalists. The Vincent government refused to agree to the department's plan for gradual Haitianization, and Munro reported in June: "It is obvious, however, that we cannot permit this internal political situation to prevent us from executing our own policy of withdrawal. I assume that what the Department desires is Haitianization either by agreement or by our own action." [53]

Shortly after this Stimson instructed Munro to back down in a controversy over the promotion of a Haitian Garde officer, noting that the alternative was "virtual military occupancy of Haiti," which would not be tolerated by public opinion in the United States.[54] In March, Assistant Secretary of State Francis White had written Munro that discouraging news from Haiti had resulted in "a desire, on the part of the President [Hoover], to withdraw from Haiti bag and baggage immediately if possible." [55]

The State Department abandoned the gradual withdrawal plan in favor of a new policy described by W. R. Scott of the Division of Latin American Affairs as follows: "It was decided that, since we could no longer exert a proper control over the Treaty Services for which we were responsible, it would be better to turn over all American activities in Haiti in so far as this could be done consistently with our treaty obligations and our good faith toward the holders of Haitian bonds." [56]

Ernest Gruening, a long-time critic of the Occupation, lamented that "Just at a time when the United States might conceivably render some genuine assistance to the Haitians, the cumulative errors of the past render the possibility of cooperation difficult." [57] Actually there was little possibility of rendering effective assistance since demoralization of personnel and fiscal limitations precluded new development activities. In any case the United States sacrificed what little was left of the uplift programs to the exigencies of a policy that stressed rapid withdrawal. Munro concluded a Haitianization agreement with the Vincent government in August, 1931, after threats and concessions on both sides, and as an act of goodwill the United States made the gesture of formally ending martial law.

The crucial issue, however, was not Haitianization but rather the problem of redefining the status of American financial interests. The State Department abandoned its earlier encouragement and supervision of American investments in view of the new policy of "narrowing American activities in Haiti." [58] An ironic indication of the reversal in American policy with respect to private investments was the decline and fall of Roger L. Farnham, who, as Bryan's confidant, had played a major role in engineering the 1915 intervention and in securing unflinching State Department support for the National Railway and for National City Bank. By the late 1920s his influence with the department had declined considerably. American financial advisers rejected several earlier exploitative railway contracts proposed by Farnham, and in 1930 he was reduced, in a futile attempt to procure department backing, to threatening American officials with British and French military intervention on behalf of the National Railway, with a French embargo on Haitian coffee, and with personal disclosures to the American press about conditions in Haiti that would presumably upset the chairman of the Republican party.[59] Financial Adviser de la Rue characterized the threats as "wild," and Munro reported that Farnham's desperate tactic of shutting down the railway was of little consequence since motor trucks were already carrying on a destructive competition and were entirely able to handle any additional traffic. Munro confided to Francis White that Farnham had "aged a great deal . . . but his capacity for mischief seems, if anything, to be increasing rather than decreasing." [60]

The State Department's policy against extending extraordinary assistance to American businessmen became more systematic and stringent after 1929. The department insisted that American financial control continue after the pending troop withdrawal in order to safeguard the existing commitments to holders of the 1922 bonds but new commitments were strictly forbidden. The United States refused to grant the Vincent government permission to float a new development loan, stipulating that an agreement on post-1936 financial arrangements would have to be reached first, and that even then the United States could not "in any sense urge or recommend to bankers that they undertake this business for Haiti." [61] In an April, 1933, policy memorandum, the chief of the Division of Latin American Affairs noted that the United States did not want to "extend in any way the period of its financial stewardship. This principle must be borne in mind in connection with any attempts on Haiti's part to obtain further foreign financing." [62] Thus Haiti's vaunted credit standing, achieved through ten years of diligent attentiveness to the interests of American bondholders, came to naught, since the attractiveness of Haiti as an investment opportunity ultimately rested on the extent of United States government involvement.

The department's new policy of narrowing American activities in Haiti had an immediate effect on National City Bank, whose branch, the Banque Nationale, served as the Haitian government treasury and was inextricably tied to the problem of safeguarding the interests of American bondholders. Assistant Secretary of State Francis White, after a conversation with a National City Bank representative in July, 1930, recorded: "The Bank fears that President Hoover is going to abandon the Caribbean area on behalf of better relations in the larger Central American countries and that we will scuttle from Haiti, in which event the Bank wants to scuttle also." [63]

White added that the Bank was interested in selling out and was concerned about public attacks in Congress and elsewhere that the marines were in Haiti to protect its interests. In 1933 National City Bank made an unsolicited offer to sell the Banque Nationale to the Haitian government. Chairman of the Board James H. Perkins explained the offer to Secretary of State Cordell Hull by asserting that, while the Banque Nationale was capable of returning "moderate profits," it was "an anomalous element in our organization on account of its governmental character and functions" and had caused National City Bank to be "subjected to criticism from public and private sources for controlling a bank in another country which has such functions." * Perkins, in what amounted to a final panegyric on the long collaboration in Haiti, expressed the bank's "warm appreciation of the support and many courtesies" it had received from the State Department since the time it originally bought out the French interests in the Banque Nationale "at the suggestion of the Honorable William Jennings Bryan." [64]

The final sale of the Banque Nationale to the Haitian government was not concluded until 1935, by which time, after various

---

* The American manager of the Banque Nationale, Walter Voorhies, told Minister Armour that the offer of sale was intended by Perkins as a gesture to silence critics, such as those writing in the *Nation* and *New Republic,* but that Perkins really intended to hold on to the Banque, which had made a steady return even during the worst years of the Depression. 838.516/275, Norman Armour to Hull, Nov. 15, 1933.

difficulties in obtaining ratification by the Haitian legislature, the transaction included a plan to transfer the functions of American financial supervision to the Banque, which was to be controlled by a board of directors dominated by representatives of the American bondholders.[65] This plan, which proved to be unacceptable to the bondholders, was the last in a series of State Department attempts to reduce the responsibility of the United States government for direct supervision of Haitian finances in fulfillment of obligations to protect the interests of the bondholders. In 1933 Edwin C. Wilson, chief of the Division of Latin American Affairs, noted that the department had rejected various Haitian proposals for continued American financial control because "they would have meant merely supervision over the collection of customs duties in Haiti, with no effective control over the Haitian budget in order to see that expenditures are kept in line with receipts. This is the crux of the problem of maintaining Haiti's finances in healthy condition."

Wilson described the American counterproposal, which became the basis for the subsequent Executive Accord of August 7, 1933, as calling for the replacement of the American financial adviser, whose powers were "exceedingly broad and are exercised over all phases of the Haitian Government's finances," with an American fiscal representative whose powers, according to Wilson, would be much more limited. The fiscal representative would continue to collect customs but would "merely supervise" the Internal Revenue Service and have custody over only those funds necessary for service of the foreign debt. There would be no "broad general grant of powers as under the 1915 treaty" and controls over the Haitian government budget would be limited to those "necessary to see that expenses are kept within the Government's revenues." [66] The department hoped that the new agreement would be more palatable to Haiti and would still contain the essential features of control necessitated by existing obligations to American bondholders.

The Vincent government, itself increasingly bold and under pressure from extreme Haitian nationalists to procure immediate Haitianization and withdrawal of the marines, also wanted to procure necessary American approval for use of cash reserves plus authorization for a new foreign developmental loan and agreed to the American plan for continued financial control in September, 1932.[67]

The Haitian legislature, however, rejected the new treaty by a unanimous vote in an outburst of nationalistic fervor. The United States continued to withhold approval on accelerated Haitianization and advance withdrawal of the marines pending the financial settlement, and in January, 1933, American Minister Norman Armour, who had replaced Munro in October, 1932, reported that it might be possible "to trade our approval of the $400,000 credit now offered for a ratified accord on the question of future financial administration and other pending issues." [68] The department refused to consider the proposed loan project, which never materialized anyhow, until after conclusion of financial negotiations, while Vincent offered to agree to a future financial settlement after the termination of the current obstructive legislative session in return for present American concessions on Haitianization and troop withdrawal. [69] Ultimately the problem of securing ratification from the legislature, which opposed all forms of continued American control, was eliminated by bypassing the legislature entirely, and Vincent and the United States reached a mutually satisfactory agreement embodied in the Executive Accord of August 7, 1933. Under Secretary of State William Phillips wrote President Roosevelt that he was "highly gratified at the successful outcome" of the negotiations and pointed out that the early withdrawal of American marines would "greatly enhance the prestige" of the United States throughout Latin America and would be "a signal example of practical application of your policy of the 'good neighbor.'" [70]

The Accord provided for continued American financial control by a fiscal representative as stipulated in previous American-sponsored versions. The fiscal representative would control customs, inspect the Internal Revenue Service, set limitations on the Haitian government budget, and be able to set up and control reserve funds. The Haitian government was forbidden to increase its indebtedness, change tariffs and taxes, or dispose of investments without his consent. This financial supervision was to continue until all the outstanding bonds, scheduled to expire in 1952, were liquidated. The United States, in turn, agreed to withdraw American troops by October, 1934, one and one half years before the 1936 date stipulated in the 1915 treaty, and to limit the number of Americans employed by the fiscal representative. [71]

President Vincent and his supporters defended the accord as the best possible under the circumstances, but the agreement aroused bitter protests from Haitian nationalists, who considered it a disastrous capitulation that entailed substantial continuation of the control previously exercised by the financial adviser.[72] American critics, such as Ernest Gruening, charged that the accord validated the "old deal" of the State Department acting as a collecting agent for American financial interests.[73] In November, 1933, Vincent, reacting to political dissatisfaction in Haiti and trying to regain his stature as the champion of Haiti's Second Independence, wrote President Roosevelt requesting that the United States give new proof of its Good Neighbor policy by renouncing "useless financial control in Haiti." Roosevelt replied that the United States could not abandon its commitments to American bondholders: "Except for this obligation upon which the bondholders are entitled to insist, my Government would be only too glad to discontinue at once its connection with financial administration in Haiti." [74]

The commitments to the bondholders were moral, not legal; presumably Roosevelt's commitment to withdrawal from Haiti also was a moral one. The issue did not die with the Vincent-Roosevelt exchange. Agitation against the accord continued in the United States and caused Vincent embarrassment at home, since it appeared that American organizations were more active in championing Haitian independence than Vincent was himself. Moreover, the upcoming Seventh Inter-American Conference at Montevideo, Uruguay, held in December, 1933, provided Haiti with a perfect opportunity to apply pressure on the United States for additional concessions. This opportunity was pointed out by Ernest Gruening, himself a member of the American delegation to the conference, in a September, 1933, letter to Dantès Bellegarde, then Haitian minister to Washington.[75]

Secretary of State Hull, en route to the Montevideo Conference on board the S.S. *American Legion,* made a special effort to impress members of other delegations with the nonimperialistic aspects of the United States Good Neighbor policy. Hull later recalled:

I was as much in favor of nonintervention as any of them. I tried to put this point over as emphatically as I could in my preliminary conversations with delegations so that no representatives need feel a desire to line up for a fight against the United States. Several attacks on us did come from Cuban and Haitian delegates, but they were actually not so strong as many had expected.[76]

In wooing the Haitian delegation on the way to Montevideo, Hull made ambiguous oral references to complete withdrawal of American financial control. Justin Barau, head of the Haitian delegation, reported to Vincent that Hull had been disposed to give "full satisfaction" to Haiti and that he recognized that the continued financial control was "unjust," while Hull said that he had told the Haitian delegation "that the American Government would agree to and would welcome an arrangement which would result in withdrawal of American Government action in financial control of Haiti" and that he had instructed the department to inform the Haitian government that a new arrangement was possible.[77]

President Vincent, attempting to assume credit for what appeared to be a great triumph for Haiti, released to local newspapers the diplomatic correspondence from Barau describing Hull's alleged new position along with what purported to be earlier instructions from Vincent to the Haitian delegation to press for new concessions. Haitian newspapers proclaimed the complete liberation of the country, while American Minister Armour was left in the embarrassing position of waiting for supposed instructions from Washington to inform the Haitian government of a new United States desire to change the financial arrangements.[78] Barau soon complained to Hull that Armour had not communicated the promised new proposal, and Hull replied that there was nothing more to say.[79] All the confusion was finally resolved after the Montevideo conference, when Hull made it clear that there were no new concessions and that, while he had reaffirmed the "anxious desire" of the United States "to get released from this special relationship with Haiti," the State Department would do no more than lend moral support to Haitian efforts to secure a refunding loan to cover the remaining $11 million debt to American bondholders. In January, 1934, Hull publicly declared that "When the debts are eliminated, we will immediately pull out. . . . We are just as anxious to withdraw as the Haitians are in wanting us to withdraw." [80]

Given the scarcity of investment capital in the mid-1930s and the unwillingness of the United States government to "extend in any way the period of its financial stewardship," [81] there was little hope for a refunding loan. During the Montevideo discussions Hull had also suggested another possible alternative, that of having National City Bank insure the collection of the outstanding debt through its control of the Banque Nationale.[82] This idea became the basis of the aforementioned 1935 sale of the Banque Nationale to the Haitian government, which included provisions for the transfer of the functions of American financial supervision to the Banque. American bondholders were to be protected by virtue of the fact that their representatives would control the six-man board of directors of the Banque, two of whom were to be selected by the Haitian government, two by National City Bank, and two by the Foreign Bondholders Protective Council. The council, however, refused to cooperate with the plan despite strong urging from the State Department. Francis White, who had formerly played a leading role in shaping United States financial policy in Haiti as assistant secretary of state and was now representing the American bondholders as executive vice-president of the Foreign Bondholders Protective Council, wrote Hull that the new arrangement "would not provide guarantees as satisfactory to the holders of the bonds" as those currently in force.[83] This left the accord of August 7, 1933, in effect and an American fiscal representative continued to supervise Haitian finances until 1941, when his functions were transferred by a new agreement to the fiscal department of the Banque Nationale, which remained under United States supervision until full redemption of the 1922 loan was completed in 1947.

While the United States government's commitments to American bondholders persisted as a source of contention until the bonds were fully paid, the withdrawal of American military and civilian personnel proceeded smoothly according to the Haitianization agreement incorporated in the accord of August 7, 1933. A 1934 Haitian newspaper article stated that in recent years Haitians had grown apathetic to the presence of the marines, who were accepted, though unwelcome.[84] In the accord the United States had agreed to withdraw the last marines in October, 1934. As an extra goodwill gesture, President Roosevelt, on a personal visit to Cap Haïtien in

July, 1934, announced that the last marines would leave by August 15. Roosevelt's visit, and his speech, which was partly in French, created a highly favorable impression in Haiti. It was the first time in Haitian history that the chief of a foreign state had visited the country. Roosevelt's personal graciousness continued to warm Haitian-American relations in subsequent years and he retained a special affection for Haiti. In a 1943 dinner speech on the occasion of a visit by Haitian President Elie Lescot, Roosevelt remarked: "I think it was a certain Queen of England who said that after her death 'Calais' would be written on her heart. When I die, I think 'Haiti' is going to be written on my heart because for all these years I have had the most intense interest in the Republic of Haiti and the development of its people in a way that will never mean exploitation by any other nation." [85] As a final gesture of goodwill in 1934 the United States donated leftover buildings and military equipment valued at $120,000 to the Haitian government.

The ceremony transferring the Garde on August 1 and the departure of the marines on August 15 were dignified and cordial. A crowd of 10,000 applauded wildly as the American flag was lowered, and the marine embarkation was accompanied by cheering, but there were no hostile incidents.[86] A "Festival of the Second Independence" took place on August 21, and President Vincent styled himself the "Second Liberator" in the tradition of Toussaint Louverture and Jean Jacques Dessalines.

12

Epilogue

The series of American military interventions in Caribbean countries that had begun with the landing of United States forces in Cuba in 1898 ended with the termination of the military occupation of Haiti in August, 1934. While the withdrawal of the marines from Haiti reflected a new policy of noninterventionism and Good Neighbor conviviality, the basic objectives of American policy remained unchanged. In 1927 Henry L. Stimson alluded to a special American "Isthmian Policy," distinct from the Monroe Doctrine, which was based upon the "principle of national self-determination": "The national safety of our own country has, however, imposed upon us a peculiar interest in guarding from foreign influence the vital sea route through the Caribbean Sea and the Panama Canal, and therefore in seeing to it that no cause for foreign intervention may arise along the borders of that route." [1]

For the time being, recently established American naval hegemony in the Caribbean barred any immediate foreign military threat, and the United States correspondingly de-emphasized the overt military facets of its presence in favor of achieving more friendly relations with all of Latin America.

The Good Neighbor policy of the 1930s was, in terms of means if not ends, the antithesis of the previous policy of force diplomacy. The occupation of Haiti had been a grave embarrassment to the United States in its efforts to convince Latin-American nations that it was genuinely repudiating Theodore Roosevelt's Big Stick policy, and the memory of the occupation served to cast doubts on subsequent American protestations of respect for the sovereignty and political independence of those nations. Indeed, when situations eventually arose in which the United States decided that its vital interests could not be secured through peaceful means, the nonintervention doctrine was scrapped. The 1961 Bay of Pigs invasion of Cuba, the Johnson Doctrine, and the 1965 marine intervention in the Dominican Republic demonstrated the continuity of the same principles of national security and assumptions of regional hegemony that governed the 1915 marine intervention in Haiti. In 1963, at the expiration of Haitian President François Duvalier's constitutional term of office, a marine expeditionary brigade stood off Port-au-Prince in anticipation of political disorders, which failed to materialize.[2]

Irrespective of the shift to the Good Neighbor policy in the late 1920s and early 1930s, American officials continued to view Haiti as a special United States preserve. In 1932 Minister to Haiti Dana G. Munro, arguing against permitting a new French loan because it would probably lead to either French control or new American intervention, noted that "The Monroe Doctrine is still just as essential as it ever was to our safety and comfort."[3] The United States continued to play a dominant role in Haiti after the withdrawal of the marines, with financial control continuing until 1947 while the American share of the Haitian import trade regained its previous level of 75 percent after a period of decline in the 1930s.[4] After World War II the United States exercised great influence through control of government loans and foreign aid projects.* The American embassy in Port-au-Prince continues to play a major role, many Haitians believe a dominant role, in Haitian internal and external politics.

In view of the international phenomenon of growing disparity in wealth between rich industrial nations and impoverished underdeveloped nations, Haiti profited little from almost twenty years of direct and complete American control. Economic development

* From 1945 to the mid-1960s the United States provided Haiti with $62 million in grants and $33 million in loans. Leslie F. Manigat, *Haiti of the Sixties, Object of International Concern* (Washington: Washington Center of Foreign Policy Research, 1964), p. 19.

was stymied by the mutually exclusive factors of Haiti's lack of natural resources and the prerequisite expectation of lucrative profits insisted upon by American investors and entrepreneurs. In the 1960s low wages, themselves an index of impoverishment, were still the major basis for attracting American capital. American efforts to uplift Haiti through the example of superior moral and technical attainment failed, partly because of racial and cultural barriers which prevented the development of sympathetic relations between Haitians and Americans. American civil service reform, for instance, had little impact. After the occupation, Haitian politics reverted to the "spoils system" whereby successive administrations installed their own partisans in public office.[5]

Even the substantial material accomplishments of the Occupation proved to be largely ephemeral. Notable progress had been made in the fields of sanitation and public health. The Occupation cleaned up the streets and built hospitals and rural health clinics. An American author who investigated various colonial situations stated that the public health services under the Occupation in Haiti compared satisfactorily with those in the British colonies of Kenya, Uganda, British East Africa, and British West Africa, and with the American facilities in Puerto Rico.[6] These facilities, however, were inadequate during the occupation, and with the subsequent swelling of the population became even more so.

Public works projects, such as the construction of bridges, schools, and communications systems, have since fallen into decay. In a recent paper on the impact of the occupation, Marine Colonel Robert D. Heinl, Jr., who served as head of the United States military mission to Haiti from 1958 to 1963, describes the current state of Occupation "infrastructural" achievements as follows:

Telephones are gone. Roads are approaching non-existence. The satellite ports are obstructed by silt and wrecks, their docks crumbling away. Urban improvements are in decay and collapse; sanitation and electrification are, to say the least, in precarious decline. Curiously, the only effective survivor of the occupation's infrastructural benefits is the modest network of grass air-strips which, unchanged since 1934, now provide Haiti with its sole pervasive system of transport—other than the *bourrique* [donkey].[7]

The network of roads, potentially the most significant legacy of the occupation, didn't last long because almost all roads were unpaved and required elaborate maintenance.

The Occupation's policy of retiring the Haitian debt to American bondholders in advance of contract requirements deprived Haiti of surplus revenues which might have been used for development projects during the prosperous 1920s and did not result in any countervailing subsequent advantages. In 1932 former Financial Adviser W. W. Cumberland, who had promoted advance debt retirement during the mid-1920s, remarked:

It seems to me that all of us who have handled Haitian finances have reason for complacence and even a little pride, in view of what has happened elsewhere. . . . Haitian bonds are now selling higher than those of any other Latin American country, I think, with the exception of Cuba. And I predict that Cuba will soon go into default and that Haiti will continue to pay. This is the direct result of our policy of diminishing the debt as rapidly as possible and accumulating generous cash balances.[8]

The excellent record of debt payment may have been a source of great satisfaction to American bondholders, but the alleged benefits to Haiti, in terms of higher credit standing, failed to materialize. Despite the fact that Haiti had an exemplary record of debt payment, Haitian bonds fell to a low of 68¼ on the depressed New York Stock Exchange in 1933, and any residual aura of financial soundness that might have procured favorable loan terms after the world depression was destroyed with the relinquishment of further American financial responsibility.[9] Occupation financial policy, like most facets of the occupation, looked first to American interests. On the positive side, American fiscal reforms strengthened the Banque Nationale and created a sound national currency.

The occupation resulted in a number of important changes in Haitian economic, social, and political life. The century-long isolation of the country from the outside world was rudely terminated as Haiti was drawn into a close relationship, both economic and political, with the United States. American businessmen subsequently played leading roles in local sugar, banana, and sisal industries, and the beginnings of a tourist industry. The use of Port-au-Prince as a liberty port for United States Navy ships brought additional contact with foreigners. Haiti's sisal plantations played a crucial role in supplying naval cordage for the United States military effort during World War II, and the country received substantial American technical assistance in the postwar era.

Politically, the development of the Garde d'Haïti as an efficient military organization plus the building of functioning communications networks resulted in a decisive centralization of Haitian political authority in the aftermath of the occupation. The Garde, conceived of as a nonpartisan peacekeeping force that would dominate politics and ensure orderly constitutional processes, became an instrument of political domination. As in the Dominican Republic and Nicaragua, American-sponsored constabularies fell far short of the nonpartisan ideal but did have the desired effect of stabilizing politics.[10] While the creation of a powerful, centralized military force in Haiti did not result in long-term dictatorships comparable to the Somoza and Trujillo regimes in Nicaragua and the Dominican Republic, political strongmen in Port-au-Prince were able to control the entire country more effectively than ever before. The high degree of centralization under the authoritarian rule of a high commissioner had been based on the Garde and on an extensive government bureaucracy. Under the Americans, Haitian Garde personnel were deliberately shifted from district to district in order to break down local prejudices and associations. Remnants of the centralized governmental institutions and chains of command were taken over by successive Haitian governments. In time the Garde deteriorated along with the roads and telephone system, but the pattern of central political domination persists.

American racism and instances of boorish military dictation spurred the development of a new kind of national and racial pride. The ideology of négritude, a direct reaction to white American domination, has become an important factor in Haitian politics. President François Duvalier, who as a young man contributed to the black-nationalist literature of the *génération de l'occupation,* changed the national flag from blue and red to black and red, and attempted to establish ties with emerging African nations. Duvalier, self-professed heir to the "black revolution" of 1946, promoted his regime as embodying the victory of the masses over the oligarchy.[11]

The triumph of black politicians after the period of mulatto ascendancy associated with the occupation can itself be partly attributed to forces generated during the occupation. Aside from the obvious impact of négritude, the Occupation contributed to the social mobility which resulted in serious inroads into the privileged position of the elite. Blacks were recruited as soldiers for the Garde and students for the Service Technique. While the Service Technique proved less successful in this respect, the Garde was an important avenue of social mobility for illiterate blacks, who were able to obtain secondary education and opportunity for promotion in the Garde. For the first time education, however limited in scope and purpose, was open to the population at large. Also, the nineteen-year presence of the marine brigade created a progeny of nonelite mulattoes. Since the occupation, a new "brown" middle class, consisting of civil servants, skilled workers, and shopkeepers, has emerged to challenge the previously exclusive position of the elite.[12] The American presence similarly contributed to advances in the emancipation of women. Haitian women had been subject to the Napoleonic Code, with few legal rights and limited social functions; under the stress of the occupation, women took jobs as teachers and secretaries and became active in patriotic political movements.[13]

The occupation also played a significant role in the development of the Marine Corps. With the rapid expansion of the corps during World War II many veterans of Haitian service rose to top ranks, including three who became commandants.

In general the occupation did not directly alter the lives of most Haitians. Financial Adviser Sidney de la Rue reported in 1931 that the Depression was having little effect on the mass of Haitian peasants, who were able to supply their usual wants through subsistence agriculture and were not grievously injured by the decline of marginal cash crops.[14] In the same fashion the occupation failed to work fundamental social and economic changes in the daily lives of the masses. American anthropologist Melville J. Herskovits, who studied the Mirebalais Valley in 1934, noted that "as concerns the inner life of this valley it [the occupation] seems to have passed without any discernible effect."[15] The pessimistic assessments by officials of the occupation in the early 1930s that Haiti had made little fundamental economic or political progress were borne out by subsequent developments. By the mid-1960s Haiti had the lowest life expectancy, the lowest per capita calory intake, the lowest per capita gross national product, the lowest literacy rate (10 percent), and the lowest percentage of children in school of any Latin-American country; [16] the morbid specter of expending population and inadequate food supply envisioned by the Occupation officials was becoming a reality.

Notes

Abbreviations used in the notes are listed below. In addition, military ranks are abbreviated according to common United States military usage: thus, Colonel, United States Marine Corps is abbreviated COL, USMC; and Rear Admiral, United States Navy is abbreviated RADM, USN.

Beach MS
Edward L. Beach, CAPT, USN, "Admiral Caperton in Haiti," unpublished MS, Jan. 13, 1920, National Archives, Naval Records Collection, RG45, Box 850.

CR
U.S., *Congressional Record* (various volumes).

Cumberland MSS
Reminiscences of Dr. William W. Cumberland, 1951, Oral History Research Office, Columbia University.

Daniels MSS
Papers of Josephus Daniels, Library of Congress.

Forbes Commission Papers
Records of the President's Commission for the Study and Review of Conditions in the Republic of Haiti, 1930, National Archives, RG220.

FR
U.S., Department of State, *Papers Relating to the Foreign Relations of the United States* (Washington, various years and volumes).

LC
Library of Congress, Washington, D.C.

Lejeune MSS
Papers of John A. Lejeune, Library of Congress.

MARCORPS HQ Haiti MSS
Haiti MSS, U.S. Marine Corps Headquarters Historical Section, Alexandria, Va.

MARCORPS MUS
U.S. Marine Corps Museum, Quantico, Va.

NA
National Archives, Washington, D.C.

NA, RG45
National Archives, Naval Records Collection, Record Group 45.

NA, RG80
National Archives, General Records of the Department of the Navy, Record Group 80.

NA, RG127
National Archives, Records of the U.S. Marine Corps, Record Group 127.

NYT   *New York Times* (various dates).
RG   Record Group (referring to the Record Groups in the National Archives).
Roosevelt MSS   Papers of Franklin D. Roosevelt, Franklin D. Roosevelt Library, Hyde Park, N.Y.
SD   State Department Decimal File, National Archives, Record Group 59.
Senate Hearings,   U.S. Senate, Inquiry into Occupation and Ad-
1922   ministration of Haiti and Santo Domingo, *Hearings Before a Select Committee on Haiti and Santo Domingo,* 67th Cong., 1st and 2d Sess., 1922.
White MSS   Papers of Francis White, National Archives, General Records of the State Department, Record Group 59.

CHAPTER 1

1. William Appleman Williams, *The Tragedy of American Diplomacy* (New York: Dell Publishing Co., 1962, rev. ed.). Arno J. Mayer, *Politics and Diplomacy of Peacemaking: Containment and Counterrevolution at Versailles, 1918–1919* (New York: Alfred A. Knopf, 1967). N. Gordon Levin, Jr., *Woodrow Wilson and World Politics* (New York: Oxford Univ. Press, 1968).

2. Testimony of Robert P. Hughes, BRIG GEN, USA, before the Senate Committee on the Philippines (1902), quoted in Henry F. Graff (ed.), *American Imperialism and the Philippine Insurrection* (Boston: Little, Brown & Co., 1969), p. 65.

3. Allan Reed Millett, *The Politics of Intervention: The Military Occupation of Cuba, 1906–1909* (Ohio State Univ. Press, 1968), p. 7.

4. See Samuel P. Hays, *Conservation and the Gospel of Efficiency: The Progressive Conservation Movement, 1890–1920* (Cambridge: Harvard Univ. Press, 1959); Gabriel Kolko, *The Triumph of Conservatism* (New York: Free Press, 1963); and Samuel Haber, *Efficiency and Uplift: Scientific Management in the Progressive Era, 1890–1920* (Chicago: Univ. of Chicago Press, 1964).

5. See Roland Sarti, "Fascist Modernization in Italy: Traditional or Revolutionary?" *American Historical Review,* LXXV, No. 4 (April, 1970), 1029–45.

6. Littleton W. T. Waller, COL, USMC, to John A. Lejeune, COL, USMC, Oct. 13, 1915; Lejeune MSS, Container 4.

CHAPTER 2

1. The following discussion of Haiti before 1915 is based largely on secondary sources which are not specifically cited when information is of a general or uncontroversial nature. These sources include C. L. R. James, *The Black Jacobins* (New York: Vintage Books, 1963); James G. Leyburn, *The Haitian People* (New Haven: Yale Univ. Press, 1966); Rayford W. Logan, *Haiti and the Dominican Republic* (New York: Oxford Univ. Press, 1968), and *The Diplomatic Relations of the United States with Haiti: 1776–1891* (Chapel Hill: Univ. of North Carolina Press, 1941); Ludwell Lee Montague, *Haiti and the United States; 1714–1938* (Durham: Duke Univ. Press, 1940); Dana G. Munro, *Intervention and Dollar Diplomacy in the Caribbean; 1900–1921* (Princeton: Princeton Univ. Press, 1964); H. P. Davis, *Black Democracy: The Story of Haiti* (New York: Dial Press, 1928); Louis Morpeau, "Un Dominion intellectuel français: Haïti (1789–1924)," *Revue de l'Amérique latine*, 3e Année, VIII (1924), 332–41; and Leslie F. Manigat, "La Substitution de la prépondérance américaine a la prépondérance française en Haïti au début du XXe siècle: la conjoncture de 1910–1911," *Revue d'histoire moderne et contemporaine* XIV (October–December, 1967), 321–55. There never had been a systematic census of Haitian population or literacy. The above estimates are taken from Carl Kelsey, "The American Intervention in Haiti and the Dominican Republic," *Annals of American Academy of Political and Social Science*, C (March, 1922), 109 ff.

2. Davis, pp. 23–26. Montague, p. 5.

3. James, p. 50.

4. Leyburn, 18n.

5. Generic definition of a plural society by J. S. Furnivall, quoted in H. Hoetink, *The Two Variants of Caribbean Race Relations* (London: Oxford Univ. Press, 1967), p. 91.

6. For a critique of Leyburn's *Haitian People,* see Jean Price-Mars, "Classe ou caste? Etude sur 'The Haitian People' de James G. Leyburn," *Revue de la Société d'Histoire et de Géographie d'Haïti* XIII, No. 46 (July, 1942), 1–50.

7. Jean Price-Mars quoted in O. Mennesson-Rigaud, "Le Rôle du Vaudou dans l'indépendance d'Haïti," *Présence Africaine* (Paris) XVIII–XIX (February–May, 1958), 43–67.

8. Logan, *Haiti and the Dominican Republic,* pp. 96–97. George Séjourné, "Etablissement de la propriété et de la famille au lendemain de l'indépendance," *Revue de la Société d'Historie et de Géographie d'Haïti* VI, No. 17 (January, 1935), 9–32.

9. Melville J. Herskovits, *Life in a Haitian Valley* (New York: Octagon Books, 1964), chaps. iv, xiii. Sidney W. Mintz, "Peasant Markets," *Scientific American*, CCIII, No. 2 (August, 1960), 112 ff.

10. See Logan, *Diplomatic Relations* . . . , pp. 141–51, for a historiographic discussion of the relative importance of various factors leading to the French decision to sell Louisiana.

11. *Ibid.*, pp. 47, 53.

12. Navy Department Memorandum submitted to U.S. Senate, Select Committee on Haiti and Santo Domingo; *Senate Hearings, 1922*, p. 63.

13. Adee quoted in Logan, *Diplomatic Relations* . . . , p. 399.

14. Arthur C. Millspaugh, *Haiti Under American Control: 1915–1930* (Boston: World Peace Foundation, 1931), 18n.

15. Republic of Haiti, *Annual Report of the Financial Adviser-General Receiver, 1926*, p. 32. Referred to hereafter as *Annual Report, Financial Adviser* (various years).

16. Samuel Guy Inman, *Through Santo Domingo and Haiti; A Cruise with the Marines* (New York: Committee on Cooperation in Latin America, 1919?), p. 73.

17. Alfred Nemours, *Ma campagne française* (Port-au-Prince, 1925), p. 261, quoted in Auguste Viatte, *Histoire littéraire de l'Amérique française; des origines a 1950* (Paris: Presses universitaires de France, 1954), p. 429. My translation.

18. Quoted in SD 838.42/-, H. Furniss to Knox, Apr. 30, 1912.

19. "'D' Confidential Tentative Plans for Employment of Naval Forces Stationed in Haitien Ports—Port-au-Prince" (*ca.* July, 1914); NA, RG45, WA-7, Box 631.

20. SD 838.00/1667, J. H. Stabler to W. J. Bryan, May 13, 1914. Roger L. Farnham, vice-president of National City Bank, estimated that 90% of Haitian business was controlled by Germans on the eve of American intervention; *Senate Hearings, 1922*, p. 110.

21. Manigat, *Revue d'histoire moderne et contemporaine*, XIV, 321–55.

22. Davis, p. 151. Munro, p. 326.

23. Testimony of the Reverend L. Ton Evans; *Senate Hearings, 1922*, p. 156. Evans told of a 1911 conversation with a German banker who financed Haitian revolutions from Berlin.

24. Rates of interest were as high as 35%. SD 838.51/283, Furniss to Knox, Sept. 26, 1911; also 838.00/1667, Stabler to Bryan, May 13, 1914.

25. Montague, p. 163.

26. *Ibid.*, p. 172. Max Winkler, *Investments of United States Capital in Latin America* (Boston: World Peace Foundation Pamphlets, XI, No. 6, 1928), 274.

27. Montague, p. 199.

28. *Ibid.*

29. Millspaugh, p. 21.

30. Charles M. DuPuy, "La Compagnie Nationale des Chemins de Fer d'Haïti," *La Revue de l'Association Internationale des Hommes d'Affaires d'Haïti* (Port-au-Prince), 1ere Année, No. 4 (October–November, 1923), 74–78.

31. SD 838.51/81, Speyer & Co. to Huntington Wilson, Aug. 12, 1910.

32. Testimony of Roger L. Farnham, vice-president of National City Bank and president of the National Railway of Haiti; *Senate Hearings, 1922,* pp. 106–7.

33. SD 838.77/399, list of stockholders submitted to the department by Farnham in 1924, attached to W. R. Scott Memorandum, Mar. 30, 1931.

34. Munro, p. 332.

35. "La Substitution de la préponderance américaine a la préponderance française en Haïti au début du XXe siècle: la conjoncture de 1910–1911," *Revue d'histoire moderne et contemporaine* XIV (October–December, 1967), 321–55.

36. SD 838.51/81, Speyer & Co. to Huntington Wilson, Aug. 12, 1910. SD 838.51/72, M. E. Ailes, representing National City Bank, to Knox, June 4, 1910. Also SD 838.51/74, H. M. Hoyt to Huntington Wilson, July 6, 1910.

37. Memorandum "Banque Nationale de la République d'Haïti," submitted to the Forbes Commission by National City Bank on Feb. 12, 1930; Forbes Commission Papers, Box 1.

38. See SD 838.00/1377 for a copy of the 1910 Banque Contract.

39. SD 838.51/198, Hoyt to Knox, Oct. 14, 1910. For a listing of the department's objections, see 838.51/119a, A. A. Adee to American Legation, Port-au-Prince, Oct. 12, 1910.

40. SD 838.51/204, agreement signed by representatives of the American participants in the National Bank of Haiti, addressed to the Secretary of State (Knox), Jan. 10, 1910, and Knox to American participants, Jan. 11, 1911.

41. SD 838.51/240, F. A. Vanderlip to Knox, May 1, 1911. Philip W. Henry to Vanderlip, Nov. 1, 1910; Frank A. Vanderlip Papers, Columbia Univ. Library.

42. See SD 838.51/218, Walter T. Rosen, on behalf of American participants, to Attorney General George W. Wickersham, asking him to prod the State Department for approval of the contract, Dec. 18, 1910.

43. SD 838.51/240, Vanderlip to Knox, May 1, 1911.

44. United Nations, Department of Economic and Social Affairs, *Foreign Capital in Latin America,* Sales No.: 1954, II.G.4 (1954), 6.

45. Winkler, *Investments of United States Capital in Latin America,* p. 275.

CHAPTER 3

1. Testimony of John A. McIlhenny, Financial Adviser-General Receiver of the Republic of Haiti; *Senate Hearings, 1922,* p. 1225.

2. SD 838.51/2393, State Department Press Release, Feb. 10, 1932.

3. Council of the Corporation of Foreign Bondholders, *Forty-Second Annual Report, 1915* (London: Wertheimer, Lea & Co., 1916?), pp. 375–76.

4. Root to H. M. Flagler, Jan. 3, 1905, quoted in Philip C. Jessup, *Elihu Root* (New York: Dodd, Mead & Co., 1938), I, 471.

5. For a description of how the loan-default syndrome led to American intervention in the Dominican Republic, see Melvin M. Knight, *The Americans in Santo Domingo* (New York: Vanguard Press, 1928), pp. v–xi.

6. Knox speech, Apr. 3, 1912; *FR, 1912,* p. 545.

7. *The Messages and Papers of Woodrow Wilson,* ed. Albert Shaw, Vol. I (New York: Review of Reviews Corp., 1924), p. 401.

8. Bryan speech, 1900, quoted in Louis L. Snyder (ed.), *The Imperialism Reader* (Princeton: D. Van Nostrand Co., 1962), p. 401.

9. Arthur S. Link, *Wilson, The New Freedom* (Princeton: Princeton Univ. Press, 1956), p. 329.

10. Bryan speech at banquet given in honor of Uruguayan delegation to the Pan-American Financial Conference, May 27, 1915, enclosed in Bryan letter to Vanderlip, May 27, 1915; Frank A. Vanderlip Papers, Columbia Univ.

11. Arthur S. Link, *Wilson, The Struggle for Neutrality: 1914–1915* (Princeton: Princeton Univ. Press, 1960), p. 498.

12. John H. Allen, "An Inside View of Revolutions in Haiti," *Current History,* XXXII (May, 1930), 325–29.

13. Link, *Wilson, The Struggle for Neutrality,* p. 499. Professor Link says, "In Caribbean policy, therefore, it was a case of the blind leading the blind."

14. Bryan to Walter W. Vick, Receiver General of Customs, Dominican Republic, Aug. 20, 1913, quoted in *NYT,* Jan. 15, 1915, p. 6.

15. SD 838.00/1151a, Bryan to A. Bailly-Blanchard, Mar. 26, 1915; also 838.00/1152, Bailly-Blanchard to Bryan, Mar. 27, 1915. Also Bryan to Wilson, Apr. 3, 1915; NA, Bryan-Wilson Correspondence.

16. Link, *Wilson, The Struggle for Neutrality,* p. 523. Also Munro, *Intervention and Dollar Diplomacy,* pp. 332, 338.

17. Bryan to Wilson, July 1, 1914; NA, Bryan-Wilson Correspondence.

18. Memorandum "Banque Nationale de la République d'Haïti," submitted to the Forbes Commission by National City Bank, Feb. 12, 1930; Forbes Commission Papers, Box 1.

19. Office of Naval Intelligence memorandum "The Bank," unsigned, undated, *ca.* 1915, annotated "Confidential, Written by a Naval Officer," by E. H. Durell, CAPT, USN, Commanding Officer, U.S.S. *Connecticut,* in Haitian waters August–September, 1915; NA, RG45, WA-7, Box 631. Also, for assurances given the department by the bankers, see SD 838.51/204, agreement signed by American participants in the National Bank of Haiti, addressed to the Secretary of State (Knox), Jan. 10, 1911.

20. SD 838.77/95, Furniss to Bryan, July 24, 1913. Also 838.51/290, Furniss to Knox, Nov. 7, 1911.

21. SD 838.51/266, Furniss to Knox, Aug. 18, 1911. Also Office of Naval Intelligence memorandum "The Bank"; NA, RG45, WA-7, Box 631.

22. SD 838.51/291, Furniss to Knox, Nov. 9, 1911. Also 838.51/298, Division of Latin American Affairs memorandum, J. A. Doyle to Huntington Wilson, Dec. 28, 1911.

23. O. Ernest Moore, "Monetary-Fiscal Policy and Economic Development in Haiti," *Public Finance,* IX, No. 3 (1954), 230–53. The exchange rate of the gourde rose from 5.63 to the dollar in 1909 to 3.5 gourdes to the dollar in 1912.

24. Office of Naval Intelligence memorandum "The Bank"; NA, RG45, WA-7, Box 631. Also Paul H. Douglas, "The Political History of the Occupation," in Emily G. Balch and others, *Occupied Haiti* (New York: Writers Publishing Co., 1927), pp. 15–36.

25. Joseph Chatelain, *La Banque Nationale; son histoire—ses problèmes* (Port-au-Prince: Collection du Tricinquantenaire de l'indépendance d'Haïti, 1954), p. 105. SD 838.516/50, Solon Menos, Haitian minister to Washington, to Bryan, Jan. 11, 1915. The search was made after $500,000 had been removed from the vaults and taken to New York on the U.S.S. *Machias.*

26. SD 838.51/350, Bailly-Blanchard to Bryan, Aug. 31, 1914.

27. M. R. Smith to Bryan, June 9, 1914; *FR, 1914,* pp. 345–46.

28. Bailly-Blanchard to Bryan, Dec. 24, 1914; *ibid.,* pp. 373–75.

29. SD 838.51/494, unsigned memorandum to Bryan, June 23, 1914.

30. Office of Naval Intelligence memorandum "The Bank"; NA, RG45, WA-7, Box 631.

31. "Confidential Memorandum in Respect to American Interests in the National Bank of Haiti," dictated by Farnham at the State Department, Mar. 27, 1915, enclosed in Bryan to Wilson, Mar. 27, 1915; NA, Bryan-Wilson Correspondence.

32. Munro, p. 332.

33. Farnham, "Confidential Memorandum in Respect to American Interests in the National Bank of Haiti"; NA, Bryan-Wilson Correspondence. Also "Confidential Memorandum Concerning the National Railroad of Haiti," dictated by Farnham at the State Department, Mar. 27, 1915, enclosed in Bryan to Wilson, Mar. 27, 1915; NA, Bryan-Wilson Correspondence. Also SD 838.00/801, Farnham to Bryan, Feb. 3, 1914; 838.00/809, Farnham to Bryan, Feb. 5, 1914; 838.00/933, Farnham to Bryan, June 19, 1914.

34. German investments in Cuba, Haiti, and the Dominican Republic in 1918 amounted to only $1 million. J. Fred Rippy, "German Investments in Latin America," *Journal of Business*, XXI, No. 2 (April, 1948), 63–73.

35. SD 838.00/1667, Stabler to Bryan, May 13, 1914.

36. Farnham, "Confidential Memorandum in Respect to American Interests in the National Bank of Haiti," and "Confidential Memorandum Concerning the National Railroad of Haiti"; NA, Bryan-Wilson Correspondence.

37. Bryan to Wilson, Mar. 27, 1915; NA, Bryan-Wilson Correspondence.

38. *Ibid.* Also testimony of Farnham, *Senate Hearings, 1922,* p. 106.

39. Bryan to Wilson, Apr. 3, 1915; NA, Bryan-Wilson Correspondence.

40. *Ibid.* Wilson to Bryan, Mar. 31, 1915; NA, Bryan-Wilson Correspondence.

41. For a sanguine assessment of Haiti's economic potential as seen by a former governor of West Virginia, see William A. MacCorkle, *The Monroe Doctrine in Its Relation to the Republic of Haiti* (New York: Neale Publishing Co., 1915), pp. 25–26.

42. Bryan to Bailly-Blanchard, Dec. 19, 1914; *FR, 1914,* pp. 370–71.

43. Bryan to Wilson, Apr. 3, 1915; NA, Bryan-Wilson Correspondence.

44. *Ibid.*

45. Bryan to Wilson, June 20, 1913, and Wilson to Bryan, June 23, 1913; NA, Bryan-Wilson Correspondence. Also Bryan to Wilson, June 14, 1913, quoted in Ray Stannard Baker, *Woodrow Wilson, Life and Letters: 1915–1917,* VI (Garden City: Doubleday, Doran & Co., 1937), p. 87.

46. SD 838.00/1668, Stabler memorandum, May 14, 1914.

47. *Ibid.* Also Bryan to Wilson, Apr. 3, 1915; NA, Bryan-Wilson Correspondence.

48. For a discussion of relative naval power in the Caribbean on the eve of World War I, see Montague, *Haiti and the United States,* pp. 181–83, 210–11.

49. Robert Lansing, "Drama of the Virgin Islands Purchase," *NYT,* July 19, 1931, Pt. V, p. 4.

50. SD 838.00/1275A, Lansing to Wilson, Aug. 2, 1915.

51. Lansing memorandum, July 11, 1915, in Robert Lansing, *War Memoirs of Robert Lansing* (New York: Bobbs-Merrill Co., 1935), pp. 19–21. Also Logan, *Haiti and the Dominican Republic,* p. 125.

52. Lansing to Senator Medill McCormick, May 4, 1922; *CR,* 67th Cong., 2d Sess., 1922, LXII, Pt. 6, 6485–88.

53. SD 838.00/2006, Francis White to C. E. Hughes, Apr. 17, 1922.

54. Lansing, *War Memoirs,* p. 310.

55. Lansing memorandum "Present Nature and Extent of the Monroe Doctrine and Its Need of Restatement," June 11 and Nov. 24, 1915; *FR: The Lansing Papers, 1914–1920,* II, 460–70.

56. *Ibid.*

57. Wilson to Lansing, Nov. 29, 1915; *ibid.,* p. 470.

58. Daniels to William Allen White, Feb. 18, 1930; Daniels MSS.

59. For a detailed discussion of State Department activities leading up to armed intervention, see Munro, pp. 333–51.

60. Farnham, "Confidential Memorandum in Respect to American Interests in the National Bank of Haiti"; NA, Bryan-Wilson Correspondence.

61. Banque Nationale de la République d'Haïti to Bryan, Dec. 8, 1914; *FR, 1914,* p. 365. Also Farnham testimony, *Senate Hearings, 1922,* p. 122.

62. Chatelain, *La Banque Nationale,* pp. 105–6.

63. SD 838.00/793, Farnham to Bryan, Jan. 31, 1914.

64. Bryan to Wilson, Mar. 24, 1914, and Wilson to Bryan, Mar. 26, 1914; LC, Wilson Papers.

65. Munro, p. 337. Also SD 838.00/947a, Bryan to L. W. Livingston, July 10, 1914. 838.00/948, Livingston to Bryan, July 12, 1914.

66. Bryan to Bailly-Blanchard, July 2, 1914; *FR, 1914,* pp. 347–50.

67. Bailly-Blanchard to Bryan, Dec. 4, 1914; *ibid.,* p. 363.

68. Bailly-Blanchard to Bryan, Dec. 2, 1914; *ibid.* Also Smith to Bryan, Feb. 28, 1914; *ibid.,* p. 340.

69. Bryan to Bailly-Blanchard, Nov. 12, 1914; *ibid.,* p. 359.

70. SD 838.00/1197, William Phillips memorandum, June 22, 1915.

71. SD 838.51/354, E. V. Haniel von Haimhausen to Phillips, July 25, 1914.

72. SD 838.00/1352, Phillips memorandum of visit of de Laboulaye, secretary of the French Embassy in Washington, July 29, 1915.

73. Bryan to Wilson, Apr. 3, 1915; NA, Bryan-Wilson Correspondence.

74. Munro, pp. 341–42.

75. Lansing to J. H. Oliver, RADM, USN, governor of Virgin Islands, Jan. 30, 1918; LC, Papers of Robert Lansing, quoted in Logan, *Haiti and the Dominican Republic*, p. 126.

76. Girard to Delcassé, Apr. 17, 1915; No. 26. France Aff. Etr. Haïti Pol. Etr. II (1909–18), 94–102, quoted in Manigat, "La substitution de la prépondérance américaine a la prépondérance française . . . ," 323. (My translation.)

77. SD 838.00/1391, Phillips memorandum "Notes and Recommendations on the Political Situation in Haiti," *ca.* Aug., 1915.

CHAPTER 4

1. Radiogram Daniels to U.S.S. *Connecticut,* July 21, 1914; NA, RG45, WA-7, Box 631.

2. "War Portfolio No. 1, Reference No. 5-D: Republic of Haiti," Nov. 9, 1914; NA, RG45, WA-7, Box 636.

3. "Tentative Plans for Employment of Naval Forces Stationed in Haitien Ports—Port-au-Prince," undated, *ca.* July, 1914; NA, RG45, WA-7, Box 633.

4. Office of Naval Intelligence Register No. 4801A, "Haiti and Santo Domingo—Plan of Occupation," October to December, 1914; NA, RG45, WA-7, Box 633.

5. SD 838.00/1426, Stabler to Lansing, Aug. 5, 1915.

6. For an eyewitness account of these events by the secretary of the U.S. legation, see R. B. Davis, Jr., to Lansing, Jan. 12, 1916; *FR, 1916,* pp. 310–20. Davis visited the prison after the massacre and saw Sam's body being paraded in the streets. For a defense of Sam, see also Jean Price-Mars, *Ebauches . . . Vilbrun Guillaume-Sam, ce méconnu* (Port-au-Prince: Imp. de l'Etat, 1961).

7. Lansing to Daniels, July 28, 1915; *FR, 1915,* p. 475.

8. Dantès Bellegarde, *L'occupation américaine d'Haïti: ses conséquences morales et économique* (Port-au-Prince: Imp. Chéraquit, 1929), p. 5.

9. *CR,* 71st Cong., 2d Sess., 1929, LXXII, Pt. 1, 910.

10. SD 838.00/1275B, Lansing to Wilson, Aug. 3, 1915.

11. *NYT,* Aug. 14, 1915, p. 3. Also SD 838.00/1226, R. B. Davis to Lansing, July 30, 1915.

12. Report of Operations from July 28 to Aug. 4, 1915, W. B. Caperton, RADM, USN, to Secretary of the Navy (Operations), July 18, 1916; NA, RG45, WA-7, Box 633.

13. Beach MS.

14. Faustin Wirkus and Taney Dudley, *The White King of La Gonave* (New York: Garden City Publishing Co., 1931), p. 17. Wirkus, a private in the Marine Corps at the time of the 1915 landings, was subsequently promoted to sergeant and, in this capacity, became the white king of the island of La Gonave in Port-au-Prince Bay.

15. *Ibid.*, pp. 28–29.

16. Caperton to Secretary of the Navy and Commander in Chief, Aug. 19, 1915; *Senate Hearings, 1922*, p. 335.

17. Daniels to Wilson, Aug. 2, 1915; Daniels MSS, Container No. 12, Correspondence Daniels to Wilson, 1911–23.

18. "An Account of the Red Cross Relief Work in Port-au-Prince, Haiti, January to April, 1916," Apr. 30, 1916, by P. A. Surgeon H. A. May, USN; NA, RG45, WA-7, Box 633.

19. Frederick M. Wise, *A Marine Tells It to You* (New York: J. H. Sears & Co., 1929), p. 134.

20. Fred E. McMillen (CAPT, SC, USN), "Some Haitian Recollections," *U.S. Naval Institute Proceedings*, LXII, No. 398 (April, 1936), 522–36.

21. Wise, p. 135.

22. SD 838.00/1275B, Lansing to Wilson, Aug. 3, 1915. SD 838.00/1418, Wilson to Lansing, Aug. 4, 1915.

23. See Daniels to William Allen White, Feb. 18, 1930; Daniels MSS. Daniels states that Wilson personally dictated instructions that were cabled by the Navy Department to Admiral Caperton on Aug. 7, 1915, in which Caperton was ordered to inform the Haitians that the United States intended to retain troops in Haiti only until a firm and stable government was established.

24. Lansing to Wilson, Aug. 9, 1915; *FR: The Lansing Papers, 1914–1920*, II, 524.

25. See "Admiral Caperton in Haiti," by Edward L. Beach, CAPT, USN, referred to herein as Beach MS, submitted to the Historical Section, Office of Naval Intelligence on Jan. 13, 1920, but refused publication by the Navy Department "as containing political matters which it was not desirable to publish." Beach was Caperton's chief of staff and undertook all negotiations with Haitian politicians ashore during the months following the intervention. Beach was in constant communication with "X," a prominent Haitian politician, probably J. N. Leger, whose advice was highly valued by the Americans. Reference to "X"s advice on preventing the election of Bobo is found in a separate, undated memorandum in Beach's handwriting; NA, RG45, WA-7, Box 632. See also Caperton to Daniels, Aug. 2, 1915; *FR, 1915*, pp. 477–78.

26. Beach MS, pp. 98, 140–44.

27. *Ibid.*, p. 129. After having been barred from the Haitian presidency by the Americans, Bobo went to Cuba, where he worked for four years as a medical missionary; G. A. Roberts, president of the Jamaica Conference of the Seventh Day Adventists, to President Harding, June 6, 1921, SD 838.51/1105.

28. SD 838.00/1182, Livingston to Bryan, May 1, 1915.

29. *NYT*, July 29, 1915, p. 4. SD 838.00/1156, Bailly-Blanchard to Bryan, Apr. 6, 1915.

30. Caperton to Daniels, Report of Operations, Aug. 13–19, 1915; NA, RG45, WA-7, Box 636. Also SD 838.00/1275B, Lansing to Wilson, Aug. 3, 1915.

31. Beach MS, pp. 122, 133–34.

32. Undated memorandum in Beach handwriting, *ca.* Aug. 15, 1915; NA, RG45, WA-7, Box 632.

33. Beach memorandum, undated, *ca.* Aug. 15, 1915; NA, RG45, WA-7, Box 635. The United States was no longer interested in acquiring the Môle at this point.

34. See "Memorandum re. Haitien Situation," August, 1915; Frank A. Vanderlip Papers, Columbia Univ., Haiti file. At this time Vanderlip was president of National City Bank, which controlled the Banque Nationale and the National Railway in Haiti.

35. Beach memorandum, Aug. 10, 1915; NA, RG45, WA-7, Box 635.

36. Beach conference with Bobo, Aug. 8, 1915, *ibid.*

37. *Ibid.*

38. Daniels to Caperton, Aug. 10, 1915; *Senate Hearings, 1922*, p. 315. Daniels to William Allen White, Feb. 18, 1930; Daniels MSS.

39. Lansing to Wilson, Aug. 13, 1915; *FR: The Lansing Papers, 1914–1920*, II, 526.

40. Josephus Daniels, "The Problem of Haiti," *Saturday Evening Post*, CCIII, No. 2 (July 12, 1930), 32 ff. Daniels to F. D. Roosevelt, July 15, 1933; Roosevelt MSS, Container OF237.

41. Daniels to W. A. White, Feb. 18, 1930; Daniels MSS, Container 642.

42. Beach memorandum, Aug., 1915; NA, RG45, WA-7, Box 635. Also interview with Harry R. Long, comptroller of the Haitian-American Sugar Co. from 1916 to 1918, Apr. 22, 1967.

43. Censorship Promulgation of Sept. 3, 1915; *Senate Hearings, 1922*, p. 70.

44. Davis to Lansing, Sept. 3, 1915; *FR, 1915*, p. 442.

45. Lansing to Wilson, Aug. 13, 1915; *FR: The Lansing Papers, 1914–1920*, II, 526–27. Lansing to Davis, Aug. 12, 1915; *FR, 1915*, pp. 431–33.

46. Caperton to E. H. Durell, CAPT, USN, Aug. 25, 1915; *Senate Hearings, 1922*, pp. 341–43. Durell was the commander of United States forces at Cap Haïtien.

47. Beach MS, p. 184.

48. B. Danache, *Le Président Dartiguenave et les américains* (Port-au-Prince: Imp. de l'Etat, 1950), pp. 46–47. Danache was Dartiguenave's cabinet secretary. See also Caperton testimony, *Senate Hearings, 1922*, p. 397.

49. R. B. Davis to Lansing, Sept. 29, 1915; *FR, 1915*, pp. 524–25.

50. Caperton testimony, *Senate Hearings, 1922*, p. 401. Caperton to Daniels, Report of Operations for Nov. 18, 1915, dated Nov. 20, 1915; NA, RG45, WA-7, Box 637.

51. Acting Secretary of State F. L. Polk to Davis, Sept. 27 and Oct. 2, 1915; *FR, 1915*, pp. 524–26.

52. Daniels to Caperton, Dec. 31, 1915; *Senate Hearings, 1922*, pp. 405–7.

53. SD 838.51/408a, Lansing to American Legation, Port-au-Prince, Aug. 18, 1915.

54. Caperton testimony, *Senate Hearings, 1922*, pp. 405–7.

55. The treaty, signed Sept. 16, 1915, is reprinted in *FR, 1916*, pp. 328–32.

56. SD 838.00/2484, "Intervention in Haiti," Division of Latin American Affairs memorandum, unsigned, Feb. 11, 1927.

57. Danache, p. 45.

58. Beach to Chief of Naval Operations, June 3, 1916; NA, RG45, WA-7, Box 632.

59. *NYT*, Oct. 6, 1920, p. 2.

60. "Order No. 1" of Aug. 10, 1915, Headquarters Naval Landing Force, Cap Haïtien; NA, RG45, WA-7, Box 634.

61. Conversation of H. F. Bryan with A. T. Ruan, May 8, 1921, Confidential Report, Commander Special Service Squadron (H. F. Bryan) to Chief of Naval Operations, May 10, 1921; NA, RG80, Box 135, File No. 238-8.

62. Waller to John A. Lejeune, COL, USMC, May 15 and July 1, 1916; Lejeune MSS, Container 4.

63. Waller to Butler, July 7, 1916; MARCORPS HQ Haiti MSS, Box 25, quoted in John C. Chapin, "The Marines' Role in the U.S. Occupation of Haiti: 1915–1922," unpublished M.A. thesis, George Washington Univ. (1967), p. 44.

64. Waller to Lejeune, Aug. 26 and Oct. 13, 1915; Lejeune MSS, Container 4.

65. Waller to Lejeune, Aug. 18 and 26, 1915, and July 1, 1916; *ibid.*

66. Danache, pp. 53–54.

67. Waller to Lejeune, July 1, 1916; Lejeune MSS, Container 4.

68. Butler to Thomas S. Butler, July 15, 1916; Smedley Darlington Butler Papers, MARCORPS MUS.

69. Testimony of Butler, BRIG GEN, USMC; *Senate Hearings, 1922,* p. 517.

70. Butler to Lejeune, July 13, 1916; Lejeune MSS, Container 4.

71. Butler to Lejeune, Aug. 13, 1916; *ibid.* Waller to H. S. Knapp, RADM, USN, U.S. Military Governor of Santo Domingo and Military Representative of the U.S. in Haiti, June 23, 1917; NA, RG45, WA-7, Box 632.

72. Cumberland MSS, pp. 162–63.

CHAPTER 5

1. Undated memorandum fragment by W. B. Caperton, RADM, USN, *ca.* Aug. 1915; NA, RG45, WA-7, Box 635.

2. Report for Nov. 20, 1915, Caperton to Secretary of the Navy (Operations), Dec. 7, 1915, Office of Naval Intelligence Register No. 4326E; NA, RG45, WA-7, Box 634.

3. Caperton personal letter to E. H. Durell, CAPT, USN, Sept. 26, 1915; NA, RG45, WA-7, Box 631.

4. Daniels to Caperton, Sept. 5 and Nov. 20, 1915; *FR, 1915,* pp. 486, 493. Also Daniels to Caperton, Nov. 19, 1915; *Senate Hearings, 1922,* p. 398.

5. *Senate Hearings, 1922,* pp. 399, 451. For the Butler version of the attack on Fort Rivière, see Lowell Thomas, *Old Gimlet Eye: The Adventures of Smedley D. Butler as Told to Lowell Thomas* (New York: Farrar & Rinehart, 1933), pp. 201–8.

6. Chandler Campbell, LT COL, USMC, quoted in unidentified newspaper clipping, Apr. 29, 1931; New York Public Library, Schomburg Collection, Scrapbook "Haiti," Vol. III. See also *NYT,* Apr. 26, 1931, p. 26.

7. Thomas, *Old Gimlet Eye,* p. 195.

8. Eli K. Cole, COL, USMC, personal letter to E. H. Durell, CAPT, USN, Oct. 27, 1915; NA, RG45, WA-7, Box 633.

9. Butler testimony, *Senate Hearings, 1922,* p. 514.

10. James H. McCrocklin, *Garde d'Haïti: 1915–1934* (Annapolis: U.S. Naval Institute, 1956), pp. 92, 145, 187. This work is largely taken from a 1934 official Marine Corps history by Franklin A. Hart, MAJ, USMC, located in MARCORPS HQ Haiti MSS. See *NYT,* Mar. 10, 1969, p. 34.

11. Maurice De Young, "Class Parameters in Haitian Society," *Journal of Inter-American Studies*, I (1959), 449–58.

12. A. S. Williams, LT COL, USMC to Lansing, Dec. 12, 1918; NA, RG127, Records of Adjutant and Inspector's Office, General Correspondence 1913–1932, Box 81.

13. SD 838.105/251, Neville, MAJ GEN, USMC, to Francis White, Aug. 10, 1922.

14. Commandant Marine Corps to Secretary of the Navy, Dec. 2, 1918; NA, RG127, Adjutant and Inspector's Office, General Correspondence L913-32, File No. 1375-20.

15. Josephus Daniels, *The Cabinet Diaries of Josephus Daniels: 1913–1921*, ed. E. David Cronon (Lincoln: Univ. of Nebraska Press, 1963), p. 332.

16. Butler to Lejeune, July 13, 1916; Lejeune MSS, Container 4.

17. Butler testimony, *Senate Hearings, 1922*, p. 516.

18. Butler quoted in the *Nation*, CXXXVI, No. 3524 (Jan. 18, 1933), 49. A. A. Vandegrift, *Once a Marine: The Memoirs of General A. A. Vandegrift*, as told to Robert B. Asprey (New York: W. W. Norton & Co., 1964), p. 49. General Vandegrift, a commandant of the Marine Corps during World War II, served as Butler's adjutant in Haiti.

19. Daily Diary Report, Brigade Commander (Cole), July 3, 1917; NA, RG45, WA-7, Box 632.

20. John H. Craige, *Black Bagdad* (New York: Minton, Balch & Co., 1933), p. 39.

21. Wirkus and Dudley, *The White King of La Gonave*.

22. Inman, *Through Santo Domingo and Haiti*, p. 68.

23. George Marvin, "Healthy Haiti," *World's Work*, XXXIV, No. 1 (May, 1917), 33–51.

24. " 'D' Confidential Tentative Plans for Employment of Naval Forces Stationed in Haitien Ports—Port-au-Prince," *ca.* July, 1914; NA, RG45, WA-7, Box 631.

25. SD 838.00/1275B, Lansing to Wilson, Aug. 3, 1915. McMillen, *U.S. Naval Institute Proceedings*, LXII, No. 398, 524.

26. SD 838.00/1403, Waller to J. B. Wright, May 26, 1916. *New York Herald*, Apr. 29, 1916.

27. Undated report on article appearing in the *Times* (San Juan, Puerto Rico), June 6, 1916; NA, Records of the Bureau of Insular Affairs, RG350, File No. 22843-9.

28. Daily Diary Reports (Cole), Feb. 9 and Mar. 28, 1917; NA, RG45, WA-7, Box 632.

29. Cole personal letter to H. S. Knapp, RADM, USN, Military Governor of Santo Domingo, Apr. 8, 1917; NA, RG45, WA-7, Box 632. SD 838.00/1453, Marston, Office of Civil Administrator, Port-au-Prince, to Cole, Apr. 16, 1917.

30. See, for example, intelligence reports in Confidential File, MARCORPS HQ Haiti MSS, Box 23.

31. English translation of German message from L. Cappel, German minister at Port-au-Prince, to the German Imperial Chancellor, Berlin, via M. Bieler, The Hague, dateline Mar. 31, 1917, intercepted and sent to the State Department by the British Ambassador, June 9, 1917; NA, RG45, WA-7, Box 632.

32. Brigade Commander (Russell) to Office of Naval Intelligence, Feb. 5, 1918; *ibid.* Daily Diary Reports, Brigade Commander (Russell), Dec. 25 and 26, 1917; *ibid.*

33. Butler to John A. Lejeune, BRIG GEN, USMC, June 22, 1917; Smedley Darlington Butler Papers, MARCORPS MUS.

34. Vandegrift, *Once A Marine*, pp. 52–53.

35. Cole to Knapp, Military Governor of Santo Domingo, Apr. 8 and 13 and July 24, 1917; NA, RG45, WA-7, Box 632.

36. McMillen, *U.S. Naval Institute Proceedings*, LXII, No. 398, 525.

37. Butler to John A. McIlhenny, Dec. 31, 1917, and Jan. 29, 1918; Smedley Darlington Butler Papers, MARCORPS MUS.

38. Daily Diary Report, Brigade Commander (Cole), May 12, 1917; NA, RG45, WA-7, Box 632.

39. Dartiguenave Decree of July 24, 1918; *ibid.*, Box 634.

40. Daily Diary Reports, Brigade Commander, Mar. 30, July 20, Aug. 21, and Dec. 22, 1917, Jan. 31, 1918; *ibid.*, Box 632. The American blacklists for World War I included 12 Haitian firms out of a total of 1,019 for all of Latin America; Rippy, *Journal of Business*, XXI, No. 2 (April, 1948), 65.

41. Emily G. Balch (ed.), *Occupied Haiti* (New York: Writers Publishing Co., 1927), 55.

42. SD 838.105/122, "Memorandum Concerning the Replacing of the Present Occupation of Haiti by a Legation Guard," by John H. Russell, *ca.* March, 1919.

43. Brigade Commander to Secretary of the Navy (Operations), July 16, 1919; NA, RG127, Miscellaneous Records, Haiti, Filecase 70.

44. Daily Diary Reports, Brigade Commander (Russell), Jan. 23 and Feb. 21, 1920; NA, RG45, WA-7, Box 632.

45. Message draft, Brigade Commander to Marine Corps Head-

quarters, December, 1920; NA, RG127, Miscellaneous Records, Haiti, Filecase 70. Also copies of the deportation agreements, along with intelligence reports on Germans, *ibid.*

46. Marine Corps Headquarters to Brigade Commander, Dec. 1920; *ibid.*

47. SD 838.00/2382, S. W. Morgan to Kellogg, May 5, 1927.

48. SD 838.011/69, "The New Haitian Constitution of 1918," by F. Mayer, Jan. 3, 1921.

49. For Butler's behind-the-scenes account of American manipulation of the Dartiguenave government and the dissolution of the Assembly, see Thomas, *Old Gimlet Eye*, pp. 214–16.

50. SD 838.011/23, Bailly-Blanchard to Lansing, June 21, 1917.

51. SD 838.00/1675a, Lansing to Wilson, June 23, 1917.

52. Daily Diary Report, Brigade Commander (Cole), June 21, 1917; NA, RG45, WA-7, Box 632.

53. SD 838.011/69, "The New Haitian Constitution of 1918," by Mayer, Jan. 3, 1921.

54. SD 838.011/61, Bailly-Blanchard to Lansing, June 18, 1918.

55. Testimony of Alexander S. Williams, LT COL, USMC; *Senate Hearings, 1922*, pp. 566–68. SD 838.011/57, Bailly-Blanchard to Lansing, May 29, 1918, enclosing Commandant Gendarmerie d'Haiti Circular Letter of May 20, 1918.

56. Brigade Commander (Russell) to Chief of Naval Operations, June 17, 1918; NA, RG45, WA-7, Box 632.

57. Daniels to Roosevelt, July 15, 1933, quoted in D. David Cronon, *Josephus Daniels in Mexico* (Madison: Univ. of Wisconsin Press, 1960), p. 68. At this time Daniels was Roosevelt's ambassador to Mexico.

58. For a copy of the constitution, see *FR, 1918*, pp. 487–502.

59. SD 838.154/4, Bailly-Blanchard to Lansing, Nov. 16, 1918, enclosing report on corvée submitted by Williams, Nov. 9, 1918.

60. Butler to Roosevelt, Dec. 28, 1917, quoted in Frank Freidel, *Franklin D. Roosevelt: The Apprenticeship* (Boston: Little, Brown & Co., 1952), 282n.

61. Knapp to Daniels, Nov. 2, 1920; NA, RG45, WA-7, Box 632.

62. Testimony of A. S. Williams, commandant of the Gendarmerie, 1918–19; *Senate Hearings, 1922*, pp. 555–56. Testimony of Rev. L. Ton Evans; *ibid.*, pp. 164–67. Also SD 838.00/1551, Monsignor F. Kersuzan, Bishop of North Haiti, to Lansing, Sept. 17, 1918.

63. Proclamation of Aug. 22, 1918, quoted in Daily Diary Report, Brigade Commander (Little), Aug. 23, 1918; NA, RG45, WA-7, Box 632.

64. John H. Russell, COL, USMC, to Major General Commandant, Nov. 14, 1918; NA, RG127, Adjutant and Inspector's Office, General Correspondence, 1913–22, Box 243.

65. Major General Commandant (Lejeune) to Secretary of the Navy (Daniels), Nov. 1, 1920; NA, RG 80, File No. 5526-321.

66. Testimony of Albertus W. Catlin, BRIG GEN, USMC; *Senate Hearings, 1922*, pp. 649–69.

67. Report of Hooker to Catlin, Feb. 15, 1919; *ibid.*, pp. 654–55. Testimony of Hooker; *ibid.*, pp. 469–70.

68. Testimony of A. S. Williams, Commandant of the Gendarmerie, 1919; *ibid.*, p. 598.

69. Letter from Peralte to British consul, Port-au-Prince, quoted in Daily Diary Report, Brigade Commander (Catlin), June 25, 1919; NA, RG45, WA-7, Box 632. Also Russell to Barnett, Oct. 17, 1919; *Senate Hearings, 1922*, p. 428.

70. *Ibid.*, p. 1728.

71. Russell to Barnett, Oct. 17, 1919; *Senate Hearings, 1922*, p. 428.

72. Wise, *A Marine Tells It to You*, p. 309.

73. Waller to Lejeune, Oct. 13, 1915; Lejeune MSS, Container 4.

74. Heinl, *Soldiers of the Sea*, p. 242.

75. *Senate Hearings, 1922*, p. 451.

76. Millett, *The Politics of Intervention*, p. 9.

77. Herbert J. Seligmann, "The Conquest of Haiti," *Nation*, CXI, No. 2871 (July 10, 1920), 35–36. Franck, 180. Drake Scottman, "A Marine Remembers Haiti," *Leatherneck*, XXVI, No. 2 (February, 1943), 22 ff.

78. *Senate Hearings, 1922*, pp. 813–932.

79. "Report of investigation of certain irregularities alleged to have been committed by officers and enlisted men in the Republic of Haiti," by T. C. Turner, MAJ, USMC, Nov. 3, 1919; *ibid.*, pp. 461–73.

80. Lejeune to Daniels, Nov. 1, 1920; NA, RG80, File No. 5526-321.

81. *Senate Hearings, 1922*, p. 429.

82. Daniels to W. A. White, Feb. 18, 1930; Daniels MSS, Container 642.

83. H. C. Haines, BRIG GEN, USMC, Adjutant and Inspector of the Marine Corps, to Russell, Brigade Commander, Port-au-Prince, Dec. 24, 1919; NA, RG80, File No. 5526-321:5.

84. Daniels, *Cabinet Diaries*, p. 553.

85. Lejeune to Daniels, Nov. 1, 1920; NA, RG80, File No. 5526-321.

86. For the record of the Mayo court, see *Senate Hearings, 1922*, pp. 1585–1668.

87. Wise, *A Marine Tells It to You*, p. 334.

88. *NYT,* Oct. 14, 1920, p. 1.

89. Barnett to Russell, Oct. 20, 1919; *Senate Hearings, 1922,* pp. 1722–23.

CHAPTER 6

1. One noted Wilson scholar has stated that "Wilson gave only casual attention to the task in Haiti after 1916"; Arthur S. Link, *Wilson, The Struggle for Neutrality; 1914–1915* (Princeton: Princeton Univ. Press, 1960), p. 538.

2. Expeditionary Commander (Cole) to Commander, Cruiser Force, Atlantic Fleet (Knapp), Dec. 17, 1916; NA, RG45, WA-7, Box 632.

3. Commander Cruiser Force (Knapp) to Daniels, Dec. 20, 1916; *ibid.*

4. Chief of Naval Operations to Comander Cruiser Force (Knapp), Jan. 11, 1917; *ibid.*

5. For a detailed account of Roosevelt's visit, see Frank Freidel, *Franklin D. Roosevelt: The Apprenticeship* (Boston: Little, Brown & Co., 1952), pp. 277–83.

6. Daniels to Roosevelt, July 15, 1933; Roosevelt MSS, OF 237.

7. Freidel, p. 283.

8. Roosevelt, "Trip to Haiti and Santo Domingo, 1917," unpublished travel diary; Roosevelt MSS, RG10, Box 155. Armour to Roosevelt, July 7, 1934; Roosevelt MSS, PPF1710. McIlhenny was financial adviser to the Haitian government from 1919 to 1922.

9. H. L. Roosevelt to F. D. Roosevelt, Feb. 17, 1917; Roosevelt MSS, RG10, Box 145.

10. H. L. Roosevelt to F. D. Roosevelt, Feb. 17 and Mar. 24, 1917. H. L. Roosevelt to J. A. McIlhenny, Mar. 4, 1917; *ibid,* Boxes 145, 155.

11. H. L. Roosevelt to F. D. Roosevelt, Feb. 17, 1917; *ibid.,* Box 145.

12. H. L. Roosevelt to F. D. Roosevelt, Mar. 24, 1917; *ibid.,* Box 155.

13. Louis Howe to F. D. Roosevelt, Jan. 16, 1919, quoted in Alfred B. Rollins, Jr., *Roosevelt and Howe* (New York: Alfred A. Knopf, 1962), p. 173.

14. F. D. Roosevelt to McIlhenny, Aug. 11 and Oct. 14, 1922. McIlhenny to Roosevelt, July 13 and Oct. 18, 1922; Roosevelt MSS, Group 14. Also undated McIlhenny proposal, 9 pp., *ibid.*

15. Roosevelt to McIlhenny, Oct. 14, 1922; Roosevelt MSS, Group 14.

16. McIlhenny to Roosevelt, July 13, 1922; *ibid.*

17. SD 838.51/578b, Lansing to A. T. Ruan, financial adviser to Haiti, Dec. 20, 1916.

18. Daily Diary Report, Brigade Commander (Cole), Feb. 27, 1917; NA, RG45, WA-7, Box 632.

19. Daily Diary Report, Brigade Commander (Cole), Feb. 25, 1917; *ibid.* For a copy of the treaty extension, see FR, 1917, pp. 807–8.

20. Woodrow Wilson, "The Mexican Question," *Ladies' Home Journal,* XXXIII, No. 10 (October, 1916), 9.

21. *NYT,* Apr. 26, 1916, p. 11.

22. Daniels to W. A. White, Feb. 18 and 26, 1930; Daniels MSS, Containers 641, 642. Also Daniels, *Saturday Evening Post,* CCIII, No. 2, 32 ff. Also Josephus Daniels, *The Wilson Era: Years of Peace, 1910–1917* (Chapel Hill: Univ. of North Carolina Press, 1944), p. 179.

23. Haitian Minister of Foreign Affairs to Haitian Minister in France, Jan. 22, 1919; *FR, 1919,* II, 314. Dantès Bellegarde, *Pour une Haïti heureuse* (Port-au-Prince: Imp. Chéraquit, 1929), II, 102–5.

24. SD 838.00/1563, American Mission, Paris, to State Department, Mar. 14, 1919.

25. Bailly-Blanchard to Acting Secretary of State, Apr. 5, 1919; *FR, 1919,* II, 330–31. Also SD 838.105/122, "Memorandum Concerning the Replacing of the Present Occupation of Haiti by a Legation Guard," by John H. Russell, COL, USMC, *ca.* March, 1919. Also SD 838.00/1574, Acting Secretary of the Navy (Roosevelt) to Lansing, Mar. 31, 1919.

26. SD 838.00/1569, Acting Secretary of State (Phillips) to Bailly-Blanchard, Mar. 22, 1919. SD 838.00/1568, American Mission, Paris (Lansing), to State Department, Mar. 23, 1919.

27. McIlhenny to Roosevelt, May 2, 1919; Roosevelt MSS, RG10, Box 127.

28. N. T. McLean, SURGEON, USN, to H. S. Knapp, RADM, USN, Aug. 7, 1917; NA, RG45, WA-7, Box 632. Butler to John A. Lejeune, BRIG GEN, USMC, June 22, 1917; Smedley Darlington Butler Papers, MARCORPS MUS.

29. Knapp to Chief of Naval Operations, June 27 and Sept. 9, 1917; NA, RG45, WA-7, Box 632. Knapp to Secretary of the Navy (Daniels), Jan. 10, 1921; NA, RG80, File No. 5526-39:299:1.

30. Testimony of Richard E. Forrest, president of the West Indies Corporation; *Senate Hearings, 1922,* p. 757.

31. Montague, *Haiti and the United States,* p. 225.

32. McIlhenny to Roosevelt, May 2, 1919, and Roosevelt to McIlhenny, May 23, 1919; Roosevelt MSS, RG10, Box 127.

33. Testimony of Roger L. Farnham; *Senate Hearings, 1922,* pp. 115, 120.

34. SD 838.51/911, F. Mayer memorandum, March, 1918. SD 838.00/ 1666, Munro memorandum, Aug. 11, 1920.

35. Defense of the Wilson administration's Haitian policies by Secretary of State Bainbridge Colby, *NYT*, Sept. 21, 1920, p. 16.

36. *NYT*, Aug. 19, 1920, p. 15.

37. Harding speech, Aug. 28, 1920, quoted in *NYT*, Aug. 29, 1920, pt. II, p. 12. *NYT*, Sept. 18, 1920, p. 14.

38. James Weldon Johnson, *Along This Way; The Autobiography of James Weldon Johnson* (New York: Viking Press, 1933), 358–60.

39. For an undocumented inside story explaining the release of the Barnett letter during the heat of the election campaign, see John H. Craige, *Cannibal Cousins* (New York: Minton, Balch & Co., 1934), pp. 84–87. See also testimony of George Barnett, MAJ GEN, USMC; *Senate Hearings, 1922*, pp. 425–34.

40. *Public Ledger* (Philadelphia), *Tribune* (New York), *Eagle* (Brooklyn) quoted in "Probing the Haitian Scandal," *Literary Digest*, LXVII, No. 5 (Oct. 30, 1920), 16–17.

41. *NYT*, Oct. 15, 1920, p. 17. Franck blamed President Wilson and Secretary Daniels for failing to take steps to change the prevailing low value placed on Haitian lives. For a different perspective on the ethos of marine air operations, see Irwin R. Franklyn, *Knights of the Cockpit: A Romantic Epic of the Flying Marines in Haiti* (New York: Dial Press, 1931).

42. SD 838.51/954, McIlhenny to Colby, Sept. 1, 1920, and Colby to McIlhenny, Sept. 4, 1920. See also Marvin, *World's Work*, XXXIV, No. 1 (May, 1917), 33–51. Marvin had been a traveling companion of Franklin D. Roosevelt and McIlhenny during Roosevelt's 1917 tour of Haiti, and was currently unemployed in Haiti.

43. John W. Blassingame, "The Press and American Intervention in Haiti and the Dominican Republic, 1904–1920," *Caribbean Studies*, IX, No. 2 (July, 1969), 27–43.

44. Seligmann, *Nation*, CXI, No. 2871, 35–36. James Weldon Johnson, "Self-Determining Haiti," *Nation*, CXI, Nos. 2878, 2879, 2880, and 2882 (Aug. 28 through Sept. 25, 1920), 4 parts.

45. Blassingame, *Caribbean Studies*, IX, No. 2, 27–43.

46. Johnson, *Along This Way* . . . , 345–58. Georges Sylvain, *Dix années de lutte pour la liberté: 1915–1925* (Port-au-Prince: Editions Henri Deschamps, 195–?), I, 4–6, 76–78, 98–99. Also Danache, *Le Président Dartiguenave et les américains*, pp. 97–102.

47. Gruening to Sylvain, Sept., 1921, quoted in Sylvain, *Dix années* . . . , I, 125–28.

48. Oswald Garrison Villard, *Fighting Years; Memoirs of a Liberal Editor* (New York: Harcourt, Brace & Co., 1939), pp. 478–86. Memoir of the Union Patriotique reprinted in *Nation*, CXII, No. 2916 (May 25, 1921), 751–75.

49. *Ibid.*, No. 2920 (June 22, 1921), 861. For comments on the memoir in the American press, which were generally favorable to the Occupation, see "Haiti Charges Us with Misrule," *Literary Digest*, LXIX, No. 12 (June 18, 1921), 12.

50. Interview with Ernest Angell, counsel representing the Union Patriotique, the Haiti-Santo Domingo Independence Society, and the NAACP before the Senate Inquiry; New York City, July 28, 1970.

51. Secret alliance between Ch. Emmanual Kernizan and Rosalvo Bobo, represented by Marc Raphael Séjour, Paris, Jan. 8, 1921; Boston Public Library, Special Collections (Haiti), Rare Book Department. This was an elaborate alliance providing for mutual support for the presidency, with diplomatic posts going to the losers along with guarantee of presidential succession.

52. For example, intelligence reports on 65 important Haitians in Cap Haïtien, 1921; NA, RG127, Miscellaneous Records (Haiti), Filecase 70.

53. My interview with Senator Ernest Gruening, Washington, D.C., Aug. 4, 1967.

54. Senate Report No. 794, 67th Cong., 2d Sess., 1922, reprinted in *CR*, 67th Cong., 4th Sess., 1923, LXIV, Pt. 2, 1121–31.

55. Medill McCormick, "Our Failure in Haiti," *Nation*, CXI, No. 2891 (Dec. 1, 1920), 615–16.

56. Senate Report No. 794.

57. *Senate Hearings, 1922*, pp. 858–59, 1694–95.

58. Senate Report No. 794.

59. SD 838.00/1825½, McCormick to Hughes, Dec. 14, 1921.

60. Hughes to Denby, Oct. 18, 1921; NA, RG80, File No. 5526-321:37.

61. Interview between John C. Chapin and Dana G. Munro, Feb. 15, 1967; John C. Chapin, "The Marines' Role in the U.S. Occupation of Haiti: 1915–1922," unpublished M.A. thesis, George Washington Univ. (1967), p. 103.

62. John H. Russell, "History of Haiti," unpublished MS (n.d.), 1; MARCORPS MUS, MS File No. 4-50.

63. SD 838.00/1842, Russell memorandum, Oct. 1, 1921.

64. SD 838.105/122, "Memorandum Concerning the Replacing of the Present Occupation of Haiti by a Legation Guard," by Russell, *ca.* March, 1919. U.S., Department of State, *Report of the American High Commissioner at Port-au-Prince, Haiti, 1925.* (Referred to hereafter as *Annual*

Report, High Commissioner, various years.) "Memorandum on the Judicial System of Haiti," by Russell, Mar. 17, 1920; NA, RG80, Box 135, File No. 238-1.

65. Danache, pp. 125–26. Paul Morand, *Hiver caraïbe* (Paris: Ernest Flammarion, ed., 1929), 102–3. W. B. Seabrook, *The Magic Island* (New York: Harcourt, Brace & Co., 1929), p. 148.

66. My interview with Harry R. Long, comptroller of the Haitian-American Sugar Co. from 1916 to 1918 and vice-president of the West Indies Trading Co., Port-au-Prince, from 1918 to 1920; Somerville, N.J., Apr. 22, 1967. Long and other members of the board favored admitting the Swiss. W. Cameron Forbes, "Journal of W. Cameron Forbes," Second Series, III, 1930–34, unpublished journal, pp. 32, 37; LC, W. Cameron Forbes Papers.

67. For Russell's formal instructions, see Hughes to Russell, Feb. 11, 1922; *FR, 1922,* II, 461–66.

68. Arthur C. Millspaugh, "Our Haitian Problem," *Foreign Affairs,* VII, No. 4 (July, 1929), 556–70.

69. SD 883.01/42, Russell to Hughes, Nov. 15, 1924, and J. C. Grew to Russell, Dec. 19, 1924. (883 is the decimal code for Egypt.)

70. *Ibid.*

71. The Earl of Cromer, *Modern Egypt* (London: Macmillan & Co., 1911), p. 4.

72. "Memorandum No. 2," Russell to treaty officials, Brigade Commander, Chargé d'Affaires, and Commandant of the Gendarmerie, Mar. 24, 1922; NA, Records of the Bureau of Insular Affairs, RG350, File No. 26778. "Instruction Memorandum No. 8," Russell to General Receiver of Customs, Apr. 21, 1923; *ibid.* SD 838.51/1555, Russell to Hughes, Apr. 9, 1923. SD 838.105/300, Munro to Francis White, Apr. 26, 1924. Also SD 838.105/319, Russell to Kellogg, Apr. 28, 1927. SD 838.105/317, Russell to Kellogg, Apr. 26, 1927. SD 838.51A/190, W. R. Scott to W. C. Thurston, Feb. 3, 1931. SD 838.51A/154, S. de la Rue to W. R. Castle, May 8, 1929.

73. Millspaugh, *Foreign Affairs,* VII, No. 4, 557–58. For information on Millspaugh's dismissal, see SD 838.51A/190, Scott to Thurston, Feb. 3, 1931, and SD 838.51A/189, Millspaugh to Stimson, Jan. 31, 1931.

74. J. S. Turrill, COL, USMC, to Lejeune, Mar. 14, 1927; Lejeune MSS, Container 4.

75. Dartiguenave's former Cabinet secretary implies that Dartiguenave voluntarily declined reelection and personally selected Borno as his successor, then changed his mind and decided to run, but was prevented from doing so by Russell; Danache, pp. 135–48.

76. For a laudatory description of Borno, plus quotations of his poetry, see Pierre-Louis Damase, *Les mensonges de notre démocratie* (Paris: Imp. des Presses Universitaires de France, 1933).

77. Littleton W. T. Waller, BRIG GEN, USMC, to John A. Lejeune, BRIG GEN, USMC, June 26, 1916; Lejeune MSS, Container 4. SD 838.00/ 1424, Stabler memorandum, Nov. 22, 1916. Daily Diary Report, Brigade Commander (Russell), Nov. 23, 1918; NA, RG45, WA-7, Box 632.

78. References to Mussolini in Clarence K. Streit, "Parting of the Ways Faces Us in Haiti," *NYT*, Mar. 18, 1928, Pt. III, p. 6, and John H. Craige, CAPT, USMC, "Haitian Vignettes," *National Geographic*, LXVI (1934), 435–85. Borno quotes are in Louis Borno, "Problems of Interest to Haiti and the United States," *Bulletin of the Pan American Union*, LX, No. 9 (Sept., 1926), 845–51. Borno Circular of Oct. 8, 1925, is quoted in Raymond Leslie Buell, "The American Occupation of Haiti," *Foreign Policy Association Information Service*, V, No. 15 (Oct. 2, 1929), 387. *Annual Report, High Commissioner, 1928*, pp. 4–6.

79. Millspaugh, chap. iv.

80. Cumberland MSS, pp. 165–69. See also Vilfort Beauvoir, *Le contrôle financier du Gouvernement des Etats-Unis d'Amérique sur la République d'Haïti* (Bordeaux: Imp. Cadoret, 1930), for another incident of Cumberland holding up pay checks.

81. Danache, p. 101.

82. SD 838.105/122, "Memorandum Concerning Replacing of the Present Occupation of Haiti by a Legation Guard," by Russell, *ca.* March, 1919.

83. Pencil draft of Butler letter to J. Butler Wright, State Department, Oct. 13, 1916; Smedley Darlington Butler Papers, MARCORPS MUS.

84. McIlhenny to Roosevelt, May 2, 1919; Roosevelt MSS, RG10, Box 127.

85. McIlhenny to chief, Division of Latin American Affairs (Rowe), July 21, 1920; *FR, 1920*, II, 762–67.

86. SD 838.516/117, Mayer memorandum, Jan. 19, 1918.

87. SD 838.516/105, Bailly-Blanchard to Lansing, Feb. 6, 1918.

88. "Banque Nationale de la République d'Haïti," memorandum submitted to Henry P. Fletcher by National City Bank on Feb. 12, 1930; Forbes Commission Papers, Box 1.

89. SD 838.516/180, Minutes of Conference, Division of Latin American Affairs, Mar. 9, 1922, statement by J. A. McIlhenny. Testimony of H. M. Pilkington, vice-president, American Development Co. of Haiti; *Senate Hearings, 1922*, p. 796.

90. Haitian chargé (Blanchet) to Colby, July 30, 1920, and Bailly-Blanchard to Colby, Aug. 5, 1920; *FR, 1920,* II, 767–71.

91. Colby to Bailly-Blanchard, Aug. 6 and 7, 1920; *ibid.,* pp. 771–72. SD 838.00/1666, "The Present Situation in Haiti," by Munro, Aug. 11, 1920.

92. SD 838.51/1417, Welles to Hughes, Mar. 8, 1922.

93. SD 838.516/180, Minutes of Conference in Latin American Division, Mar. 9, 1922, and Welles to Assistant Secretary of State F. M. Dearing, Mar. 14, 1922.

94. SD 838.516/181, Munro to Welles, Mar. 8, 1922. For a detailed comparison of the two charters, see Marc E. Malval, *La politique financière extérieure de la République d'Haïti depuis 1910* (Paris: Université de Paris, 1932), pp. 75–88.

95. SD 838.51/578½, Wilson to Lansing, Dec. 3, 1916.

96. SD 838.51/628, Division of Latin American Affairs memorandum of Farnham visit, May 24, 1917.

97. SD 838.51/1126, Maumus to McIlhenny, July 1, 1921, and McIlhenny to F. Mayer, July 26, 1921.

98. SD 838.51/1204, Division of Latin American Affairs memorandum, Oct. 21, 1920.

99. SD 838.51/1262, Division of Latin American Affairs memorandum to Welles, Nov. 16, 1921. SD 838.51/1263, Russell (?) to Hughes, April 26, 1922.

100. Hughes to J. C. Dunn, Sept. 28, 1922; *FR, 1922,* II, 514. *New York Journal of Commerce and Commercial Bulletin,* Oct. 10, 1922.

101. See Sténio Vincent, *Outline of Financial History of the Republic of Haiti* (Port-au-Prince: Imp. de l'Etat, 1939), pp. 17–21. Malval, pp. 99–101.

102. SD 838.51/1336, Harding to Hughes, July 31, 1922. 838.51/1323, Frank McIntyre to Maumus, June 16, 1922.

103. SD 838.00/2004, Hughes to Medill McCormick, Feb. 21, 1924. Joseph C. Grew, *Turbulent Era; A Diplomatic Record of Forty Years* (Boston: Houghton, Mifflin Co., 1952), I, 634. Charles Evans Hughes, *Our Relations to Nations of the Western Hemisphere: The Stafford Little Lecture Series for 1928* (Princeton: Princeton Univ. Press, 1928), p. 79.

104. Howard H. Quint and Robert H. Ferrell (eds.), *The Talkative President; The Off-the-Record Press Conferences of Calvin Coolidge* (Amherst: Univ. of Massachusetts Press, 1964), p. 223. Collidge statement of Mar. 13, 1925, *ibid.,* p. 232.

105. *CR,* 67th Cong., 2d Sess., 1922, LXII, Pt. 9, 8974.

CHAPTER 7

1. Paul Reboux, *Blancs et noirs* (Paris: E. Flammarion, ed., 1915), p. 98. Marvin, *World's Work*, XXXIV, No. 1, 47. Marvin visited Haiti before and after the American intervention and observed that by 1917 the previous Haitian attitudes of racial equality and superiority were no longer in evidence and that the people were more subdued.

2. Thomas, *Old Gimlet Eye*, p. 231.

3. *Ibid.*

4. See, for instance, Harry L. Foster, *Combing the Caribbees* (New York: Dodd, Mead & Co., 1929), p. 255. Robert Herrick article in the *New York World,* Apr. 10, 1927; Seabrook, *Magic Island,* pp. 147–48, 156; Frazier Hunt, *The Rising Temper of the East* (Indianapolis: Bobbs-Merrill Co., 1922), p. 192; E. W. Hutter, "A Jim-Crow Situation in Haiti," *Plain Talk* (March, 1929), pp. 349–56; Ernest H. Gruening, "Haiti Under American Occupation," *Century* (April, 1922), pp. 836–45.

5. Testimony of H. M. Pilkington, vice-president and manager, American Development Co. of Haiti; *Senate Hearings, 1922,* p. 794.

6. Gunnar Myrdal, and others, *An American Dilemma* (New York: McGraw-Hill Book Co., 1964), I, 60. Originally published in 1944.

7. Foster, p. 255.

8. Daniels, *Cabinet Diaries . . . ,* p. 553. Harold N. Denny, "Proud Haiti Demands Her Old Freedom," *NYT,* Oct. 9, 1932, Pt. VI, p. 8.

9. Franck, *Roaming Through the West Indies,* p. 118.

10. Gruening, *Century* (April, 1922), pp. 836–45. Also *NYT*, Dec. 22, 1929, p. 20. Also Testimony of Ernest Gruening, *Senate Hearings, 1922,* p. 1220. Also Seabrook, p. 134.

11. Marvin, *World's Work,* XXXIV, No. 1, 51.

12. Harry L. Foster, "That Colorful Black Republic," *Independent,* CXXI, No. 4079 (Aug. 4, 1928), 111–13. Also Danache, *Le Président Dartiguenave . . . ,* p. 65.

13. Edna Taft, *A Puritan in Voodoo-Land* (Philadelphia: Penn Publishing Co., 1938), chap. ii.

14. Hutter, *Plain Talk* (March, 1929), p. 355.

15. SD 838.00/2870, Brigade Commander (R. M. Cutts) to American chargé (S. E. Grummon), Aug. 8, 1930, and Grummon to Stimson, Aug. 14, 1930.

16. Helena Hill Weed, "Fresh Hope for Haiti," *Nation,* CXXX, No. 3376 (Mar. 19, 1930), 342–44. Seabrook, pp. 156–57.

17. *Brigade Manual, 1932* (Port-au-Prince), chap. x; MARCORPS HQ Haiti MSS, Box 30. Secretary of the Navy Daniels to H. S. Knapp,

RADM, USN, May 28, 1918; NA, RG80, File No. 5526-129. Testimony of Rev. L. Ton Evans; *Senate Hearings, 1922*, p. 181. Wise, *A Marine Tells It to You*, p. 334. Clement Wood, "The American Uplift in Haiti," Pt. I, *Crisis*, XXXV, No. 5 (May, 1928), 152 ff. Scottman, *Leatherneck*, XXVI, No. 2, 22 ff.

18. Craige, *Cannibal Cousins*, p. 78. Testimony of H. M. Pilkington; *Senate Hearings, 1922*, p. 794. J. W. Johnson, *Along This Way*, pp. 348–49. Robert Herrick article in the *New York World*, Apr. 10, 1927. K. S. Angell, *New Republic*, XXX, No. 381, 108. Seabrook, p. 24.

19. Cumberland MSS, pp. 163–64.

20. SD 838.00/2402, Lejeune to S. W. Morgan, Sept. 19, 1927.

21. *Brigade Manual, 1932*, chap. x; MARCORPS HQ Haiti MSS, Box 30.

22. Taft, p. 94. See also Weed, *Nation*, CXXX, No. 3376, 343. Seabrook, pp. 156–57.

23. *Ibid.* Also interview with Harry R. Long, comptroller of the Haitian-American Sugar Co., 1916–18, Somerville, N.J., Apr. 22, 1967.

24. Taft, p. 105.

25. Weed, *Nation*, CXXX, No. 3376, 343. Seabrook, p. 139. Rayford W. Logan, "Haiti: The Native Point of View," *Southern Workman* (Hampton Institute), LVIII, No. 1 (January, 1929), 36–40. K. S. Angell, *New Republic*, XXX, No. 381, 108.

26. SD 838.00/2007, Munro memorandum, Jan. 14, 1924. SD 838.4237/48, Russell to Hughes, Dec. 22, 1922. For the Haitian minister's appraisal, see 838.61/63a, Hughes to Coolidge, Dec. 14, 1923. SD 838.4237/50, Harry Daugherty (Attorney General) to Harding, Oct. 7, 1922. SD 838.4237/43, Medill McCormick to Hughes, Oct. 18, 1922, and Hughes to McCormick, Oct. 21, 1922. SD 838.4237/45, Harding to Hughes, Oct. 9, 1922. Padgett, *Journal of Negro History*, XXV, No. 3, 330.

27. Seabrook, p. 128. Wise, pp. 310–12.

28. Seabrook, p. 133.

29. Lothrop Stoddard, *The Rising Tide of Color Against White World-Supremacy* (New York: Charles Scribner's Sons, 1921), pp. 100, 227.

30. Charles E. Chapman, "The Development of Intervention in Haiti," *Hispanic-American Historical Review*, VII (1927), 299–319.

31. "Supplementary Report on Haiti," H. S. Knapp, RADM, USN, to Secretary of the Navy (Denby), Jan. 13, 1921; NA, RG45, WA-7, Box 632.

32. Russell, "A Marine Looks Back on Haiti" (n.d., *ca.* 1934), unpublished MS, pp. 61, 67; MARCORPS MUS, MS File No. 4-50.

33. Wise, *A Marine Tells It to You*, p. 308.

34. SD 838.105/122, "Memorandum Concerning the Replacing of the Present Occupation of Haiti by a Legation Guard," *ca.* March, 1919, by Russell.

35. "Report of the President's Commission for the Study and Review of Conditions in the Republic of Haiti"; *FR, 1930,* III, 217–37.

36. SD 838.00/2373, W. M. Wilson to S. W. Morgan, Aug. 12, 1927.

37. Francis White to Dana G. Munro (American minister to Haiti), Feb. 24, 1932; White MSS, Box 5.

38. SD 838.00/2881, S. E. Grummon to Stimson, Aug. 29, 1930.

39. James Weldon Johnson, "Self-Determining Haiti," Pt. I, *Nation,* CXI, No. 2878 (Aug. 28, 1920), 238. M. McCormick, *Nation,* CXI, No. 2891, 616.

40. SD 838.51/448a, Lansing to Wilson, Dec. 13, 1915. 838.51/449, Wilson to Lansing, Dec. 16, 1915. Also 838.51/1323, Frank McIntyre (chief, Bureau of Insular Affairs) to Maumus, June 16, 1922. Also 838.51/1336, Harding to Hughes, July 31, 1922. See speech by Senator George W. Norris criticizing appointment of McIlhenny as financial adviser; *CR,* 67th Cong., 2d Sess., 1922, LXII, Pt. 9, 8968–69. Norris argued that McIlhenny was a political appointee who had no experience in financial administration and was otherwise unsuited for the job.

41. SD 838.00/2373, W. M. Wilson to Morgan, Aug. 12, 1927, quoted above. Paul H. Douglas, "The American Occupation of Haiti," Pt. II, *Political Science Quarterly,* XLII, No. 3 (1927), 368–96. Hunt, *Rising Temper of The East,* p. 192. Hutter, *Plain Talk* (March, 1929), 349. Franck, *Roaming Through the West Indies,* p. 118.

42. Franck E. Coombs (trade commissioner) to Dr. Julius Klein (director, Bureau of Foreign and Domestic Commerce), Aug. 30, 1922; NA, Records of the Bureau of Foreign and Domestic Commerce, RG151, File No. 430.37.

43. Leyburn, 103n. In response to a 1964 inquiry Leyburn stated that he did not recall what his authority was for making this assertion; Leyburn letter to Ann Hurst, 1964, quoted in Ann Hurst letter to Robert D. Heinl, Jr., COL, USMC (Ret.), June 29, 1964, copy in my possession.

44. SD 838.00/1825½, McCormick to Hughes, Dec. 14, 1921.

45. Ann Hurst, "Southerners to Handle Haitians?" unpublished undergraduate term paper, Wellesley College, May 4, 1964. Ann Hurst letter to Robert D. Heinl, Jr., June 29, 1964, copy in my possession. Hurst based her conclusions on an examination of the *Register of the Commissioned and Warrant Officers of the United States Navy and Marine Corps* for the years in question. There is no comparable publication covering the places of birth and duty stations of enlisted men.

46. *Recruiter's Bulletin* (Marine Corps), VI, No. 9 (November, 1921), 2. Memorandum, Headquarters Eastern Recruiting Division to all districts, Apr. 18, 1924; NA, RG127, General Correspondence, Recruiting, 1924–25, Box 3.

47. SD 838.00/2881, Grummon to Stimson, Aug. 29, 1930.

48. SD 838.42/81, Russell to Stimson, Dec. 3, 1929.

49. Cole to H. S. Knapp, RADM, USN, Military Governor of Santo Domingo, May 17, 1917; *Senate Hearings, 1922*, pp. 1777–85.

50. *Ibid.* Daily Diary Report, Brigade Commander (Cole), Feb. 25, 1917; NA, RG45, WA-7, Box 632.

51. Testimony of Smedley D. Butler, BRIG GEN, USMC; *Senate Hearings, 1922*, 517. Thomas, *Old Gimlet Eye*, p. 240.

52. John Houston Craige, *Black Bagdad* (New York: Minton, Balch & Co., 1933), 133.

53. Supplement to Daily Diary Report, Brigade Commander (Russell), Apr. 4, 1921; NA, RG45, WA-7, Box 632.

54. Francis White to Kellogg, May 10, 1926; Forbes Commission Papers, Box 1, "Elections."

55. Louis Borno, Circulaire aux Préfets, May 19, 1922; *Le Moniteur* (Port-au-Prince), May 20, 1922. Also Damase, *Les Mensonges de notre démocratie*, pp. 155–64.

56. K. S. Angell, *New Republic*, XXX, No. 381, 108.

57. SD 838.00/2881, Grummon to Stimson, Aug. 29, 1930. Danache, 68–69.

58. Danache, p. 69. Cumberland MSS, p. 157.

59. SD 838.00/1825½, McCormick to Hughes, Dec. 14, 1921.

60. Testimony of H. M. Pilkington; *Senate Hearings, 1922*, p. 794.

61. Marthe Oulié, *Les Antilles, filles de France* (Paris: Fasquelle Editeurs, 1935), p. 305

62. Arthur Lescouflair, "Je n'aime pas les américains, mais . . ." *La Plume* (Port-au-Prince), Nov. 6, 1915. Beaugé Bercy, *Les Péripéties d'une démocratie* (Paris: Librairie L. Rodstein, 1941).

63. Lobb, *American Journal of Sociology*, XLVI, No. 1, 33. Murdo J. MacLeod, "The Haitian Novel of Social Protest," *Journal of Inter-American Studies*, IV, No. 2 (April, 1962), 207–21.

64. Lorimer Denis and François Duvalier, "La Civilisation haïtienne; notre mentalité est-elle africaine ou gallo-latine?" *Revue de la Société d'Histoire et de Géographie d'Haïti*, VI, No. 23 (May, 1936), 1–29.

65. Jean-Paul Sartre, "Orphée Noir" in Léopold Sédar-Senghor (ed.), *Anthologie de la nouvelle poésie nègre et malgache* (Paris: Presses Universitaires de France, 1948), pp. ix–xliv.

66. G. R. Coulthard, "The French West Indian Background of 'Négritude,'" *Caribbean Quarterly*, VI, No. 3 (December, 1961), 128–36.

67. Stephen Alexis, *Le Nègre Masqué* (Port-au-Prince: Imp. de l'Etat, 1933), 56–57, 67, 96.

68. Virgile Valcin, *La Blanche Négresse* (Port-au-Prince: Imp. V. Valcin, 1934?).

69. See Jean Brierre's poem "Me revoici Harlem," quoted in Pan American Union, *An Introduction to Haiti*, p. 110. See Maurice Casseus, *Viejo* (Port-au-Prince: Editions La Presse, 1935), for a proletarian novel about Haitian workers being exploited in Cuba. For a biography of a Haitian "engagée" writer of the period, see Bonnard Posy, *Roussan Camille* (Port-au-Prince: Imp. des Antilles, 1962).

70. See Harry L. Foster, "American Haters of Haiti," *Independent*, CXXI, No. 4080 (Aug. 11, 1928), 128–30, for a discussion of the martyr complex attributed to Haitian journalists. Dantès Bellegarde, *Dessalines a parlé* (Port-au-Prince: Société d'Editions et de Librairie, 1948), pp. 21–22. Also Bellegarde speech opposing the Occupation given at the Assembly of the League of Nations, September, 1930, quoted in *La Presse* (Port-au-Prince), Oct. 15, 1930.

71. G. J. O'Shea, chief of Police Office, Port-au-Prince, to Garde d'Haïti, July 6, 1929; NA, RG127, Filecase 251-450.

72. Foster, pp. 144, 254. Franck, p. 116.

73. Vandegrift, p. 58. Harold N. Denny, "Proud Haiti Demands Her Old Freedom," *NYT*, Oct. 9, 1932, Pt. VI, p. 8. "Living and Office Operating Costs in Haiti," June 4, 1927, Bureau of Foreign and Domestic Commerce, Special Circular No. 77; NA, Records of the Bureau of Foreign and Domestic Commerce, RG350, File No. 27843-6. In 1927 four servants cost a total of $31 monthly; Seabrook, p. 10.

74. Rayford W. Logan, "Education in Haiti," *Journal of Negro History*, XV, No. 4 (October, 1930), 401–60.

CHAPTER 8

1. Thomas, *Old Gimlet Eye*, p. 241. Vandegrift, *Once a Marine*, p. 58.

2. *Annual Report, High Commissioner, 1926*, pp. 2–3.

3. SD 838.00/2108, Francis White to Kellogg, Feb. 25, 1925.

4. Bellegarde, *L'Uccupation américaine* . . . , 21n. Bellegarde points out the irony of the Occupation permitting Haitians to vote in constitutional plebiscites while simultaneously arguing that they were too ignorant to choose elected representatives.

5. Ulysses B. Weatherly, "Haiti: An Experiment in Pragmatism," *American Journal of Sociology*, XXXII, No. 3 (November, 1926), 353–66.

6. *Annual Report, Financial Adviser, 1927,* p. 104.

7. Eve E. Sorensen article in *New York World,* Dec. 15, 1929, quoted in *CR,* 71st Cong., 2d Sess., 1929, LXXII, Pt. 1, 913–14.

8. Millspaugh, *Foreign Affairs,* VII, No. 4, 556–70.

9. See, for instance, Sidney W. Mintz, "Peasant Markets," *Scientific American,* CCIII, No. 2 (August, 1960), 112 ff.

10. Charles John Erasmus, "Agricultural Change in Haiti: Patterns of Resistance and Acceptance," *Human Organization,* XI, No. 4 (Winter, 1952), 20–26.

11. Republic of Haiti, *Report of the Receivership of Customs, 1918* (Washington, 1919), p. 52; *ibid.* (1917), p. 36.

12. McCrocklin, *Garde d'Haïti,* p. 122.

13. SD 838.00/2881, Grummon to Stimson, Aug. 29, 1930.

14. For American scrutiny of Haitian payrolls, see Caperton to Waller, Jan. 14, 1916; MARCORPS HQ Haiti MSS, Box 25. Also Vandegrift, p. 52. A notable exception to high American standards of honesty was the 1933 case of the American collector of customs at Port-au-Prince accepting bribes from local merchants; Department of State press release, Apr. 13, 1933; *FR, 1933,* V, 788–89.

15. Beauvoir, *Le Contrôle financier du Gouvernement des Etats-Unis sur la République d'Haïti,* pp. 124–35.

16. Russell to Stimson, Apr. 2, 1929; *FR, 1929,* III, 211–15.

17. Some Haitians contended that the loans were forced on them by the United States; see testimony of Georges N. Leger, U.S., Congress, Senate, Committee on Finance, *Sale of Foreign Bonds or Securities in the United States, Hearings,* 72d Cong., 1st Sess., 1931–32, Pt. 4, 2127–61. The Dartiguenave client-government had refused to pass loan authorizations.

18. Millspaugh, *Haiti Under American Control,* 119–20. Montague, *Haiti and the United States,* p. 245.

19. Protocol between the United States and Haiti, Oct. 3, 1919; *FR, 1919,* II, 347–52.

20. Millspaugh, p. 120.

21. *NYT,* June 23, 1920, p. 21. *New York World,* Feb. 19, 1924. Balch, pp. 44–45. *Annual Report, Financial Adviser, 1927,* pp. 73–74.

22. SD 838.51/1332, Munro memorandum, May 31, 1922. 838.51/1308, McIlhenny to Munro, June 1, 1922. 838.51/1500½, "History of the Haitian Loan Negotiations, 1915–," by Lucile Atcherson, Division of Latin American Affairs, February, 1923.

23. *Ibid.* Also SD 838.51/2801, Harefort Beaumont (Shearman & Sterling, representing National City Bank) to de la Rue, Feb. 8, 1934.

24. U.S., Department of Commerce, Bureau of Foreign and Domestic Commerce, *American Underwriting of Foreign Securities in 1931* (Trade Information Bulletin No. 802), p. 14.

25. U.S., Congress, Senate, Committee on Finance, *Sale of Foreign Bonds or Securities in the United States, Hearings,* 72d Cong., 1st Sess., 1931–32, Pt. I, facing p. 162.

26. SD 838.51/2396, Cumberland to W. R. Scott, Feb. 16, 1932. See also 838.51/2376, Dantès Bellegarde, Haitian minister to Washington, to Stimson, Jan. 15, 1932, commenting on statement made by Charles Mitchell, president of National City Bank, to the Senate Finance Committee to the effect that large profit spreads on Latin-American loans included bribes to Latin-American officials. Bellegarde implied that this might have accounted for exorbitant Series C profits.

27. Malval, *La Politique financière extérieure de la Républic d'Haïti depuis 1910,* p. 97. First National City Bank, successor to National City Bank, informed me in 1967 and again in 1970 that it no longer has records of National City Bank Haiti transactions.

28. Chatelain, *La Banque Nationale,* p. 186.

29. SD 838.516/223, Munro to L. Harrison, Apr. 23, 1924. 838.516/225, C. E. Mitchell to Russell, Jan. 22, 1925. 838.51/1648, Cumberland to Russell, Apr. 12, 1924. National City Bank, as privileged depository for Haitian government funds, paid 2.25% on Haitian deposits totaling $4 million while the National Bank of Commerce offered 3.25% and 3.75%.

30. *FR, 1919,* II, 347–51.

31. SD 838.51/1129, Mitchell to Hughes, Aug. 12, 1921.

32. SD 838.51/1517, Munro to Francis White, Mar. 23, 1923.

33. SD 838.51/1132, Harding to Hughes, Aug. 20, 1921.

34. National City Bank flier on Haitian bonds, 1922; NA, Records of the Bureau of Insular Affairs, RG350, File No. 27770-13.

35. W. W. Cumberland, "Haiti's Foreign Commerce," *Bulletin of the Pan American Union,* LIX, No. 11 (November, 1925), 1133–36.

36. Cumberland MSS, p. 181.

37. Cumberland, *Bulletin of the Pan American Union,* LIX, No. 11, 1133–36. SD 838.51/2254½, Cumberland to W. R. Scott, Apr. 13, 1931.

38. Republic of Haiti, *A Review of the Finances of the Republic of Haiti; 1924–1930,* by S. de la Rue, submitted to the American High Commissioner, Mar. 3, 1930, p. 27. *Annual Report, Financial Adviser, 1927,* p. 95. A portion of the supplemental debt reduction was the result of supplemental amortization requirements stipulated in the three loan contracts; *ibid.* (1930), p. 97. These requirements indicated that conservative, extractive financial policies were intended from the outset.

39. Millspaugh, *Haiti Under American Control*, 125.

40. U.S., Department of State, *Report of the President's Commission . . .* , p. 12.

41. SD 838.51/2254½ Cumberland to Scott, Apr. 13, 1931. Cumberland had himself invested in Haitian bonds.

42. *Annual Report, Financial Adviser, 1927*, p. 104.

43. Republic of Haiti, *A Review of Finances . . .* , p. 28.

44. *Ibid.*, p. 29.

45. Millspaugh, p. 120. My interview with Dana G. Munro, Princeton, N.J., Feb. 28, 1968.

46. Millspaugh, p. 156.

47. *Annual Report, Financial Adviser, 1927*, p. 95. SD 838.00/2440, "Annual Report of the Financial Adviser-General Receiver, 1927."

48. For a clear statement of this hypothesis by a former Assistant Secretary of State, see Huntington Wilson, "The Relation of Government to Foreign Investment," *Annals of the American Academy of Political and Social Science*, LXVIII (November, 1916), 298–311.

49. SD 838.00/1859, Mayer to Welles, Jan. 31, 1921.

50. *Annual Report, Financial Adviser, 1927*, p. 108.

51. SD 838.00/2602, Munro to Francis White, Oct. 26, 1929. See also 838.153C73/23, "Matters in Controversy Between the Haytian American Corporation and the Haitian Government," submitted by the corporation to the Department of State, July 22, 1920, 37 pp.

52. Daniels to Lansing, Feb. 8, 1916; NA, RG45, WA-7, Box 632. SD 838.63/51, Munro to S. K. Hornbeck, Oct. 5, 1922.

53. *Ibid.*, A. N. Young memorandum, Apr. 29, 1923.

54. SD 838.00/1948, Harding to Hughes, June 18, 1923. Harding was referring to a proposed logwood concession. Sinclair Oil interests were notoriously involved in the Teapot Dome scandal.

55. "Wards of the United States: Notes on What Our Country Is Doing for Santo Domingo, Nicaragua, and Haiti," *National Geographic*, XXX (July–December, 1916), 143–77. West India Management and Consultation Co., *Haitian Investigation; Plains of Cul de Sac and Leogane* (New York: May 10, 1916), p. 8.

56. MacCorkle, *The Monroe Doctrine in Its Relation to the Republic of Haiti*, pp. 25–26.

57. West India Management and Consultation Co., *Haitian Investigation*, pp. 26–27. Roger W. Babson article in the *New York Sun*, Sept. 19, 1915.

58. West India Management and Consultation Co., *Haitian Investigation*, p. 26. J. W. DuB. Gould, *General Report on Haiti* (Chicago: P. W.

Chapman, 1916), p. 11. G. Padmore, *Haiti, An American Slave Colony* (Moscow: Centrizdat, 1931), pp. 16–20. "Memorandum in connection with the raising of a subscription by the Patriotic Union," Brigade Command, Port-au-Prince, Jan. 9, 1922; NA, RG127, Miscellaneous Reports, Haiti, Filecase 83.

59. *Annual Report, Financial Adviser, 1930*, p. 117.

60. SD 837.5538/7, Office of Economic Adviser Memorandum, Apr. 23, 1928. Also 838.5637/6MP, M. P. Dunlap to Kellogg, Sept. 10, 1925. Padmore, pp. 24–25.

61. *Senate Hearings, 1922*, pp. 111–12, 749–58, 789–812.

62. Testimony of Roger L. Farnham; *ibid.*, pp. 111–12.

63. Candelon Rigaud, *Promenades dans les campagnes d'Haïti: la Plaine de la Croix des Bouquets dite "Cul-de-Sac," 1789–1928* (Paris: L'Edition Française Universelle, 192?), pp. 189–91. For a comprehensive description of American capital investments, see Winkler, *Investments of United States Capital in Latin America*, pp. 214–16, 274–78. See also H. P. Davis, *Black Democracy*, pp. 282–84.

64. Cleona Lewis, *America's Stake in International Investments* (Washington: Brookings Institution, 1938), p. 590. Wilhelm Koch, *Beiträge zur Landschaftskunde und zur Geschichte der Landschaftsumwandlungen der Republik Haiti* (Hamburg: A. Preilipper, 1937), pp. 58–61. H. P. Davis, *Black Democracy*, p. 282.

65. "Intelligence Monograph on the Republic of Haiti," by First Marine Brigade, Port-au-Prince, Sept. 8, 1930, sections 401-300, 401-400; NA, RG127, Subject File I, Haiti, Filecase 39.

66. H. P. Davis, *Black Democracy*, 2d ed. rev. (1936), p. 282.

67. SD 838.61/21, "Agricultural Survey of Haiti," by O. W. Barrett, 1922.

68. Republic of Haiti, Department of Public Works, *Geology of the Republic of Haiti*, by P. Woodring, John S. Brown, and Wilbur S. Burbank (1924).

69. U.S., Department of Commerce, Bureau of Foreign and Domestic Commerce, *Haiti: An Economic Survey* (Trade Information Bulletin No. 264, 1924), pp. 13–16.

70. *Annual Report, High Commissioner, 1925*, p. 7.

71. C. S. Butler, CAPT, USN, quoted in Cumberland MSS, pp. 209–10.

72. Millspaugh, *Foreign Affairs*, VII, No. 4, 556–70.

CHAPTER 9

1. Note by Russell, undated *ca.* 1920–21; NA, RG127, Miscellaneous Records, Haiti, Filecase 83.

2. SD 838.04/10, Munro to Kellogg, Mar. 18, 1925.

3. Walter Gerling, *Wirschaftsentwicklung und Landschaftswandel auf den west-indischen Inseln Jamaika, Haiti und Puerto Rico* (Freiburg im Breisgau: Verlag Sintermann, 1938), pp. 142–44.

4. See especially monthly reports from the district commander at Les Cayes, 1921, which show constant concern over the welfare of the population and economic development; NA, RG127, Report of Conditions, Haiti, Z No. 1, Filecase 31.

5. See *Annual Report, Financial Adviser, 1928*, p. 76.

6. SD 838.63/52, S. K. Hornbeck memorandum, Sept. 11, 1923. Also 837.5538/7, Office of Economic Adviser memorandum, Apr. 23, 1928.

7. Cumberland MSS, pp. 196–200.

8. SD 838.51A/75, Russell to Kellogg, Dec. 19, 1927.

9. *Ibid.*

10. *Annual Report, Financial Adviser, 1926*, p. 32. Republic of Haiti, *Annual Report of the Fiscal Representative, 1934*, pp. 99–100. The latter document will be referred to hereafter as *Annual Report, Fiscal Representative* (various years).

11. Hughes quoted in *NYT*, Oct. 16, 1924, p. 8.

12. Malval, *La Politique financière extérieure de la Republic d'Haïti depuis 1910*, pp. 67–68, 99–103. Alain Turnier, *Les Etats-Unis et le marché haïtien* (Montreal: Imp. Saint-Joseph, 1955), pp. 308–10.

13. *Annual Report, Fiscal Representative, 1934*, pp. 99–100.

14. Freeman to W. M. Jardine, Secretary of Agriculture, June 25, 1925; NA, Records of the Bureau of Plant Industry, Soils, and Agricultural Engineering, RG45, Correspondence No. 4895.

15. Interview with Dana G. Munro, chief, Division of Latin American Affairs in 1929, Princeton, N.J., Feb. 28, 1968.

16. W. W. Cumberland, "Notable Commercial and Financial Progress in Haiti," *Bulletin of the Pan American Union*, LXI, No. 4 (April, 1927), 316–19. Raymond Leslie Buell, "The American Occupation of Haiti," *Foreign Policy Association Information Service*, V, No. 15 (Oct. 2, 1929), 327–92.

17. United Nations, *Foreign Capital in Latin America*, 102. See also United Nations, Mission of Technical Assistance to Haiti, *Mission to Haiti* (New York, 1949), p. 212.

18. Millspaugh, *Foreign Affairs*, VII, No. 4, 556–70. Also SD 838.52/ German, Russell to Stimson, Jan. 21, 1929.

19. Clarence K. Streit, "Haiti: Intervention in Operation," *Foreign Affairs*, VI, No. 4 (July, 1928), 615–32.

20. SD 838.00/2313, Coolidge to Kellogg, May 3, 1927, *Annual Report,*

Financial Adviser, 1928, p. 76. Rigaud, p. 200. My interview with Harry R. Long, Somerville, N.J., Feb. 3, 1968.

21. SD 838.00/2382, Morgan to Kellogg, May 5, 1927.

22. Georges Séjourné, "Etablissement de la propriété et de la famille au lendemain de l'indépendance," *Revue de la Société d'Historie et de Géographie d'Haïti,* VI, No. 17 (January, 1935), 9–32.

23. Republic of Haiti, Direction générale des travaux publique, *The Public Works of Haiti* (1931), p. 44.

24. SD 838.00/2382, Morgan to Kellogg, May 5, 1927.

25. SD 838.52/87, W. R. Scott to Munro, May 6, 1929.

26. *Annual Report, Financial Adviser, 1928,* p. 76.

27. *CR,* 67th Cong., 2d Sess., 1922, LXII, Pt. 9, 8958.

28. Erasmus, *Human Organization,* XI, No. 4, 20–26.

29. *Annual Report, Financial Adviser, 1927,* p. 53.

30. SD 838.42/68, Scott memorandum of conversation with Freeman, June 28, 1929.

31. Streit, *Foreign Affairs,* VI, No. 4, 615–32. Report of District Commander, Aux Cayes, to chief, Gendarmerie d'Haïti, Sept. 1, 1921; NA, RG127, Report of Conditions, Haiti, Z No. 1, Filecase 31.

32. U.S., Department of State, *Report of the President's Commission . . . ,* p. 7.

33. Colby to Bailly-Blanchard, Sept. 29, 1920; *FR, 1921,* II, 188–90. Samuel Guy Inman, "Hard Problems in Haiti," *Current History,* XIII (1921), 338–42. Buell, *Foreign Policy Association Information Service,* V, No. 15, 364.

34. "Intelligence Monograph on the Republic of Haiti," by the First Marine Brigade, Port-au-Prince, Sept. 8, 1930, sections 204-100, 206-200; NA, RG127, Subject File I, Haiti, Filecase 39.

35. *Annual Report, Financial Adviser, 1927,* p. 83. Also Cumberland, *Bulletin of the Pan American Union,* LXI, No. 4, 316–19.

36. Logan, *Journal of Negro History,* XV, No. 4, 443.

37. U.S., Department of State, *Report of the United States Commission on Education in Haiti, October 1, 1930* (1931), p. 15. Forbes Commission interview with Dr. George F. Freeman, Port-au-Prince, Mar. 13, 1930; Forbes Commission Papers, Box 1.

38. *Annual Report, High Commissioner, 1925,* pp. 6–7.

39. *Ibid.* République d'Haïti, Service Nationale de la Production Agricole et de l'Enseignement Rural, *Rapport Annuel, 1931–1932,* pp. 1–6. SD 838.42/38, conversation B. Thaw with Freeman, Oct. 2, 1926.

40. Logan, *Journal of Negro History,* XV, No. 4, 401–60. *La Presse* (Port-au-Prince), Apr. 25, 1930. Also H. P. Davis, "Haiti After 1936: So

Far Intervention Has Failed," *Outlook,* CLIV, No. 12 (Mar. 19, 1930), 443 ff.

41. Forbes Commission interview with Freeman, Mar. 13, 1930; Forbes Commission Papers, Box 1.

42. SD 838.42/77, Russell to Stimson, Nov. 27, 1929. Eve E. Sorensen article, *New York World,* Dec. 15, 1929, quoted in *CR,* 71st Cong., 2d Sess., 1929, LXXII, Pt. 1, 913–14. Scholarships were $25 per month, so Sorensen was undoubtedly exaggerating their relative munificence, but this was still a very attractive sum.

43. SD 838.4237/64, Freeman speech, Mar. 25, 1925.

44. For enrollment statistics, see SD 838.42/68, Scott memorandum of conversation with Freeman, June 28, 1929.

45. My interview with Munro, Princeton, N.J., Feb. 28, 1968.

46. SD 838.6113/80, Thurston memorandum of conversation with Farnham, Mar. 17, 1931.

47. SD 838.5045/34, Scott memorandum of conversation with Guy Wadsworth, assistant in the Office of the Financial Adviser, Dec. 18, 1929.

48. Logan, *Journal of Negro History,* XV, No. 4, 401–60. Also SD 838.5045/46, Hoover to J. P. Cotton, Jan. 18, 1930. Eve E. Sorensen article in *New York World,* Dec. 15, 1929, quoted in *CR,* 71st Cong., 2d Sess., 1929, LXXII, Pt. I, 913–14. Also SD 838.5045/47, Russell to Cotton, Feb. 4, 1930.

49. SD 838.42 Moton Commission/12, Munro to Cotton, Feb. 20, 1930. My Munro interview, Princeton, N.J., Feb. 28, 1968.

50. SD 838.42 Moton Commission/62, Grummon to Stimson, July 7, 1930.

51. U.S., Department of State, *Eighth Annual Report of the American High Commissioner at Port-au-Prince, Haiti, 1929* (Washington, 1930).

CHAPTER 10

1. *Annual Report, High Commissioner,* 1922–29.

2. Cumberland MSS, pp. 158, 164.

3. *NYT,* Mar. 13, 1927, p. 1, and Mar. 26, 1927, p. 9. Also *Le Moniteur* (Port-au-Prince), Mar. 17, 1927. Grew to Russell, Mar. 9, 1927; *FR, 1927,* III, 81–82.

4. Cumberland MSS, pp. 215–17. See also J. S. Turrill, COL, USMC, to John A. Lejeune, Commandant, Marine Corps, Mar. 14, 1927; Lejeune MSS, Container 4.

5. Wood, *Crisis,* XXXV, No. 5 (May, 1928), 152 ff.

6. SD 838.203/2, "The Use of Military Tribunals in Haiti," by D. G. Munro, Dec. 11, 1929.

7. Russell to Kellogg, Jan. 7, 1926; *FR, 1926,* II, 396.

8. Millspaugh, *Current History,* XXXI, No. 5 (Feb., 1930), 919–26.

9. SD 838.51A/154, de la Rue to W. R. Castle, May 8, 1929.

10. SD 838.00/2319, Russell to Kellogg, May 14, 1927.

11. *Ibid.,* S. W. Morgan to Francis White, June 14, 1927.

12. Russell to Kellogg, June 1, 1927; *FR, 1927,* III, 48–50.

13. Kellogg to Christian Gross, Aug. 16, 1927; *ibid.,* 65–66.

14. SD 838.011/89, W. M. Wilson to Francis White and Morgan, June 27, 1927.

15. *Ibid.*

16. *Annual Report, High Commissioner, 1928,* p. 2.

17. Stimson to Russell, Apr. 11, 1929; *FR, 1929,* III, p. 170. Russell to Stimson, Mar. 14, 1929; *ibid.,* pp. 166–69.

18. SD 838.00/2519½, Munro to Francis White, Apr. 23, 1929. Stimson to Russell, Aug. 22, 1929; *FR, 1929,* III, 171–72. Russell to Stimson, Mar. 14, 1929; *ibid.,* pp. 166–69.

19. SD 838.00/2519½, Munro to White, Apr. 23, 1929.

20. *La Presse* (Port-au-Prince), Nov. 4, 1929, "English Section," translation of Borno circular of Oct. 6, 1929, canceling legislative elections scheduled for Jan. 10, 1930.

21. SD 838.42/40, Russell to the *Nation,* Jan. 24, 1927.

22. Foster, *Independent,* CXXI, No. 4080, 128–30. Wood, *Crisis,* XXXV No. 5, (June, 1928), 152. Bellegarde, *L'Occupation américaine . . . ,* 14n.

23. SD 838.00/2354, Gross to Kellogg, July 13, 1927.

24. Buell, *Foreign Policy Asociation Information Service,* V, No. 15, 385. Also *Le Nouvelliste* (Port-au-Prince), July 4, 1929. See also Arthur Ruhl, "Muzzling Editors in Haiti," *American Mercury,* V, No. 20 (August, 1925), 468–71.

25. File on press censorship, 1916–21; MARCORPS HQ Haiti MSS, Box 28. 838.00/1894, Hughes to Russell, Oct. 4, 1922. Also, 838.00/1999, Munro to Francis White, Dec. 15, 1925.

26. Republic of Haiti, Garde d'Haïti, *Annual Report, 1929,* p. 7. *Le Nouvelliste,* Nov. 8 and 14, 1929. "Student Strike" file; MARCORPS HQ Haiti MSS, Box 29.

27. Forbes Commission interview with Freeman, Mar. 13, 1930; Forbes Commission Papers, Box 1.

28. John H. Russell, "A Marine Looks Back on Haiti," unpublished MS (n.d., *ca.* 1934), 27; MARCORPS MUS, MS File 4-50. *Annual Report, High Commissioner, 1929,* p. 6.

29. *Le Nouvelliste,* Oct. 9–Dec. 4, 1929.

30. Russell to Stimson, Nov. 25, 27, 29, 1929; *FR, 1929,* III, 178–82.

31. Russell to Stimson, Dec. 2 and 3, 1929; *ibid.*, pp. 174, 188.

32. Garde d'Haïti, *Annual Report, 1929*, pp. 7–8.

33. SD 838.5045/37, de la Rue to W. R. Castle, Dec. 10, 1929. See also 838.5045/34, Scott conversation with Guy Wadsworth, Dec. 18, 1929.

34. C. F. Wood to Stimson, Dec. 4, 1929; *FR, 1929*, III, 190. Also SD 838.00/2673, personal letter from Margaret Scoville, Cap Haïtien, to her mother, Dec. 8, 1929. Also 838.5045/12, Russell to Stimson, Dec. 7, 1929. Also "Student Strike" file; MARCORPS HQ Haiti MSS, Box 29.

35. SD 838.5045/21, Brigade Commander to Major General Commandant, Dec. 4, 1929.

36. *Le Nouvelliste,* Dec. 5 and 16, 1929. Republic of Haiti, *Monthly Bulletin,* VI, No. 12 (December, 1929), 1.

37. SD 838.5045/4, Stimson to Russell, Dec. 4, 1929. 838.00/2613, Stimson to Russell, Dec. 5, 1929.

38. SD 838.00/2615A, Stimson to Russell, Dec. 4, 1929.

39. Garde d'Haïti, *Annual Report, 1929*, p. 8.

40. *Annual Report, High Commissioner, 1929*, p. 10. L. J. De Bekker, "The Massacre at Aux Cayes," *Nation,* CXXX, No. 3376 (Mar. 19, 1930), 308–10. Also Russell to Stimson, Dec. 5, 1929; *FR, 1929*, II, 190–91.

41. Account of Lester N. Gillaspey and William T. Myers, privates, USMC, quoted in *New York Telegram,* Dec. 9, 1929, p. 9.

42. *NYT,* Dec. 8, 1929, p. 2.

43. *Ibid.* Also SD 838.5045/6, Russell to Stimson, Dec. 6, 1929, in which Russell added that "Magistrate at Cayes reported whole countryside in revolt." Also SD 838.5045/47, Russell to Cotton, Feb. 4, 1930.

44. De Bekker, *Nation,* CXXX, No. 3376 (March 19, 1930), 308–10.

45. SD 838.5045/45, Cotton to Francis White, Jan. 20, 1930. 838.5045/46, Hoover to Cotton, Jan. 18, 1930. Also SD 838.5045/47, Russell to Cotton, Feb. 4, 1930.

46. *Ibid.*

47. *Nation,* CXXX, No. 3386 (May 28, 1930), 612.

48. Hoover message to Congress, Dec. 3, 1929, quoted in *New York Telegram,* Dec. 3, 1929, p. 8. Alexander De Conde, *Herbert Hoover's Latin-American Policy* (Stanford: Stanford Univ. Press, 1951), p. 79.

49. SD 838.00/2627, Stimson to Russell, Dec. 9, 1929.

50. Stimson to Russell, Dec. 9, 1929; *FR, 1929*, III, 198–99.

51. *NYT,* Dec. 13, 1929, p. 13.

52. Russell to Stimson, Dec. 9, 1929; *FR, 1929*, III, 197–98.

53. SD 838.5045/38, Munro to White, Dec. 26, 1929.

54. SD 838.5045/39, Stimson to Russell, Dec. 31, 1929.

55. *Annual Report, High Commissioner, 1928*, p. 1.

56. *Annual Report, High Commissioner, 1929*, p. 7. See also SD 838.42/74, Russell to Stimson, Nov. 29, 1929.

57. *Annual Report, High Commissioner, 1929*, p. 9.

58. SD 838.00 General Conditions/37, Russell to Stimson, Jan. 7, 1930. Also 838.00/2802, Russell to Stimson, Apr. 19, 1930. Also Russell to Stimson, Feb. 12, 1930; 838.113/19.

59. Russell, "A Marine Looks Back on Haiti," p. 28; MARCORPS MUS, MS File 4–50.

60. For a sampling of over 600 intelligence reports on individual Haitians, see NA, RG127, Filecases 1-250, 66-HE-108-HC, 251-450, 1-JFF-29-LS, 30-PGJ-65-VJ, 6-10-1-6-17-1, 76-JBT P Au P 107-SN, and 81.

61. *NYT*, Dec. 15, 1929, p. 1. See also *New York Telegram*, Dec. 14, 1929, and *Le Nouvelliste*, Dec. 16, 1929.

62. *CR*, 71st Cong., 2d Sess., 1929, LXXII, Pt. 1, 316–18, 677–78, 917. Also *NYT*, Dec. 13 (p. 30) and 19 (p. 3), 1929.

63. Speech by Representative Robert Crosser (D-Ohio), Dec. 18, 1929; *CR*, 71st Cong., 2d Sess., 1929, LXXII, Pt. 1, 910.

64. Speech by Representative George Huddleston (D-Ala.), Dec. 9, 1929; *ibid.*, pp. 317–18.

65. *Ibid.*, pp. 817, 922.

66. "What is News in Haiti?" *Nation*, CXXVI, No. 3282 (June 6, 1928), 627. SD 838.00/2735, L. J. De Bekker to Hoover, Feb. 6, 1930. John H. Craige, CAPT, USMC, had been a Marine publicity officer during World War I. See also letter of Don Glassman published in the *Nation*, CXXX, No. 3390 (June 25, 1930), 734, which states that the Commandant of the Garde (Evans), who served as AP correspondent, was an honest person with previous newspaper experience.

67. "The Hate of Haiti," *Literary Digest*, CIII, No. 12 (Dec. 21, 1929), 6–7. *Baltimore Sun*, Dec. 8, 1929. 1 ff.

68. Speech by Representative Loring M. Black, Jr. (D-N.Y.), Dec. 18, 1929; *CR*, 71st Cong., 2d Sess., 1929, LXXII, Pt. 1, 917.

69. Great Britain, *Parliamentary Debates* (Commons), LXXXI (1920), p. 1938; LXXXIV (1920), p. 1665; LXXXVIII (1920), p. 1170.

70. Samuel Guy Inman, "Imperialistic America," *Atlantic Monthly*, CXXXIV, No. 1 (July, 1924), 107–16.

71. SD 838.00/2041, Sept. 26, 1924 and 838.00/2096, Mar. 29, 1925, from Paris enclosing French newspaper clippings. Also *NYT*, June 21, 1929, p. 1.

72. *NYT*, Dec. 10, 1929, p. 3, and Dec. 11, 1929, p. 4. Also SD 838.00/2684, Norman Armour (Paris) to Stimson, Dec. 12, 1929.

73. *Manchester Guardian*, Dec. 9, 1929, p. 13, quoted in Donald B.

Cooper, "The Withdrawal of the United States from Haiti, 1929–1934," *Journal of Inter-American Studies,* V, No. 1 (January, 1963), 83–101.

74. *Manchester Guardian,* Dec. 10, 1929, enclosed in SD 838.00/2648, Ray Atherton to Stimson, Dec. 10, 1929.

75. SD 838.00/2694, F. P. Hibbard (Bolivia) to Stimson, Jan. 4, 1930. Also 838.00/2716, H. F. Guggenheim (Cuba) to Stimson, Jan. 12, 1930. Also 838.00/2721, H. V. Johnson (Mexico) to Stimson, Jan. 21, 1930. Also 838.00/2723, F. L. Mayer (Peru) to Stimson, Jan. 14, 1930.

76. Hoover quoted in *NYT,* Feb. 5, 1930, p. 1.

CHAPTER 11

1. My interview with Dana G. Munro, chief, Division of Latin American Affairs (1929–30), Princeton, N.J., Feb. 28, 1968. Also SD 838.00/2519½, Munro to Francis White, Apr. 23, 1929.

2. Munro interview, Princeton, N.J., Feb. 28, 1968. The Haitian-American Sugar Co. had been embroiled in a lengthy dispute with treaty officials. See also SD 838.00/2604, Stimson to Russell, Nov. 11, 1929.

3. Walter Johnson, *William Allen White's America* (New York: Henry Holt & Co., 1947), pp. 417–18.

4. "Journal of W. Cameron Forbes, Second Series, III, 1930–1934," p. 3; LC, W. Cameron Forbes Papers (referred to hereafter as Forbes, "Journal").

5. *NYT,* Mar. 1, 1930, p. 2. Also "Report of the President's Commission for Study and Review of Conditions in the Republic of Haiti, 1930," *FR, 1930,* III, 217–37.

6. *Le Nouvelliste* (Port-au-Prince), Mar. 6, 1930, quoted in W. Johnson, *William Allen White's America,* p. 423. See also Forbes, "Journal," Second Series, III, 31.

7. *La Presse* (Port-au-Prince), Mar. 26, 1930.

8. Forbes, "Journal," Second Series, III, 32, 36.

9. SD 838.00 Commission of Investigation/106, Russell to Stimson, Mar. 17, 1930.

10. Forbes Commission interview with Freeman, Mar. 13, 1930; Forbes Commission Papers, Box 1.

11. *Ibid.* SD 838.00 Commission of Investigation/132, "Confidential Memorandum, Steps taken to solve acute political situation in Haiti," by Forbes, Mar. 26, 1930. See also Robert M. Spector, "W. Cameron Forbes in Haiti: Additional Light on the Genesis of the 'Good Neighbor' Policy," *Caribbean Studies,* VI, No. 2 (July, 1966), 28–45.

12. SD 838.00 Commission of Investigation/71, Russell to Stimson, Mar. 7, 1930.

13. Forbes, "Journal," Second Series, III, 29, 40.

14. White quoted in Walter Johnson, *William Allen White's America*, p. 421.

15. SD 838.00/2511, W. R. Scott to Munro, Mar. 29, 1929. Russell to Stimson, Oct. 24, 1929; *FR, 1929*, III, 172–73.

16. SD 838.00 Commission of Investigation/132, Forbes memorandum, Mar. 26, 1930.

17. Intelligence Reports, Secret Agent No. 2 (Paul), Reports No. 20, Jan. 6, 1930, and No. 21, Jan. 12, 1930; MARCORPS HQ Haiti MSS, Box 26.

18. Forbes to Acting Secretary of State J. P. Cotton, Apr. 17, 1930, quoted in Forbes, "Journal," Second Series, III, 87–88.

19. SD 838.00 Commission of Investigation/132, Forbes memorandum, Mar. 26, 1930. Also *NYT*, Mar. 11, 1930, p. 4.

20. SD 838.00 Elections/64, Cotton to Russell, Apr. 14, 1930. Cotton to Russell, Apr. 11, 1930; *FR, 1930*, III, 245–46.

21. U.S., Department of State, *Report of the President's Commission for Study and Review of Conditions in the Republic of Haiti, 1930.* Reprinted in *FR, 1930*, III, 217–37.

22. Forbes, "Journal," Second series, II, 68. Forbes letter to David Gray, Oct. 28, 1931; *ibid.*, pp. 103–6.

23. Forbes, "Journal," Second Series, III, 69, 103–6. Forbes later supported Russell when he was promoted to Commandant of the Marine Corps in 1934; Forbes to David I. Walsh (U.S. senator), Dec. 23, 1933; *ibid.*, p. 124.

24. White to Stimson, July 10, 1930; White MSS, Box 1.

25. *NYT*, Mar. 22, 1930, p. 3.

26. "Report of the President's Commission . . ."; *FR, 1930*, III, 217–37.

27. *Ibid.*

28. SD 838.5045/34, W. R. Scott memorandum of conversation with Guy Wadsworth, assistant in the Office of the Financial Adviser, Dec. 18, 1929.

29. SD 838.00/2636½, Russell to Stimson, May 26, 1930.

30. Russell to Forbes, Mar. 13, 1930; Forbes Commission Papers, Box 4, Russell file. Also SD 838.00/2636½, Russell to Stimson, May 26, 1930.

31. "Report of the President's Commission . . ."; *FR, 1930*, III, 217–37. Forbes, "Journal," Second Series, III, 63.

32. Irwin to Forbes, June 23, 1930, and Forbes to Irwin, Apr. 10, 1930; *ibid.*, 76–80, 98A–98B.

33. Russell, "A Marine Looks Back on Haiti," MARCORPS MUS, MS File 4-50.

34. Report on Captain D. P. Calixte, Garde d'Haiti, by Thomas S. Clarke, MAJ, USMC, Commander, Département du Centre; Clarke to Commandant, Garde d'Haïti, May 9, 1930, MARCORPS HQ Haiti MSS, Box 22, Headquarters Garde d'Haïti file.

35. Goldwert, *The Constabulary in the Dominican Republic and Nicaragua,* p. vii.

36. Frank E. Evans, COL, USMC, "Salient Haitian Facts," *Marine Corps Gazette,* XV, No. 4 (February, 1931), 14 ff. Also SD 838.00/2958, Stimson to W. H. King (U.S. senator), May 8, 1931.

37. Republic of Haiti, *A Review of the Finances of the Republic of Haiti; 1924–1930,* 31–32. SD 838.51A/188, de la Rue to Castle, Jan. 7, 1931.

38. "Memorandum of Conversation with Franklin D. Roosevelt, Monday, January 9 [1933], at Hyde Park, New York," Diary No. 25, Henry L. Stimson Papers, Yale Univ. Library.

39. *Ibid.* See also Henry L. Stimson, *On Active Service in Peace and War* (New York: Harper & Brothers, 1947), p. 184.

40. SD 838.48/53, Russell to Stimson, Apr. 29, 1930. Republic of Haiti, *Monthly Bulletin,* VII, No. 4 (April, 1930), 2–3.

41. SD 838.5045/53, Wood to Stimson, Dec. 27, 1930. Also SD 838.5045/57, Munro to Stimson, Dec. 30, 1930. Also SD 838.5045/62, Scott memorandum, Dec. 31, 1930.

42. SD 838.00 Elections/103, Grummon to Stimson, Oct. 17, 1930.

43. Intelligence Report on Jolibois, entry for Mar. 26, 1934; NA, RG127, Filecase 1-JJF-29-LS, file 1-JJF.

44. Stimson to Munro, Oct. 18, 1930; *FR, 1930,* III, 255–61.

45. Louis McCarty Little, COL, USMC, to Francis White, Mar. 5, 1931; White MSS, Box 12.

46. Munro to Stimson, Dec. 22, 1930; *FR, 1930,* III, 266–73.

47. *NYT,* June 28, 1931, Pt. III, p. 6.

48. *Annual Report, Financial Adviser, 1931,* p. 2.

49. *Ibid.,* pp. 45–46. Also *ibid.* (1932), pp. 2, 23, 25. Also Republic of Haiti, Direction Générale des Travaux Publique, *The Public Works of Haiti* (1931), pp. 49, 58–59.

50. John T. Madden, Marcus Nadler, and Harry C. Sauvain, *America's Experience as a Creditor Nation* (New York: Prentice-Hall, 1937), p. 308.

51. SD 838.51/2364½, "Policy Concerning Financial Control in Haiti," by W. R. Scott, Nov. 19, 1931.

52. Munro to Stimson, Jan. 24, 1931; *FR, 1931,* II, 406–7. Also Munro to Francis White, Jan. 9, 1931; White MSS, Box 14.

53. SD 838.00/2978, Munro to Stimson, June 3, 1931.

54. Stimson to Munro, June 22, 1931; *FR, 1931*, II, 484–85.

55. White to Munro, Mar. 5, 1931; White MSS, Box 5.

56. SD 838.51/2364½, "Policy Concerning Financial Control in Haiti," by Scott, Nov. 19, 1931. The policy change was made in a conference with the Secretary of State on Mar. 11, 1931.

57. Ernest Gruening, "Our 'Disoccupation' of Haiti Fraught With Many Problems," *NYT*, Mar. 29, 1931, Pt. IX, p. 3.

58. SD 838.6463/27, Scott to W. C. Thurston, Oct. 17, 1930.

59. SD 838.77/389, Scott to Thurston, Oct. 28, 1930. Also SD 838.77/393, Munro to Stimson, May 8, 1931. Also SD 838.77/400, Munro to Stimson, Nov. 19, 1931. Also SD 838.77/390, de la Rue to Stimson, Oct. 16, 1930.

60. *Ibid.* Also SD 838.77/393, Munro to Stimson, May 8, 1931. Also SD 838.77/391, D. R. Heath report on Haitian Railways, Nov. 28, 1930. Also Munro to White, Mar. 30, 1932; White MSS, Box 14.

61. SD 838.51/2569, White to Armour, Dec. 8, 1932.

62. "Memorandum by the Chief of the Division of Latin American Affairs," by Edwin C. Wilson, *ca.* Apr. 3, 1933; *FR, 1933*, V, 735–38.

63. SD 838.00/2852, "Conditions in Haiti," conversation between W. W. Lancaster and White, July 17, 1930.

64. SD 838.516/274, J. H. Perkins to Hull, Nov. 10, 1933.

65. Hull to Francis White, June 28, 1935; *FR, 1935*, IV, 724–26.

66. "Haiti," memorandum by E. C. Wilson, Feb. 28, 1933; NA, Records of the U.S. delegation to the Seventh International Conference of American States, 1933, RG43, E190, Box 1, "Survey: Haiti."

67. Armour to Stimson, Nov. 19, 1932; *FR, 1932,* V, 693–94. Munro to Stimson, Sept. 14, 1932, enclosing treaty signed Sept. 3; *ibid.*, pp. 671–78.

68. Armour to Stimson, Jan. 2, 1933; *FR, 1933*, V, 710–13.

69. Stimson to Armour, Jan. 9, 1933; *ibid.*, pp. 713–14. Armour to Hull, June 5, 1933; *ibid.*, pp. 745–46.

70. Phillips to Roosevelt, Aug. 3, 1933; Edgar B. Nixon (ed.), *Franklin D. Roosevelt and Foreign Affairs* (Cambridge, Mass.: Belknap Press, 1969), I, 343.

71. Executive Agreement Series No. 46: Accord of Aug. 7, 1933; *FR, 1933*, V, 755–61.

72. *L'Action Nationale* (Port-au-Prince), Aug. 10, 1933. Armour to Hull, Aug. 9, 1933; *FR, 1933*, V, 762–63. Also SD 838.51/2721, Armour to Hull, Oct. 19, 1933. Emile Cauvin, *Un Désastre; l'accord du 7 août 1933* (Port-au-Prince: Imp. Haïtienne, 1933). L'Imprimerie Haïtienne (ed.),

Pour l'histoire (Port-au-Prince: Imp. Haïtienne, 1934). Also SD 838.51/2747½, G. A. Drew to Hull, Nov. 29, 1933.

73. Ernest Gruening, "At Last We're Getting Out of Haiti," *Nation,* CXXXVIII, No. 3598 (June 20, 1934), 700–1. Also SD 838.51/2750, Harry F. Ward, Secretary, American Civil Liberties Union, to W. Phillips, Dec. 1, 1933.

74. Vincent to Roosevelt, Nov. 16, 1933, and Roosevelt to Vincent, Nov. 29, 1933; *FR, 1933,* V, 764–66, 767–68.

75. Gruening to Bellegarde, Sept. 14, 1933, quoted in Bellegarde, *Dessalines a parlé,* pp. 125–27.

76. Cordell Hull, *The Memoirs of Cordell Hull* (New York: Macmillan Co., 1948), I, 333.

77. SD 838.51/2755, Armour to Hull, Dec. 4, 1933, enclosing Barau to Vincent, Nov. 22, 1933. SD 838.51/2785, Hull to State Department, Dec. 5, 1933. See also Phillips to Armour, Dec. 1, 1933; *FR, 1933,* V, 770–71.

78. SD 838.51/2752 enclosing Haitian newspaper clippings of Dec. 1, 1933. Armour to Acting Secretary of State, Dec. 14, 1933; *FR, 1933,* V, 775–76.

79. SD 838.51/2751½, Barau to Hull, Dec. 5, 1933, and Hull to Barau, Dec. 9, 1933.

80. Hull memorandum of conversation with Albert Blanchet, Haitian minister to Washington, Jan. 27, 1934; LC, Cordell Hull Papers. *NYT,* Jan. 17, 1934, p. 12.

81, Edwin C. Wilson, "Memorandum by the Chief of the Division of Latin American Affairs," *ca.* April 3, 1933; *FR, 1933,* V, 735–38.

82. SD 838.51/2788, Hull to State Department, Nov. 22, 1933.

83. Foreign Bondholders Protective Council, Inc., *Annual Report, 1935* (New York, 1936?), pp. 124, 126. Also SD 838.516/387, White to Hull, July 15, 1935.

84. SD 838.00/3259, Armour to Hull, Aug. 30, 1934, enclosing translation of article from *Le Temps* (Port-au-Prince), Aug. 24, 1934.

85. Roosevelt quoted in Frank Freidel, "The Haitian Pilot Plant," *Politics,* I, No. 2 (March, 1944), 43–45.

86. *NYT,* Aug. 15, 1934, p. 5. Also SD 838.00/3232, Armour to Hull, Aug. 15, 1934.

CHAPTER 12

1. Henry L. Stimson, *American Policy in Nicaragua* (New York: Charles Scribner's Sons, 1927), pp. 108, 115.

2. Robert D. Heinl, Jr., COL, USMC (Ret.), "Haiti: A Case Study in Freedom," *New Republic,* CL, No. 20 (May 16, 1964), 15–21.

3. Munro to Francis White, Mar. 30, 1932; White MSS, Box 14.

4. United Nations, Mission of Technical Assistance to Haiti, *Mission to Haiti*, p. 218.

5. Leslie F. Manigat, *Haiti of the Sixties, Object of International Concern* (Washington: Washington Center of Foreign Policy Research, 1964), p. 27.

6. Buell, *Foreign Policy Association Information Service, V, No. 15* (Oct. 2, 1929), 327–92.

7. Robert Debs Heinl, Jr., COL, USMC (Ret.), "Haiti: Impacts of American Occupation, 1915–1934," unpublished paper presented to faculty seminar at Harvard University Faculty Club, Apr. 18, 1969.

8. SD 838.51/2396, Cumberland to W. R. Scott, Feb. 16, 1932.

9. *Annual Report, Fiscal Representative, 1934*, p. 77.

10. Goldwert, *The Constabulary in the Dominican Republic and Nicaragua*, pp. vi–vii.

11. François Duvalier, *Face au peuple et a l'histoire* (Port-au-Prince: Imp. de l'Etat, 1961), pp. 121–26.

12. Roland Wingfield and Vernon J. Parenton, "Class Structure and Class Conflict in Haitian Society," *Social Forces,* XLIII, No. 3 (May, 1965), 338–47.

13. Madeleine Sylvain Bouchereau, *Haiti et ses femmes* (Port-au-Prince: Imp. "Les Presses Libres," 1957), pp. 79–84. Madeleine G. Sylvain, "The Feminist Movement in Haiti," *Bulletin of the Pan American Union,* LXXIII, No. 6 (June, 1939), 315–21.

14. *Annual Report, Financial Adviser, 1931*, p. 44.

15. Herskovits, *Life in a Haitian Valley*, p. 12.

16. *NYT,* Nov. 25, 1966, p. 11.

Bibliography

Works of a general nature cited in the text are not included in this bibliography but are referred to in the notes.

Books

Alexis, Stephen. *Le Nègre Masqué*. Port-au-Prince: Imprimerie de l'Etat, 1933.

Balch, Emily Greene, and others. *Occupied Haiti*. New York: Writers Publishing Co., 1927.

Bausman, F., and others. *The Seizure of Haiti by the United States*. New York: Foreign Policy Association, 1922.

Beauvoir, Vilfort. *Le Contrôle financier du gouvernement des Etats-Unis d'Amérique sur la république d'Haïti*. Bordeaux: Imprimerie Cadoret, 1930.

Bellegarde, Dantès. *Dessalines a parlé*. Port-au-Prince: Société d'Editions et de Librairie, 1948.

———. *Un Haïtien parle*. Port-au-Prince: Imprimerie Chéraquit, 1934.

———. *L'Occupation américaine d'Haïti: ses conséquences morales et économiques*. Port-au-Prince: Imprimerie Chéraquit, 1929.

———. *Pour une Haïti heureuse*. 2 vols. Port-au-Prince: Imprimerie Chéraquit, 1928–29.

———. *La République d'Haïti et les Etats-Unis devant la justice internationale*. Paris: Librairie de Paris, 1924.

———. *La Résistance haïtienne*. Montreal: Editions Beauchemin, 1937.

Bercy, Beaugé. *Les Péripéties d'une démocratie*. Paris: Librairie L. Rodstein, 1941.

Blanchet, Jules. *Peint par lui-meme*. Port-au-Prince: V. Valcin, Imprimeur, 1937.

Bobo, R. *Pour l'histoire de la révolution haïtienne par le Parti Progressiste*. St. Thomas, D.W.I.: Lightbourn's Press, 1908.

Bouchereau, Madeleine Sylvain-. *Haïti et ses femmes*. Port-au-Prince: Imprimerie "Les Presses Libres," 1957.

Calixte, D. P. *Haiti: Calvary of a Soldier*. New York: Wendell Malliet & Co., 1939.

Cauvin, Emile. *Un Désastre: l'accord du 7 août 1933*. Port-au-Prince: Imprimerie haïtienne, 1933.

Chatelain, Joseph. *La Banque Nationale: son histoire—ses problèmes.* Collection du Tricinquantenaire de l'Independence d'Haïti. Lausanne: Imprimerie Held, 1954.

Craige, John H. *Black Bagdad.* New York: Minton, Balch & Co., 1933.

———. *Cannibal Cousins.* New York: Minton, Balch & Co., 1934.

Damase, Pierre-Louis. *Les Mensonges de notre démocratie.* Paris: Imprimerie des Presses Universitaires de France, 1933.

Danache, B. *Le Président Dartiguenave et les américains.* Port-au-Prince: Imprimerie de l'Etat, 1950.

Davis, Burke. *Marine! The Life of Lt. Gen. Lewis B. (Chesty) Puller, USMC (Ret.).* Boston: Little, Brown & Co., 1962.

Davis, H. P. *Black Democracy.* Rev. ed. New York: Dodge Publishing Co., 1936.

Dohrman, Richard. *The Cross of Baron Samedi.* Boston: Houghton Mifflin Co., 1958.

Fagg, John Edwin. *Cuba, Haiti and the Dominican Republic.* Englewood Cliffs, N.J.: Prentice-Hall, 1965.

Foster, Harry L. *Combing the Caribbees.* New York: Dodd, Mead & Co., 1929.

Franck, Harry A. *Roaming Through the West Indies.* New York: Blue Ribbon Books, 1920.

Franklyn, Irwin R. *Knights in the Cockpit: A Romantic Epic of the Flying Marines in Haiti.* New York: Dial Press, 1931.

Gation, Louis R. E. *Aspects de l'économie et des finances d'Haïti.* Port-au-Prince: Imprimerie du Collège Vertieres, 1944.

Gerling, Walter. *Wirtschaftsentwicklung und Landschaftswandel auf den west-indischen Inseln Jamaika, Haiti und Puerto Rico.* Freiburg im Breisgau: Verlag Sintermann, 1938.

Goldwert, Marvin. *The Constabulary in the Dominican Republic and Nicaragua: Progeny and Legacy of United States Intervention.* Gainesville: Univ. of Florida Press, 1962.

Gould, J. W. DuB. *General Report on Haiti.* Chicago: P. W. Chapman, 1916.

Herskovits, Melville J. *Life in a Haitian Valley.* 1937. Reprint. New York: Octagon Books, 1964.

Hurston, Zora Neale. *Tell My Horse.* New York: J. B. Lippincott Co., 1938.

L'Imprimerie Haïtienne, ed. *Pour l'histoire.* Port-au-Prince: Imprimerie Haïtienne, 1934.

Inman, Samuel Guy. *Through Santo Domingo and Haiti: A Cruise with the Marines.* New York: Committee on Cooperation in Latin America, ca. 1919.

Jolibois, Joseph, fils. *La Doctrine de Monroë*. Port-au-Prince: Imprimerie Aug. A. Héraux, 1932.

Kernisan, Ch. Emmanuel. *La République d'Haïti et le gouvernement démocrate de M. Woodrow Wilson*. Corbeil: Imprimerie Crété, 1919.

Koch, Wilhelm. *Beiträge zur Landschaftskunde und zur Geschichte der Landschaftsumwandlungen der Republik Haiti*. Hamburg: A. Preilipper, 1937.

Kuser, J. Dryden. *Haiti: Its Dawn of Progress after Years in a Night of Revolution*. Boston: Gorham Press, 1921.

Leyburn, James G. *The Haitian People*. 1941. Reprint. New Haven: Yale Univ. Press, 1966.

Logan, Rayford W. *The Diplomatic Relations of the United States with Haiti, 1776–1891*. Chapel Hill: Univ. of North Carolina Press, 1941.

———. *Haiti and Dominican Republic*. New York: Oxford Univ. Press, 1968.

MacCorkle, William A. *The Monroe Doctrine in Its Relation to the Republic of Haiti*. New York: Neale Publishing Co., 1915.

McCrocklin, James H. *Garde d'Haïti*. Annapolis: United States Naval Institute, 1956.

Malval, Marc E. *La Politique Financière extérieure de la République d'Haïti depuis 1910*. Paris: Université de Paris, 1932.

Manigat, Leslie F. *Haiti of the Sixties, Object of International Concern*. Washington: Washington Center of Foreign Policy Research, 1964.

Mars, Jean Price-. *Ainsi parla l'oncle*. Port-au-Prince: Imprimerie de Compiègne, 1928.

———. *De Saint-Domingue à Haïti*. Port-au-Prince: Présence Africaine, 1959.

———. *Ebauches . . . Vilbrun Guillaume Sam, ce méconnu*. Port-au-Prince: Imprimerie de l'Etat, 1961.

———. *Une Etape de l'évolution haïtienne*. Port-au-Prince: Imprimerie "La Presse," ca. 1929.

———. *La Vocation de l'élite*. Port-au-Prince: Imprimerie Edmond Chenet, 1919.

Millett, Allan Reed. *The Politics of Intervention: The Military Occupation of Cuba, 1906–1909*. Columbus: Ohio State Univ. Press, 1968.

Millspaugh, Arthur C. *Haiti under American Control, 1915–1930*. Boston: World Peace Foundation, 1931.

Montague, Ludwell Lee. *Haiti and the United States, 1714–1938*. Durham: Duke Univ. Press, 1940.

Munro, Dana G. *Intervention and Dollar Diplomacy in the Caribbean, 1900–1921*. Princeton: Princeton Univ. Press, 1964.

Nicolas, Hogar. *L'Occupation américaine d'Haïti*. Madrid: Industrias Gráficas España, *ca.* 1954.

Niles, Blair. *Black Haiti*. New York: Grosset & Dunlap, 1926.

Padmore, George. *Haiti, An American Slave Colony*. Moscow: Centrizdat, 1931.

Paret, Timothée. *Dans la mêlée* . . . Paris: Jouve et Cie. 1932.

Posy, Bonnard. *Roussan Camille*. Port-au-Prince: Imprimerie des Antilles, 1962.

Reboux, Paul. *Blancs et noirs*. Paris: E. Flammarion, 1915.

Rigaud, Candelon. *Promenades dans les campagnes d'Haïti: la Plaine de la Croix des Bouquets dite "Cul-de-Sac," 1789–1928*. Paris: L'Edition Française Universelle, *ca.* 1928.

Rodman, Selden. *Haiti: The Black Republic*. New York: Devin-Adair Co., 1954.

Rosemond, Ludovic J. *Le Réveil de la conscience nationale*. Port-au-Prince: Bibliothèque Haïtienne, 1932.

Seabrook, William B. *The Magic Island*. New York: Harcourt, Brace & Co., 1929.

Séjourné, Georges. *Essaie sur le problème économique d'Haïti*. Port-au-Prince: Imprimerie du Séminaire Adventiste, 1948.

Slyvain, Georges. *Dix Années de lutte pour la liberté: 1915–25*. 2 vols. Port-au-Prince: Editions Henri Deschamps, *ca.* 1950.

Taft, Edna. *A Puritan in Voodoo-Land*. Philadelphia: Penn Publishing Co., 1938.

Thomas, Lowell. *Old Gimlet Eye: The Adventures of Smedley D. Butler as Told to Lowell Thomas*. New York: Farrar & Rinehart, 1933.

Turnier, Alain. *Les Etats-Unis et le marché haïtien*. Montreal: Imprimerie Saint-Joseph, 1955.

Valcin, Virgile. *La Blanche Négresse*. Port-au-Prince: Imprimerie V. Valcin, *ca.* 1934.

Vincent, Sténio. *Efforts et résultats*. Port-au-Prince: Imprimerie de l'Etat, 1938.

———. *En posant les jalons* . . . Port-au-Prince: Imprimerie de l'Etat, 1939, 5 vols.

———. *Outline of the Financial History of the Republic of Haiti*. Port-au-Prince. Imprimerie de l'Etat, 1939.

———. *Sur la route de la seconde indépendance*. Port-au-Prince: Imprimerie de l'Etat, 1934.

West India Management and Consultation Company. *Haitian Investigation: Plains of Cul-de-Sac and Leogane*. New York, May 10, 1916.

Wirkus, Faustin, and Dudley, Taney. *The White King of La Gonâve.* New York: Garden City Publishing Co., 1931.

Wise, Frederick M. *A Marine Tells It to You* (as Told to Meigs O. Frost). New York: J. H. Sears & Co., 1929.

Articles and Periodicals

Allen, John H. "An Inside View of Revolutions in Haiti," *Current History* XXXII (May, 1930), 325–29.

———. "American Co-Operation Assures a Better Era for Haiti," *Americas* (National City Bank of New York), VI, No. 8 (May, 1920), 6–11.

American Chamber of Commerce of Haiti. *Monthly Bulletin* III, No. 1 (November, 1925).

Angell, Ernest. Letter to the Editor. *America* XXVI, No. 15 (Jan. 28, 1922), 349.

Angell, Katharine Sargeant. "The Great Ditch in Haiti," *New Republic,* XXX, No. 381 (Mar. 22, 1922), 107–9.

Ashton, Horace D. "Haiti To-day," *Scribner's Magazine* LXVII, No. 3 (March, 1920), 327–37.

Barr, W. M. "Tells How Marine Fliers Hunt Down Bandits," *Recruiters' Bulletin* (Marine Corps) V, No. 5 (June, 1919), 5.

Bastien, Rémy. "The Role of the Intellectual in Haitian Plural Society," *Annals of the New York Academy of Sciences* LXXXIII, Art. 5 (Jan. 20, 1960), 843–49.

Blassingame, John W. "The Press and American Intervention in Haiti and the Dominican Republic, 1904–1920," *Caribbean Studies* IX, No. 2 (July, 1969), 27–43.

Borno, Louis. "Problems of Interest to Haiti and the United States," *Bulletin of the Pan American Union* LX No. 9 (September, 1926), 845–51.

Bostick, Herman F. "Contemporary Haitian Literature," *Midwest Journal* VI, No. 4 (Winter, 1954–55), 49–57.

Brown, Philip Marshall. "International Responsibility in Haiti and Santo Domingo," *American Journal of International Law* XVI (1922), 433–37.

Buell, Raymond Leslie. "The American Occupation of Haiti," *Foreign Policy Association Information Service* V, No. 15 (Oct. 2, 1929), 327–92.

Campbell, H. Denny. "Aviation in Guerrilla Warfare," *Marine Corps Gazette* XV, No. 4 (February, 1931), 37 ff.

Chapman, Charles E. "The Development of Intervention in Haiti," *Hispanic-American Historical Review* VII (1927), 299–319.

Chester, Colby M. "Haiti: A Degenerating Island," *National Geographic* XIX (1908), 200–217.

Cooper, Donald B. "The Withdrawal of the United States from Haiti, 1928–1934," *Journal of Inter-American Studies* V, No. 1 (January, 1963), 83–101.

Coulthard, G. R. "The French West Indian Background of 'Négritude,'" *Caribbean Quarterly* VII, No. 3 (December, 1961), 128–36.

Craige, John H. "The Haitian Situation," *Marine Corps Gazette* XV, No. 1 (March, 1930), 16–20.

———. "Haitian Vignettes," *National Geographic* LXVI (1934), 435–85.

Cumberland, W. W. "Notable Commercial and Financial Progress in Haiti," *Bulletin of the Pan American Union* LXI, No. 4 (April, 1927), 316–19.

———. "Haiti's Foreign Commerce," *Bulletin of the Pan American Union* LIX, No. 11 (November, 1925), 1133–36.

Daniels, Josephus. "The Problem of Haiti," *Saturday Evening Post* CCIII, No. 2 (July 12, 1930), 32 ff.

Davis, H. P. "Haiti After 1936: So Far Intervention Has Failed," *Outlook* CLIV, No. 12 (Mar. 19, 1930), 443 ff.

De Bekker, L. J. "The Massacre at Aux Cayes," *Nation* CXXX, No. 3376 (Mar. 19, 1930), 308–10.

Denis, Lorimer, and Duvalier, François. "La Civilisation haïtienne; notre mentalité est-elle africaine ou gallo-latine?" *Revue de la Société d'Histoire et de Géographie d'Haïti* VII, No. 23 (May, 1936), 1–29.

Denny, Harold N. "Proud Haiti Demands Her Old Freedom," *New York Times*, Oct. 9, 1932, Pt. VI, p. 8.

DeYoung, Maurice. "Class Parameters in Haitian Society," *Journal of Inter-American Studies* I (1959), 449–58.

Douglas, Paul H. "The American Occupation of Haiti," *Political Science Quarterly* XLII, No. 2 (1927), 228–58, and No. 3 (1927), 368–96.

———. "Haiti—A Case in Point," *World Tomorrow* X, No. 5 (May, 1927), 222–24.

———. "The National Railway of Haiti," *Nation* CXXIV, No. 3211 (Jan. 19, 1927), 59–61.

Driscoll, Charles B. "The Cruise of the S.S. Henderson," *Nation* CXVIII, No. 3067 (Apr. 16, 1924), 420–21.

Dumont-Wilden, L. "Les Embarras haïtiens des Etats-Unis," *Revue Bleue* (Revue Politique et Littéraire) LXVIIA, No. 24 (Dec. 21, 1929), 757–60.

DuPuy, Charles M. "La Compagnie Nationale des Chemins de Fer d'Haïti," *La Revue de l'Association Internationale des Hommes d'Affaires d'Haïti*, 1ere Année, No. 4 (October–November, 1923), 74–78.

Erasmus, Charles John. "Agricultural Change in Haiti: Patterns of Resistance and Acceptance," *Human Organization* XI, No. 4 (Winter, 1952), 20–26.

Evans, Frank E. "Salient Haitian Facts," *Marine Corps Gazette* XV, No. 4 (February, 1931), 14 ff. and XV, No. 5 (May, 1931), 54–59.

Fletcher, Henry Prather. "Quo Vadis, Haiti?" *Foreign Affairs* VIII, No. 4 (July, 1930), 533–48.

Foster, Harry L. "The American Haters of Haiti," *Independent* CXXI, No. 4080 (Aug. 11, 1928), 128–30.

———. "That Colorful Black Republic," *Independent* CXXI, No. 4079 (Aug. 4, 1928), 111–13.

Franck, Harry. "The Death of Charlemagne," *Century Magazine* C, No. 1 (May, 1920), 23–35.

Frankfurter, Felix. "Haiti and Intervention," *New Republic* XXV, No. 315 (Dec. 15, 1920), 71–72.

Freidel, Frank. "The Haitian Pilot-Plant," *Politics* I, No. 2 (March, 1944), 43–45.

"General Butler Tells the World," *Christian Century* XLVII, No. 1 (Jan. 1, 1930), 5–6.

Girard, Pierre. "La Révolution d'Haïti, Juillet, 1915," *La Revue Hebdomadaire*, Année 34, VII (July, 1925), 429–42.

Gray, John A. "Boucan Carré," *Marine Corps Gazette* XVI, No. 3 (November, 1931), 28–32.

———. "Cul de Sac," *Marine Corps Gazette* XVI, No. 4 (February, 1932), 41–44.

Greathouse, R. H. "King of the Banana Wars," *Marine Corps Gazette* XLIV, No. 6 (June, 1960), 29–33.

Gruening, Ernest. "At Last We're Getting Out of Haiti," *Nation* CXXXVIII, No. 3598 (June 20, 1934), 700–701.

———. "Conquest of Haiti and Santo Domingo," *Current History* XV, No. 6 (March, 1922), 885–96.

———. "The Issue in Haiti," *Foreign Affairs* XI (January, 1933), 279–89.

———. "Haiti Under American Occupation," *Century* (April, 1922), pp. 836–45.

———. "Our 'Disoccupation' of Haiti Fraught with Many Problems," *New York Times*, Mar. 29, 1931, Pt. IX, p. 3.

Heinl, Robert D., Jr. "Haiti: A Case Study in Freedom," *New Republic* CL, No. 20 (May 16, 1964), 15–21.

Hinshaw, Augusta. "The American Occupation of Haiti," *World Today* LVII, No. 5 (April, 1931), 457–65.

Hinshaw, Augusta. "Haiti Takes a Day in Court," *World's Work* LIX (July, 1930), 37–41.

Holly, Alonzo P. B. "Our Future Relations with Haiti," *Annals of the American Academy of Political and Social Science* XLVI (July, 1931), 110–15.

Houzel, Roger. "Promenade en Haïti," *Revue des Deux Mondes* (Paris), 8éme période, XXVIII (Aug. 15, 1935), 940–49.

Hutter, E. W. "A Jim-Crow Situation in Haiti," *Plain Talk* (March, 1929), 349–56. See clipping file, Haiti, in the Schomburg Collection, New York Public Library.

Inman, Samuel Guy. "Hard Problems in Haiti," *Current History* XIII, Part I (1921), 338–42.

——. "Imperialistic America," *Atlantic Monthly* CXXXIV, No. 1 (July, 1924), 107–16.

Johnson, James Weldon. "Self-Determining Haiti," *Nation*, 4 parts, CXI, Nos. 2878, 2879, 2880, 2882 (Aug. 28–Sept. 25, 1920).

Kelsey, Carl. "The American Intervention in Haiti and the Dominican Republic," *Annals of the American Academy of Political and Social Science* C (March, 1922), 109 ff.

Lansing, Robert. "Drama of the Virgin Islands Purchase," *New York Times*, July 19, 1931, Pt. V, p. 4.

Lobb, John. "Caste and Class in Haiti," *American Journal of Sociology* XLVI, No. 1 (July, 1940), 23–34.

Logan, Rayford W. "Education in Haiti," *Journal of Negro History* XV, No. 4 (October, 1930), 401–60.

——. "Haiti: The Native Point of View," *Southern Workman* (Hampton Institute) LVIII, No. 1 (January, 1929), 36–40.

——. "The Haze in Haiti," *Nation* CXXIV, No. 3219 (Mar. 16, 1927), 281–83.

——. "The U.S. 'Colonial Experiment' in Haiti," *World Today* XVII, No. 10 (October, 1961), 435–46.

——. "The United States Mission in Haiti, 1915–1952," *Inter-American Economic Affairs* VI, No. 4 (Spring, 1953), 18–28.

Lubin, Maurice A. "Ou en sommes-nous avec l'élite intellectuelle d'Haïti," *Journal of Inter-American Studies* III, No. 1 (January, 1961), 121–31.

McCormick, Medill. "Our failure in Haiti," *Nation* CXI, No. 2891 (Dec. 1, 1920), 615–16.

McCormick, William B. "The Catholic Church in Haiti," *America* XXVI, No. 11 (Dec. 31, 1921), 248–50.

——. "Government in Haiti," *America* XXVI, No. 14 (Jan. 21, 1922), 319–21.

McCormick, William B. "Haiti and the Senate Commission," *America* XXVI, No. 7 (Dec. 3, 1921), 149–50.

———. "The Senate Committee in Haiti," *America* XXVI, No. 12 (Jan. 7, 1922), 269–71.

MacLeod, Murdo J. "The Haitian Novel of Social Protest," *Journal of Inter-American Studies* IV, No. 2 (April, 1962), 207–21.

McMillen, Fred E. "Some Haitian Recollections," *United States Naval Institute Proceedings* LXII, No. 398 (April, 1936), 522–36.

McNeice, William. "America and Haiti," *America* XXV, No. 7 (June 4, 1921), 150–52.

———. "America in Haiti," *America* XXV, No. 8 (June 11, 1921), 173–75.

Manigat, Leslie F. "La Substitution de la prépondérance américaine a la prépondérance française en Haïti au début du XXe siècle: la conjoncture de 1910–1911," *Revue d'Histoire Moderne et Contemporaine* XIV (October–December, 1967), 321–55.

Mars, Jean Price-. "Classe ou caste? Etude sur 'The Haitian People' de James G. Leyburn," *Revue de la Société d'Histoire et de Géographie d'Haïti* XIII, No. 46 (July, 1942), 1–50.

Marvaud, Angel. "Le Tarif douanier de Haïti et les relations commerciales avec la France," *Revue de l'Amérique Latine* (Paris), XX, No. 105 (September, 1930), 260–63.

Marvin, George. "Healthy Haiti," *World's Work* XXXIV, No. 1 (May, 1917), 33–51.

Millspaugh, Arthur C. "Haiti Under American Control," *Current History* XXXI, No. 5 (February, 1930), 919–26.

———. "Our Haitian Problem," *Foreign Affairs* VII, No. 4 (July, 1929), 556–70.

Mintz, Sidney W. "Peasant Markets," *Scientific American* CCIII, No. 2 (August, 1960), 112 ff.

Montavon, William F. "Haiti Past and Present" (Baltimore: Legal Department, National Catholic Welfare Conference, *ca.* 1930), reprinted from *National Catholic Welfare Council Review* (May, 1930).

Moore, O. Ernest. "Monetary-Fiscal Policy and Economic Development in Haiti," *Public Finance* IX, No. 3 (1954), 230–53.

Morpeau, Louis. "Un Dominion intellectuel français: Haïti (1789–1924)," *Revue de l'Amérique Latine* (Paris), 3e Année, VIII (1924), 332–41.

Munro, Dana G. "The Basis of American Intervention in the Caribbean," *Current History* XXVI, No. 6 (September, 1927), 857–61.

Padgett, James A. "Diplomats to Haiti and Their Diplomacy," *Journal of Negro History* XXV, No. 3 (July, 1940), 265–330.

Padmore, George. "The Revolt in Haiti," *Labour Monthly* (London), XII, No. 6 (June, 1930), 356–66.

Popper, David H. "Progress of American Tariff Bargaining," *Foreign Policy Reports* (Foreign Policy Association) XI, No. 6 (May 22, 1925), 58–68.

Posner, Walter H. "American Marines in Haiti, 1915–1922," *Americas* XX, No. 3 (January, 1964), 231–66.

Römer, Hans. "Die Vereinigten Staaten und Haiti," *Zeitschrift für Geopolitik* X, No. 3 (March, 1933), 141–49.

Ruhl, Arthur. "Muzzling Editors in Haiti," *American Mercury* V, No. 20 (August, 1925), 468–71.

Scottman, Drake. "A Marine Remembers Haiti," *Leatherneck* XXVI, No. 2 (February, 1943), 22 ff.

Seligmann, Herbert J. "The Conquest of Haiti," *Nation* CXI, No. 2871 (July 10, 1920), 35–36.

Simpson, George E. "Haiti's Social Structure," *American Sociological Review* VI, No. 5 (October, 1941), 640–49.

Spector, Robert M. "W. Cameron Forbes in Haiti: Additional Light on the Genesis of the 'Good Neighbor' Policy," *Caribbean Studies* VI, No. 2 (July, 1966), 28–45.

Streit, Clarence K. "Haiti: Intervention in Operation," *Foreign Affairs* VI, No. 4 (July, 1928), 615–32.

———. "Parting of the Ways Faces Us in Haiti," *New York Times,* Mar. 18, 1928, Pt. III, p. 6.

Streitberg, Th. de. "La République d'Haïti sous l'occupation américaine depuis 1915," *Bulletin de la Société Belge d'Etudes Coloniales,* 30e Année, Nos. 7–8 (July–August, 1923), 347–75.

Sylvain, Madeleine G. "The Feminist Movement in Haiti," *Bulletin of the Pan American Union* LXXIII, No. 6 (June, 1939), 315–21.

Thézan, E. "Le Cheval de Troie: l'accord du 7 août 1933," (Port-au-Prince: Imprimerie Haïtienne, 1933).

Thurston, Walter C. "Relations with Our Latin American Neighbors," *Annals of the American Academy of Political and Social Science* CLVI (July, 1931), 116–25.

Villard, Oswald Garrison. "The Rights of Small Nations in America: The Republics of the Caribbean," *Annals of the American Academy of Political and Social Science* LXXII (July, 1917), 165–71.

"Wards of the United States: Notes on What Our Country is Doing for Santo Domingo, Nicaragua, and Haiti," *National Geographic* XXX (July–December, 1916), 143–77.

Washington, Booker T. "Haiti and the United States," *Outlook* CXI (Nov. 17, 1915), 681.

Weatherly, Ulysses B. "Haiti: An Experiment in Pragmatism," *American Journal of Sociology* XXXII, No. 3 (November, 1926), 353–66.

Weed, Helena Hill. "Fresh Hope for Haiti," *Nation* CXXX, No. 3376 (Mar. 19, 1930), 342–44.

———. "Victory in Haiti," *Nation* CXXX, No. 3377 (Apr. 2, 1930), 378–80.

Welles, Sumner. "Is America Imperialistic?" *Atlantic Monthly*, CXXXIV, No. 3 (September, 1924), 412–23.

Wood, Clement. "The American Uplift in Haiti," *Crisis* XXXV, No. 5 (May, 1928), 152–53, and XXXV, No. 6 (June, 1928), 89–91.

Newspapers

Le Moniteur (Port-au-Prince). 1915–35.

The New York Times. 1910–37.

Le Novelliste (Port-au-Prince). 1915–30 (various years).

La Plume (Port-au-Prince). 1915.

La Presse (Port-au-Prince). 1929–30.

Le Temps (Port-au-Prince). 1929.

Public Documents

de la Rue, Sidney. *A Review of the Finances of the Republic of Haiti, 1924–1930.* Submitted to the American High Commissioner, Mar. 3, 1930.

Haiti, Republic of. *Annual Report of the Financial Adviser-General Receiver.* Washington, 1924–34.

———. *Annual Report of the Fiscal Representative.* Port-au-Prince, 1934–36.

———, Department of Public Works. *Geology of the Republic of Haiti.* Port-au-Prince, 1924.

———, Direction Générale des Travaux Publics. *The Public Works of Haiti.* Port-au-Prince, February, 1931.

———, Garde d'Haïti. *Annual Report.* Port-au-Prince, 1928–34.

———, Gendarmerie d'Haïti. *Annual Report,* 1927. Port-au-Prince, 1928.

———, Office of the Financial Adviser-General Receiver. *Monthly Bulletin.* Mimeographed. Port-au-Prince, 1924–34.

———. *Report of the Haitian Customs Receivership.* Washington, 1917–23.

———, Service National de la Production Agricole et de l'Enseignement Rural. *Rapport Annuel, 1931–1932.* Port-au-Prince, 1933.

United Nations, Mission of Technical Assistance to Haiti. *Mission to Haiti.* New York, 1949.

United States, American High Commissioner to Haiti. *Data on the Physical Features and Political, Financial, and Economic Conditions of the Republic of Haiti.* Port-au-Prince: Imprimeur Aug. A. Héraux, 1924.

United States. *Congressional Record.* 1915–34.

United States, Department of Commerce, Bureau of Foreign and Domestic Commerce. *Haiti: An Economic Survey* (Trade Information Bulletin No. 264). Washington, 1924.

United States, Department of the Navy. *Annual Report.* Washington, 1915–22.

United States, Department of State. *Papers Relating to the Foreign Relations of the United States.* Washington, 1909–40.

——. *Report of the American High Commissioner at Port-au-Prince, Haiti.* Washington, 1922–29.

——. *Report of the President's Commission for the Study and Review of Conditions in the Republic of Haiti.* Washington, 1930.

——. *Report of the United States Commission on Education in Haiti, Oct. 1, 1930.* Washington, 1931.

United States, Marine Corps. *Annual Report of the Major General Commandant of the United States Marine Corps.* Washington, 1930–32.

United States, Senate, Committee on Finance. *Sale of Foreign Bonds or Securities in the United States.* Hearings, 72d Cong., 1st Sess., 1931–32, 4 parts.

United States, Senate, Inquiry into Occupation and Administration of Haiti and Santo Domingo. *Hearings Before a Select Committee on Haiti and Santo Domingo.* 67th Cong., 1st and 2d Sess., 1922.

Unpublished Material

Beach, Edward L. "Admiral Caperton in Haiti." Article, Jan. 13, 1920. National Archives, Naval Records Collection, Record Group 45, Box 850.

Bryan, William Jennings, and Wilson, Woodrow. The Bryan-Wilson Correspondence. National Archives, General Records of the State Department, Record Group 59.

Bureau of Foreign and Domestic Commerce. Records. National Archives, Record Group 151.

Bureau of Insular Affairs. Records. National Archives, Record Group 350.

Butler, Smedley Darlington. The Smedley Darlington Butler Papers. U.S. Marine Corps Museum, Quantico, Va.

Chapin, John C. "The Marines' Role in the U.S. Occupation of Haiti: 1915–1922," Master's thesis. George Washington University, 1967.

Cumberland, William W. The Reminiscences of William W. Cumberland, 1951. Columbia University, Oral History Research Office.

Daniels, Josephus. The Josephus Daniels Papers. Library of Congress.

Davis, H. P. "Haiti: The National Assembly." Typewritten memorandum, November, 1923. Library of the Pan American Union, Washington.

Forbes, W. Cameron. "Journal of W. Cameron Forbes, Second Series, III, 1930–1934." The W. Cameron Forbes Papers. Library of Congress.

Heinl, Robert Debs, Jr. "Haiti: Impacts of American Occupation, 1915–1934." Paper read at Haiti seminar, Harvard University Faculty Club, Apr. 17, 1969.

Hull, Cordell. The Cordell Hull Papers. Library of Congress.

Hurst, Ann. "Southerners to Handle Haitians?" Undergraduate term paper, Wellesley College, May 4, 1964.

Lejeune, John A. The John A. Lejeune Papers. Library of Congress.

Little, Louis McCarty. The Louis McCarty Little Papers. U.S. Marine Corps Museum, Quantico, Va.

Lyon, Eunice M. "The Unpublished Papers of Major General Smedley Darlington Butler, United States Marine Corps: A Calendar." Master's thesis, Catholic University, 1962.

Marine Corps. Haiti Collection. U.S. Marine Corps Headquarters Historical Section, Alexandria, Va.

———. Records. National Archives, Record Group 127.

Navy Department. General Records. National Archives, Record Group 80.

———. Naval Records Collection. National Archives, Record Group 45.

President's Commission for the Study and Review of Conditions in the Republic of Haiti, 1930 (the Forbes Commission). Records. National Archives, Record Group 220.

Roosevelt, Franklin D. The Franklin D. Roosevelt Papers. Franklin D. Roosevelt Library, Hyde Park, N.Y.

Russell, John H. "A Marine Looks Back on Haiti." Typewritten manuscript, n.d., ca. 1934. U.S. Marine Corps Museum, Quantico, Va., MS File No. 4-50.

———. "History of Haiti." Typewritten manuscript, n.d. U.S. Marine Corps Museum, Quantico, Va., MS File No. 4-50.

State Department. General Records. National Archives, Record Group 59.

Stimson, Henry L. The Henry L. Stimson Papers. Yale University Library.

Vanderlip, Frank A. The Frank A. Vanderlip Papers. Columbia University Library.

White, Francis. The Francis White Papers. National Archives, General Records of the State Department, Record Group 59.

Wilson, Woodrow. The Woodrow Wilson Papers. Library of Congress.

Young, Lucius E. "The American Occupation of Haiti: Some Socio-Cultural Effects." Master's thesis, Howard University, 1950.

Other Sources

Angell, Ernest. Personal interview with Ernest Angell, New York City, July 28, 1970. Mr. Angell was counsel representing the Haiti-Santo Domingo Independence Society and the NAACP before the 1921–22 Senate Hearings on the Occupation.

Gruening, Ernest. Personal interview with Ernest Gruening, Washington, D.C., Aug. 4, 1967. Dr. Gruening, former U.S. senator from Alaska, was managing editor of the *Nation* during the 1920s and was one of the most dynamic and persistent critics of the Occupation from 1920 to the end.

Long, Harry R. Personal interviews with Harry R. Long, Somerville, N.J., Apr. 22, 1967, and Feb. 3, 1968. Mr. Long was comptroller of the Haitian-American Sugar Co. from 1916 to 1918 and vice-president of the West Indies Trading Co., Port-au-Prince, from 1918 to 1920.

Munro, Dana G. Personal interview with Dana G. Munro, Princeton, N.J., Feb. 28, 1968. Dr. Munro was chief of the Division of Latin American Affairs and then minister to Haiti in the late 1920s and early 1930s.

Index

About the Author

Hans Schmidt graduated from the University of California at Berkeley and secured his master's and doctor's degrees at Rutgers University, The State University of New Jersey. At present he is an associate professor of history at State University College in New Paltz, New York.

The text of this book was set in Caledonia Linotype and printed by offset on P & S Old Forge Smooth manufactured by P. H. Glatfelter Co., Spring Grove, Pa. Composed, printed and bound by Quinn & Boden Company, Inc., Rahway, N.J.

F
1927   Schmidt
.S35   The United States
          occupation of
          Haiti, 1915-1934

Date Due

Printed In U.S.A.